|| आत्मबोधः ||

SELF-KNOWLEDGE

An English Translation of Sankarācārya's Ātmabodha with Notes, Comments, and Introduction.

BY

SWĀMI NIKHILĀNANDA

SRI RAMAKRISHNA MATH
16, Sri Ramakrishna Math Road
MADRAS-600 004 :: INDIA

Published by :
The President
Sri Ramakrishna Math
Mylapore, Chennai 600 004

XI-1M 3C-8-2000
ISBN 81-7120-398-1

Printed in India at
Sri Ramakrishna Math Printing Press
Mylapore, Chennai 600 004

|| आत्मबोधः ||

SELF-KNOWLEDGE

"That which is the Pure Ātman is the Great Cause, the Cause of the cause. The gross, the subtle, the causal, and the Great Cause. The five elements are gross. Mind, buddhi, and ego are subtle. Prakrti, the Primal Energy, is the cause of all these. Brahman, Pure Ātman, is the Cause of the cause.

"This pure Ātman alone is our real nature. What is jñāna? It is to know one's own Self and keep the mind in It. It is to know the Pure Ātman'."

—SRI RAMAKRISHNA

ॐ तत् सत् ब्रह्मार्पणमस्तु

May it be dedicated to Brahman! Om Tat Sat

PUBLISHER'S NOTE

THIS volume is a reprint of the American edition of *Self-Knowledge* (*Ātmabodha*), an English translation of Sankarācārya's *Ātmabodha* with notes, comments and an elaborate introduction, by Swāmi Nikhilānanda of the Ramakrishna-Vivekananda Centre of New York. The free and metrical renderings of some of Ācārya Sankara's devotional hymns, which have been appended to his short treatise on Advaita Vedānta, serve to draw the attention of the readers to the less well-known aspect of Sankara's personality —his deep devotional approach to the 'gods and goddesses of popular religion'.

In this Indian edition the original Sanskrit texts have been added, which, we hope, will be useful to the Sanskrit-knowing readers.

15*th June* 1947

PREFACE

THE *Ātmabodha* or *Self-Knowledge,* is a short treatise on Advaita Vedānta, the philosophy of Non-dualistic Vedānta. It consists of only sixtyeight verses in melodious Sanskrit, and is believed to have been composed by Sankarācārya, the great philosopher of Non-dualism.

According to the generally accepted modern view, Sankarācārya, or Sankara, was born during the eighth century after Christ, in the village of Kālaḍi on the west coast of South India. He belonged to the simple, scholarly, and industrious Nambūdri sect of brāhmins of Malabār. After completing the study of the Vedas, he renounced the world at an early age in quest of Truth and was initiated into the monastic life by the great ascetic Govindapāda. Presently he devoted himself to the practice of spiritual austerities, meditation, and yoga. Before long Sankara's spiritual genius and intellectual acumen were acknowledged by the leading philosophers of India. He engaged himself in reforming the *Sanātana Dharma,* the Eternal Religion of the Hindus, and with that end in view wrote commentaries on the *Bhagavadgītā,* the *Brahma-sūtras,* and the principal Upaniṣads. He became the personification of the wisdom of the Vedas. He travelled the length and breadth of India, preaching the divinity of the soul and the oneness of existence. Before his death at the age of thirty-two at Kedārnāth, in the Himālayas, Sankara had established monasteries at Sringeri (Mysore) in the south, Pūri in the east, Dvārakā (Kaṭhiawad) in the west, and Joṣi Math (the Himālayas) in the north, and had placed four of his gifted disciples, each well-versed in one of the four Vedas, in charge of them. He reorganized the ancient Vedic order of sannyasis and assigned to it the spiritual leadership of Hindu society.

Sankara lived during the decadent period of Buddhism. Hinduism was beginning to reassert itself but true leadership was lacking. The country was honey-combed with conflicting sects; a spiritual confusion reigned everywhere and people were perplexed. Sankara's work, at this critical time, was the salvation of the Vedic culture. He met opponents from other schools in open debates, refuted their views, and re-established the supremacy of Non-dualistic Vedānta. In the midst of his ceaseless activities he found time to write small philosophical treatises and compose hymns in praise of the Hindu deities in order to quicken the longing of aspirants after the spiritual life. In him one finds the unusual combination of philosopher and poet, savant and saint, mystic and religious reformer, debater of rare forensic power and passionate lover of God.

There exist three great misconceptions regarding Sankara's philosophy, both in India and in the West. The first of these is that he discourages the performance of duties and advocates the discipline of non-action for the realization of Truth. Sankara's position regarding action and the performance of duties may be briefly stated. The nature of Ātman, or the Soul, is Existence-Knowledge-Bliss Absolute. It is the very embodiment of Peace, Desirelessness, Perfection, Truth, Beauty, Infinity, and Eternity. On account of māyā, or ignorance, man has forgotten his true nature and finds himself entangled in the relative world of good and evil, pain and pleasure, life and death, and the other pairs of opposites.

From the cradle to the grave, the unillumined soul engages in ceaseless action, striving to shun evil and realize the good. But his activities are influenced by love and hate, attachment and aversion, and he hopes to experience, through action, infinite and eternal happiness in the outside world. He roams aimlessly in samsara, the world of change and becoming, rising or falling according to the results of his action. Only gradually does he discover the impossibility of attaining abiding happiness through work associated with I-consciousness and the desire for results. Infinite blessedness is not possible through any finite action governed by the law of cause and effect. Then he learns from his teacher and the scriptures that karma (work), in order to produce a spiritual effect, must be performed as yoga; that is to say, the doer must regard himself as an instrument in the hand of God, surrender to God the results of action, and remain unruffled by love or hate. Work performed in this spirit purifies the heart and makes it inclined to the cultivation of meditation and Self-Knowledge. Gradually, outer action drops away, reduced to a minimum sufficient only for the maintenance of the body. The actor remains satisfied with what comes of its own accord, without feeling attachment to the agreeable or aversion for the disagreeable, devoting himself heart and soul to the contemplation of Ātman, which is the sole Reality. By means of Knowledge, or jñāna, he at last realizes the true nature of the Soul, attains peace, and is liberated from the endless suffering of the world. The liberated man engages in service to humanity, but his activities are quite different from those of an unillumined person. He is free from I-consciousness and the longing for results. He never loses the Knowledge of Ātman. In his actions he recognizes the influence of the gunas, which constitute man's physical nature. At their bidding the organs perform actions;

but the soul is always immersed in peace. Thus, though appearing to be active, he is really actionless. He sees non-action in action. If the Soul is identified with action even to the slightest degree, It has not realized its true nature.[1]

Secondly, it is contended, especially in the West, that because of Sankara's staunch loyalty to the Non-dualistic ideal of Brahman, or the Absolute, he is an enemy of the gods and goddesses of popular religion. Undoubtedly he held Ultimate Reality to be beyond name and form and of the nature of Pure Consciousness. He also stated that the direct method for realization of Brahman is not worship, but the path of knowledge, which consists in hearing the instruction of a teacher, reflecting on its meaning, and lastly, meditating on Truth with single-minded devotion. Philosophical discrimination (viveka) and renunciation of the unreal (vairāgya) constitute for Sankara the basic disciplines for realization of Brahman. Yet he was aware that few aspirants are strong enough to climb this steep path. The majority require a tangible symbol of Truth, anthropomorphic or otherwise, and also a human relationship with a Personal God. For them prayer and supplication form an indispensable part of worship. Out of compassion for these seekers Sankara composed many hymns in praise of such popular deities of Hinduism as Siva, Viṣṇu, and the Divine Mother. As one reads these hymns, one is impressed by the magnanimity of Sankara, who, having attained the highest vision of the Absolute, brought himself down to the level of ordinary worshippers smitten with the idea of many transgressions, assumed their attitude of insignificance and help-

[1] For a fuller discussion of the topic, see the present author's introduction to his translation of the Bhagavad-gītā.

lessness, and prayed to the Lord for grace to attain liberation from the many miseries of earthly life. These hymns are recited daily by countless devotees all over India at times of prayer and worship. A few of them are given in the Appendix of the present volume, along with several others of a Non-dualistic nature. They will demonstrate the grand sweep of Sankara's mind. Through all the hymns, dualistic or monistic, is expressed the longing of the devotee for freedom from ignorance, which alone is responsible for suffering in all its forms.

Even in his theistic hymns Sankara never permits one to forget that Brahman alone is the foundation of all relative ideas and that the effulgence of Pure Consciousness radiates through the vesture of name and form. The devotee catches a glimpse of the Absolute through the form of the Personal God, who is the highest manifestation of the Infinite that a finite mind can comprehend on the relative plane. Sankara reiterates this principle in his philosophy. The beginner learns the art of concentration through worship of the Personal God (Saguna Brahman) and acquires purity of heart through performance of unselfish duties. Endowed then with concentration and purity, he sets himself to the task of acquiring the Knowledge of Brahman and realizes, in the end, the Impersonal Absolute. Sankara initiated the worship of Sakti, or the Divine Mother, in his monasteries.

Thirdly, it is said by some of Sankara's Western critics that he moved away from the teachings of the seers of the Upaniṣads. The Upaniṣads, these critics contend, hold forth an optimistic and affirmative view of life, whereas Sankara, through his doctrine of māyā, describes the world as a snare and a delusion. His philosophy is regarded by them as pessimistic and negative. That this charge is without foundation will be realized by readers of the Introduction and the text of this book. It is to Sankara's everlasting glory that he points out, through unimpeachable reasoning, the spiritual nature of the world and the individual soul. Sankara takes every opportunity to insist that the true essence of man and the universe is Existence-Knowledge-Bliss Absolute. It is only when the individual sees a difference between Brahman and himself and the universe that he becomes a victim of fear, suffering, and misery. The characterization of deluding names and forms as māyā, and the injunction to renounce the unreal as a means to realization of Truth, are not new ideas of Sankara's but are both explicit and implicit in the Upanisads.

I have deemed it necessary to write a rather lengthy Introduction to the present book in order to give an outline of Non-dualistic Vedānta philosophy. Many things discussed therein may be unfamiliar to the average Western reader and therefore difficult to comprehend; but with a little labour and concentration the contents will become intelligible. It will be helpful to understand the method by which the startling conclusions of Vedānta have been reached. Some of these, such as the ideas of the divinity of the Soul and the reality of the Absolute, have become part of common human knowledge. Yet Western scholars often think that Brahman is either a dogma of the Hindu theologians or the private experience of the Vedantic mystics, and that it can never be proved by the rational and experimental methods of philosophy. Vedāntists, on the other hand, contend that Brahman, is neither a dogma of religion nor a private mystical experience, but a metaphysical truth based upon universal reason and experience. Vedānta is a systematic philosophy and aims at the demonstration of Ultimate Reality with as much reason as can possibly be brought to the understanding of the problems of transcendental Truth. A careful study of Vedānta will reveal that it not only makes room for many conflicting opinions of intellectual philosophers, but also dares to indicate their ultimate synthesis.

Vedānta is the foundation of the spiritual culture of India. It has kept Hindu society alive for the past seven thousand years. It is the philosophy of all the important religious sects and groups. In its various phases Vedānta represents the progressive thought of man, beginning with Dualism, passing through Qualified Non-dualism, and ending in absolute Non-dualism, the doctrine of the total identity of the subject and object, beyond which human reason, thought, and experience cannot go.

The conclusions of the Non-dualistic philosophy are epitomized in four statements, the importance of which is felt as keenly today as when they were first revealed to the ancient Indo-Aryan seers living on the banks of the Indus and the Ganges. They are, namely, the divinity of the Soul, the unity of existence, the Oneness of the Godhead, and the harmony of religions.

Every soul is divine, though, during the state of ignorance, it remains oblivious of its spiritual nature. While sojourning in the relative world it assumes various bodies and identifies itself with them. It is then regarded as a finite creature. But in the heart of every individual the divine light shines with undiminished lustre. Hence all men are entitled to our respect. The divinity of the Soul is the unshakable spiritual basis of democracy, self-determination, freedom, and other aspirations of modern minds. Even a noble human ideal, when guided only by expediency, can be an instrument of oppression and exploitation.

The unity of existence is the foundation of all ethical codes. Properly understood, it widens the bounds of charity beyond humanity to include the animal world as well. Self-love is the mainspring of man's action and the *raison d'etre* of his love for others. We learn from Non-dualistic Vedānta that the true Self of man is the Self of all beings. Therefore self-love finds its expressions and fulfilment in love for all. The Golden Rule of Christianity can be rationally understood and appreciated only when it is realized that by hurting others one really hurts oneself and, conversely, that by making others happy one brings happiness to oneself. Without consciousness of the unity of existence, ethics becomes a mere device for makeshift adjustments among conflicting interests: and when these interests are at any time seriously threatened, the ethical codes break down. Without a spiritual sanction, justice is in the interest of the strong.

The Oneness of the Godhead is well emphasized in the statement of the Vedas: "Truth is One, but the sages call It by various names." These names, honoured and worshipped by the various religions, are but symbols which enable finite minds to grasp the Infinite. The deities they designate are so many facets of the ineffable Reality, which is One. What is needed is steadfast loyalty to one's own ideal, and positive respect, not mere toleration, for the ideals of others.

Religion is not the goal but only a path by means of which the aspirant attains ultimate perfection. Different religions are necessary to suit different minds at varying levels of evolution. All religions are working for the good of mankind. Each religion takes up, as it were, one part of the great Universal Truth and spends its whole force in embodying and typifying it. The much sought for Universal Religion has always been in existence. It runs through all the various religions in the form of God-consciousness, which is the foundation of them all. Truth is the thread that holds together the pearls of the different faiths. Therefore religion should emphasize harmony and not dissension, unity and not discord, love and not hate, friendship and not enmity.

The introduction that I have written is based on the *Vedāntasāra* (*The Essence of Vedānta*), by Sadānanda, who probably lived during the middle of the fifteenth century. Important materials have also been taken from the *Dṛg-dṛsya Viveka* (*The Discrimination between the Seer and the Seen*) and Sankara's immortal *Vivekacūḍāmaṇi* (*The Crest-jewel of Discrimination.* I have used the English translation of the latter by Swāmī Mādhavānanda. All these books are considered by orthodox Hindus to be authoritative treatises on Non-dualistic Vedānta.

The notes and explanations given with the text are based on the traditional interpretation of Vedānta. Vedānta writers have always used analogies and illustrations to explain their points; for the subject-matter is of a supersensuous nature and cannot always be adequately explained by reason. These illustrations, culled from the daily experiences of life, help to bring home the Truth.

I am indebted to Mr. Joseph Campbell for revising and editing the manuscript, and to Mr. John Moffitt, Jr. for assistance in translating the hymns given in the Appendix. I am also grateful to Swāmi Satprakāsānanda for many valuable suggestions.

The very name of the book—*Ātmabodha*, or *Self-Knowledge*—suggests its perennial interest and universal value. Self-Knowledge is vital. All other forms of knowledge are of secondary importance; for a man's action, feeling, reasoning, and thinking are dependent upon his idea of the Self. His view of life will be either materialistic or spiritual according to his conception of himself. If he regards himself as a physical creature, and his soul (provided he believes in such a thing) as subservient to material ends, then he is a materialist; he follows the ideal of material happiness, devoting himself to the attainment of power and the enjoyment of material pleasures. Whenever a large number of people follow such an ideal, society becomes materialistic and there ensure bloodshed, war, and destruction. If, on the other hand, a man regards himself as a spiritual entity and believes that his material body should be utilized to serve a spiritual end, then he is spiritual. He follows the path of unselfishness, consecration, and love, and thus becomes a force to promote peace and happiness for all. Therefore it behoves everyone to cultivate Self-Knowledge at all times. Self-Knowledge serves the practical purpose of destroying pain and suffering (which are always caused by ignorance of the Self) and also the positive end of helping everyone enjoy supreme peace and blessedness here and always.

NIKHILANANDA

CONTENTS

INTRODUCTION

(*Vedānta : Its Theory and Practice*)

THE ORIGIN OF HINDU PHILOSOPHICAL THOUGHT

A STUDY of the early philosophical and religious writings of the Hindus indicates that the Indo-Āryans, who lived in ancient times in the valleys of the Indus and the Ganges, were keen and thoughtful observers of both the outer and the inner world. One of the things that greatly impressed them was the changeability of everything in nature. Oceans, mountains, rivers; trees, plants, herbs; birds, animals, insects; the sun, the moon, the stars—in short, all animate and inanimate objects—are subject to the law of change. And this is equally true of the states of the mind. Happiness is followed by suffering, joy by sorrow, serenity by restlessness, courage by fear, exaltation by depression. Of every experience, both subjective and objective, it may be truly said, "Even this shall pass away". And so a question naturally was raised: Is change itself the ultimate reality, or is there an unchanging essence, the ground of all change?

Like change, suffering too, was observed to be a universal phenomenon. No one escapes its cruel jaws. Rich and poor, high and low, old and young, learned and ignorant, righteous and unrighteous: all embodied beings suffer. Asked by a king about the meaning of life, a sage once replied, "A man is born, he suffers, and he dies."

Sorrow, indeed, is the price of our birth on earth. It afflicts a man's body or his mind. It may be caused by other human beings, by the denizens of the animal world, or by such uncontrollable cosmic phenomena as rain and drought, heat and cold, earthquake and storm. Twenty-five hundred years ago a great Indian seer—Buddha, the Enlightened One—declared that if all the tears that had flowed from human eyes since the beginning of creation were gathered together, they would exceed the waters of the ocean. The four Noble Truths which he discovered and announced as the basis of his religion are all related to suffering: its existence, the cause of its existence, its cessation, and the way leading to its cessation. Any glimpses of happiness that may seem to brighten our days on earth are both fugitive and deceptive. Every enjoyment is marred by a haunting fear. The rich are afraid of thieves, the beautiful of deformity, the healthy of disease, the learned of rivals, the aristocrats of dishonour, the virtuous of slander. Yet man somehow forgets this truth in the rhapsody of his fear-haunted and momentary happiness.

To illustrate the illusive nature of human happiness Buddha narrated the vivid story of a man who, while roaming in the forest, was discovered and hotly pursued by a tiger. He suddenly came to the brink of a deep precipice. The ugly beast was about to pounce. With only a split second for decision, the man perceived a vine hanging down the cliff and, catching hold of it, gave a jump. But the creeper was not long enough to land him on the ground. Looking down, he beheld, just below him, a second tiger, almost within reach, viewing him with glowering eyes. The first, meanwhile, was still roaring at him from above. And then as though his circumstances were not precarious enough, two mice, one black and one white, began to gnaw at the vine that he was clutching for his very life. It was then that he spied a strawberry growing on the side of the cliff, ripe and luscious, and just within his reach. He stretched forth his hand, plucked the fruit, put it in his mouth, and exclaimed with delight, "Ah! How perfectly delicious!"

If all our joy on earth is momentary and illusory, what is the basis of the illusion? Can there be illusion without a background or substratum? And how may one put an end to the suffering and attain peace? Or is there any peace?

The ubiquitous presence of death stirred the thoughts of the ancient Hindus. Does death mean the complete annihilation of a man, or is there something within him that survives the destruction of his body? And if death puts an end to the whole man, then why is he born at all? What purpose does one serve on earth, if the flame of life is snuffed out at a tender age? What is the meaning of death and how is it related to life? Is there any way to overcome it?

The early Indo-Āryans had an insatiable appetite for knowledge. Nothing short of omniscience would satisfy them. One reads in the Vedas of a disciple who asked his teacher, "What is it, revered sir, by the knowing of which everything in the universe can be known?" Like the Greek philosophers the Hindus first hoped to win knowledge by the analysis of external Nature. Extraordinarily detailed and poetical descriptions of the objects of nature appear in the ancient Vedic literature. But after a time the futility of such an effort to gain omniscience became apparent. One cannot adequately know an infinitesimal part of the earth through the study even of a whole lifetime. And there spread before our vision the sun, the moon, and the stars without number.

Presently, however, a clue was found to the solution of the mystery of knowledge. The Hindu philosophers observed that by knowing the nature of clay one knows the nature of everything made of clay, by knowing the nature of iron or gold one knows the nature of everything made of iron or gold. Is there not likewise, they asked, something that is the basic material of the universe, by the knowing of which everything in the universe will be known?

The *Chāndogya Upaniṣad* describes a dialogue between Nārada and Sanatkumāra. Nārada approached Sanatkumāra and said, "Teach me, sir." Sanatkumāra said to him, "Please tell me what you know; afterwards I shall tell you what is beyond." Nārada said: "I know the *Ṛg-Veda*, the *Yajur-Veda*, the *Sāma-Veda*, the *Atharva-Veda*, history and mythology, grammar, the rules for the sacrifices for the ancestors, the science of numbers, the science of portents, the science of time, logic, ethics, etymology, the science of elementals, the science of war, astronomy, the science of snake-charming, and the fine arts. All this I know, sir. But, sir, with all this I am like one who knows only the words, the sacred books. I do not know the Self. I have heard from men like you that he who knows the Self overcomes grief. Do, sir, help me over this grief of mine". Sanatkumāra said to him, "Whatever you have read is only a name."

The search for the Great Cause is linked with the search into the nature of man himself. Is man only a physical being, or has he a spiritual basis? The study of man opened before the Hindus a new vista. How does the mind think? Is the power to think inherent in the mind itself or does another extraneous power impel it to think? What has set in motion the life-breath? Who engages the tongue to speak, and the ears and eyes to hear and see?

The ancient Hindus wondered whether there was a First Principle or Ultimate Reality underlying the outside world, and also whether there was such a thing underlying man himself. If so, were the two the same?

It was apparent that the question that agitated the

Hindus, living on the banks of the Ganges and the Indus in that prehistoric time, could be adequately answered only by a true knowledge of man, the universe, and Ultimate Reality. These, then, engaged their attention and formed the subject-matter of their philosophical systems. For centuries they discussed these problems—in conferences and assemblies, in royal courts and sylvan retreats, around the sacred fires of the householders and in the hermitages of monks. They tried to work out answers through the most rigorous reasoning. They sought light in the depths of meditation. Some, inquiring about the First Cause and the ultimate explanations of things in the outside world, thought that the gods, the different personified forms of Universal Consciousness, held the key to knowledge and happiness. So they worshipped with elaborate rituals the sun, the moon, the sky, and other deities, and sought to propitiate them with appropriate oblations. But it did not take them long to discover that as everything existing in time and space is doomed to die, the gods too, must die; and as all beings living in time and space are limited, the gods too, must be limited. It is said in one of the hymns of the *Ṛg-Veda*, concerning the creation and its cause:

> Who verily knows and who can here declare it, whence
> it was born and whence comes this creation?
> The gods are later than this world's production. Who
> knows, then, whence it first came into being?
> He, the First Origin of this creation, whether He formed
> it all, or did not form it,
> Whose eye controls this world in highest Heaven, He
> verily knows it, or perhaps He knows not.

So it was clear to the Hindus that the gods cannot remove man's ignorance nor show him the way to blessedness and immortality. The problem of Ultimate Reality cannot be solved through study of, or devotion to, anything in the visible outside universe.

Other seekers directed their attention to a different world, the inner world within man himself. By means of such spiritual disciplines as severe self-control and concentration they discovered that the realm of the mind was infinitely more real, interesting, and deep than the realm of gross physical matter. There, after patient search, they at last discovered the clue to the supersensuous truths relating to the Self, the hereafter, man's destiny, and Ultimate Reality.

THE VEDAS

The supersensuous experiences of the ancient Hindu seers have been embodied in the Vedas, the sacred scriptures of Hinduism.[1] The Hindus consider that the Vedas, containing truths regarding the soul, the universe, and Ultimate Reality, are eternal (*nitya*), without beginning (*anādi*), and

[1] The religion of the Indo-Aryans is generally known as Hinduism or Brahmanism. Both these words have been coined by foreigners. The river Sindhu, flowing into the Arabian Sea and forming a part of the western boundary of India, was known by the ancient Persians as the "Hindu". The Greeks borrowed this name, changing it into "Indos", which much later was converted into the English "Indus". The Greeks called the country east of the "Indos" by the name of India. Its inhabitants became known as Hindus, and their religion as Hinduism. Early Europen travellers and Christian missionaries coined the word "*Brāhmanism*" because they found the brahmin caste dominating Hindu society and religion. But the Hindus prefer to call their religion the *Sanātana Dharma,* the Eternal Religion, because it is based upon eternal principles or the *Vaidika Dharma*, because it is based upon the teachings of the Vedas. The country of the Hindus is known to them as *Bhārata* or *Bhāratavarsa,* derived from Bharata, an ancient King of India who was the son of Dushyanta and Śakuntala immortalized by Kālidāsa in his great drama *Śākuntalam.*

not ascribable to human authorship (*apauruṣeya*). They are co-existent with the Creator and they form the very basis of creation. These truths are revealed from time to time to the hearts of men and women purified by the practice of self-control and meditation. Such fortunate souls are called rishis, or seers of Truth. Rishi-hood cannot be confined to a particular class or faith, time or country, or sex. The seers of the Vedas include both men and women, householders and sannyasis, and also people outside the brahmin caste. Many recensions of the Vedas have been lost. The Vedic teachers known to us at the present time were for the most part householders. They imparted their instructions in the crowded courts of kings as well as in retreats beyond the bustle of the city. The Vedic teachings were handed down by word of mouth. The Hindus hold the very words of the Vedas in the highest respect; for through them were revealed great spiritual truths. Therefore they would not dream of changing a single syllable of these books. Hindu boys have always been noted for their prodigious memories. These scriptures have come down to us in an undistorted form.

Much later the great sage Krishna Dvaipāyana, also known as Vyāsa, arranged the Vedas into four books called the *Ṛg-Veda*, the *Yajur-Veda*, the *Sāma-Veda* and the *Atharva-Veda*. According to the Hindu tradition he flourished at the time of the *Bhārata* and the *Bhagavadgītā*. But it must be kept in mind that the Vedas had been in existence for many centuries prior to Vyasa, who was only their compiler, not their author.

There is no agreement among Hindu or Western scholars regarding the date of the Vedas. They have been assigned dates very far apart indeed. But it would not serve any useful purpose to enter here upon a discussion regarding this highly controversial matter. According to the majority of

Hindus the age of the Vedas is not germane to the significance of their teachings. They deal with timeless Truth and hence may be called eternal and unrelated to human authorship. Likewise, next to nothing is known about the personalities of the Vedic seers. It appears that they cared more about Truth than about themselves. It is certainly true that the people of ancient India did not cultivate the sense of history as it is understood in our times.

THE DIVISIONS OF THE VEDAS

The Vedas treat of two ideals which rational minds strive to realize. These are material happiness here and hereafter (*abhyudaya*), and the Highest Good (*nihśreyasa*). Material happiness on earth or in heaven is realized through the observance of ethical laws, the performance of philanthropic works and worldly duties, and the propitiation of the gods through the offering of oblations in sacrifices as enjoined in the Vedas. These gods who were the personified forms of the Cosmic Consciousness, seemed to the ancient Hindus to control human life to a very large extent. But such happiness as one may enjoy in heaven even for millions of years is limited by time, space, and the law of causation and therefore must be considered transitory from the standpoint of Eternity. On the other hand, the Highest Good, attained through Self-Knowledge, transcends the causal law, as well as time and space, and is therefore eternal. Thus the Vedas may be roughly divided into two parts; the *Karmakāṇḍa*, which deals with rituals and sacrifices, and the *Jñanakāṇḍa*, which teaches philosophical wisdom. The purpose of the one is the attainment of material well-being here and hereafter, and that of the other, the attainment of the Highest Good. The Upanishads belong to the *Jñānakāṇḍa*.

According to orthodox Vedic scholars the Vedas consist of the *Mantras* and the *Brāhmaṇas*. The *Mantras*, which also include the *Samhitās*, are devoted to sacrifices and other types of ritualistic worship. The *Brāhmaṇas* lay down rules for the use of hymns, stating also their origin and giving detailed explanations, sometimes with lengthy illustrations in the form of legends or stories. The *Brāhmaṇas* include the *Āraṇyakās* and the *Upaniṣads*. The *Āraṇyakās* were studied by the forest-dwellers. They deal mainly with the symbolic representation of the sacrifices.[2] According to Hindu tradition the different sections of the Vedas do not represent any sequence in time. They have always existed together; for, men since the very beginning have known desires for both material happiness and spiritual felicity.

THE UPANISHADS

The Upanishads, with one or two exceptions, form the concluding chapters of the *Āraṇyakās*. Hence they are also known as Vedānta, the concluding chapters (*anta*) of the Vedas. Different families of *ṛṣis* specialized in different sections of the Vedas, and certain chapters, furthermore, had various readings followed by different schools. The teachings were transmitted orally from father to son, or from teacher to disciple. With the disappearance of the families who were their custodians many sections of the Vedas and Upanishads, together with their various readings, disappeared. One hundred and eight Upanishads remain, of which eleven are known as major Upanishads. The eleven are: *Aitareya, Taittirīya. Chāndogya, Brihadāraṇyaka, Muṇḍaka, Māṇḍūkya, Iśa, Kena, Katha, Praśna* and *S'vetāśvatara*.

As we shall presently see, the Upanishads form the basis of Vedanta, though the philosophy itself was developed later

2 See p. 20

by such thinkers as Vyasa, Gaudapada, Sankara, Ramanuja, and Madhva. There are in the main, three schools of Vedanta: the *Advaita* or Non-dualistic, the *Viśiṣṭādvaita* or Qualified Non-dualistic, and the *Dvaita* or Dualistic, their principal propounders being respectively Śankara, Ramanuja, and Madhva. Śankara has written commentaries on the major Upanishads, though it is sometimes doubted if the commentary on the *S'vetāśvatara Upaniṣad* is his. Though Ramanuja himself wrote no commentaries on the Upanishads, several of his disciples and followers have done so. Madhva has written commentaries on some of the major Upanishads.

What is the meaning of the word *Upaniṣad?* Etymologically it signifies the wisdom which, when learned from (*upa*) a competent teacher, completely (*ni*) loosens and destroys (*ṣad*) the pupil's attachment to the relative world, thus enabling him to attain Supreme Freedom and Bliss. It teaches the Knowledge of Brahman and hence is called Brahmavidya. Brahman is derived from the Sanskrit root *bṛmha,* which means to grow, increase. Brahman is the Entity to whose expansion or immensity there is no limit. It is the Absolute, the Supreme Reality, the Substratum and Ground of the visible world, the All-pervading Consciousness, the Spirit behind the universe, the Godhead, from which all beings are evolved, by which they are sustained, and to which, in the end, they are absorbed. Through the Knowledge of Brahman the aspirant attains the Highest Good, Liberation, Immortality, and Abiding Peace. When he cultivates this Knowledge with diligence, love, humility, faith, and devotion, he is freed from the round of birth in the relative world, which is associated with the pairs of opposites and also with disease, old age, death, and other forms of suffering.

The wisdom contained in the Upanishads is also called Ātmavidya, the Knowledge of Ātman, or the Self. Ātman, which is the Inmost Spirit in man, is of the nature of Pure Consciousness and, according to the Non-dualists, identical with Brahman.

It is obvious that the profound knowledge of the Upanishads can be grasped only by a competent student; not everybody is qualified. The *Chāndogya Upaniṣad* stipulates that the teacher should impart this knowledge only to his disciple or eldest son. It cannot be sold even for the whole earth and its riches; for it is much greater than the earth and all its wealth. The candidate for this knowledge should be endowed with humility, self-control, and inner serenity. Prior to the cultivation of the Knowledge of Brahman, he should have performed, either in this birth or in a previous one, the obligatory sacrifices; he should have practised devotion to the gods, and should have discharged all the duties and responsibilities of a house-holder's life. The pupil had to pass through various tests before the teacher would instruct him in the Knowledge of Brahman. We read, for example, in the *Katha Upaniṣad* that young Nachiketa approached Yama, the king of death, for the Knowledge of the Self. In order to test his sincerity and earnestness, Yama tried to dissuade him from seeking it by offering him, in its place, the possession of sons and grandsons who would live one hundred years, and of cattle, elephants, gold and horses, without number. He tempted the young aspirant with celestial dancing-girls of exquisite beauty, and with wealth, longevity, suzerainty over the whole earth, and the promise of any other acquisition he might desire. He requested Nachiketa not to bother himself with such a useless question as that of the nature of Ātman. To the king of death the boy made this spirited reply: "These are all ephemeral and only tend to the decay of the vigour of our senses. Even the longest life on earth is indeed short compared to Immortality. May the chariots, the music, and the dancing-girls remain with you." Finding him firm and unshakable in his resolve, the king of death granted Nachiketa his wished-for boon.

The *Chāndogya Upaniṣad* describes Indra, the king of the gods, and Virochana, the king of the demons, approaching the teacher Prajāpati for the Knowledge of Brahman. Prajāpati asked them to live with him thirty-two years as brahmacharis, practising continence, truthfulness, and other spiritual austerities. After the expiration of the period he gave them instruction, which they understood as identifying the Soul with the body. The king of the demons, on account of his naturally dull intellect, was satisfied and went away. But Indra, born with a purer mind, asked for higher knowledge. Prajāpati told Indra to remain with him for a second period of thirty-two years as a brahmachari. Even then Indra could not grasp the truth regarding Brahman; so he was told to spend a third period of thirty-two years. He had to lead an austere life for one hundred and five years, according to the Upanishad, before he could understand the mysteries of Brahman.

Purity of Mind, humility of spirit, and unshakable self-control were required of the seeker after Brahmavidya. Śri Krishna in the *Bhagavad-gītā* has described this Knowledge of Brahman as the "royal secret". It is the unique attainment of the Indo-Āryan culture and the permanent foundation of Hindu society.

The Upanishads cannot be called a formal and systematic philosophy in the usual sense of the term. The Hindus look upon them as containing revelations of supersensuous truths regarding the soul, the universe, and Ultimate Reality. The Vedas are called *S'ruti* (hearing), because they were taught by word of mouth. Outwardly the Upanishads contain contradictory statements, and so the texts were for a long time exhaustively discussed in order that the precise ideas of the *ṛṣis* might be ascertained. Vyasa composed a treatise known as the *Vedānta-sūtras* or *Brahma-sūtras,* in which he reconciled the many apparent contradictions. This work is now regarded as a standard treatise on Vedanta philosophy, the first successful attempt to systematize the views of the Upanishads, and has been commented on by Śankara, Ramanuja, and Madhva, as well as by other founders of religious and philosophical systems.

According to orthodox Hindu tradition none but the "twice-born", comprising the three higher castes, should be allowed to read or even to hear the *S'ruti*, or Vedas. But the members of the fourth caste were allowed to study religious books of secondary importance known as *Smṛti* (remembrance) which were ascribed to human authorship and were dependent on the Vedas for their validity. Epics like the *Rāmāyaṇa* and the *Mahābhārata,* the various *Purāṇas,* the Code of Manu, and other similar treatises, belong to this category. They deal, in concrete and popular form, with the abstruse ideas of the Upanishads. The practice of the spiritual disciplines prescribed by these books enable sincere aspirants ultimately to attain Liberation. The average Hindu derived the sanction for his religious practices from the *Smṛti.* It is the basis of the popular religious beliefs of India.

The philosophical thought of the ancient Hindus is ordered and summarized in six main systems. These are the *Pūrva Mimāmsā*, ascribed to Jaimini, the *Uttara Mimāmsā* or Vedānta, ascribed to Vyāsa, the *Sāmkhya*, to Kapila, the *Pātānjala*, to Patanjali, the *Nyāya*, to Gautama, and the *Vaiśeṣika*, ascribed to Kānada. They are called orthodox systems not because they accept God as the Creator or Ultimate Reality, but because they all derive their authority from the Vedas and maintain the existence of Atman, or the Soul as distinct from and independent of the body and mind. The Yoga system of Patanjali, no doubt, speaks of God and the need of His worship; but it does not concede the absolute necessity of such belief for the attainment of Liberation. *Saṁkhyā* does not admit the existence of God. In other systems God appears in varying roles.

Opposed to the orthodox philosophies are the four schools of Buddhism, the system of Jainism, and the materialistic system of *Cārvāka*, which are called heterodox by orthodox Hindus because they do not accept the ultimate validity of the Vedas. Even an uncompromising atheist like *Carvaka* is given the status of a philosopher or thinker.

VEDĀNTA

According to Sadananda,[3] *Vedānta* includes the Upanishads, the Brahma-Sutras, theBhaga vadgita and the commentaries elucidating these texts.

The texts of Vedanta have, in the main, given birth to two sub-systems of philosophy, namely, the Non-dualism or Absolutism of Śankara and the Theism of Ramanuja, Madhva, and other philosophers. According to the Non-dualist, Brahman, or Pure Consciousness, is the only Reality; the universe of names and forms is unreal, and man, in his true essence, is one with Brahman. The Theists accept a Personal God as Ultimate Reality; He is related to the universe and embodied souls in varying degrees. According to Ramanuja, the upholder of *Viśiṣṭādvaita*, or Qualified Non-dualism, the Reality is Brahman[4]; but the individual

3 *Vedāntasāra*, 3

4 The Brahman of Ramanuja is endowed with attributes, whereas the Brahman of the Non-dualists is attributeless Consciousness.

souls and the universe are also real, being parts of Brahman or modes of His manifestation. Brahman, with the universe and the individual souls, constitutes the whole of Reality. This is illustrated by the Philosophers of this school with the metaphor of the pomegranate fruit. The seeds are the living souls and the rind is the universe. One cannot think of the fruit without the seeds and the rind. According to Madhva, the Dualist, the Universe and the living souls are separate from God. While the universe is a material entity, the souls are spiritual in nature. The souls, though separate from God, cannot exist without Him. Their existence is entirely dependent upon God. Madhva speaks of living beings as the servants of God.

RELIGION AND PHILOSOPHY

In Sanskrit, philosophy is called *dars'ana*, derived from the root *driṣ,* meaning 'to see.' The purpose of philosophy is to enable its students to see Truth directly. Therefore, with the Hindus, philosophy is not a mere intellectual pursuit of an abstract ideal, but the actual perception or realization of Truth. In the West, especially since the beginning of the modern era, philosophy has been divorced from religion. The result seems to have been disastrous for both. But Hindu thinkers have always maintained a close alliance between the two. The one is incomplete without the other. The goal of philosophy may be Truth and the goal of religion, God; but in the final experience God and Truth are one and the same Reality. Religion insists on faith, philosophy emphasizes reason. These are two functions of our thinking mind and, if followed sincerely, often cross each other's path. The ultimate experience of Truth may be an act of faith, but its validity is judged through reason. Truth may transcend reason, but it is never illogical. One may not be able to arrive at Truth exclusively through reason, but one's experience and statement of Truth cannot be valid if they contradict reason. A direct experience that destroys one's doubts and is followed by an inner reassurance and peace is the ultimate proof of Truth, in the realization of which both faith and reason play vital parts. Religion without philosophy tends to become dogmatic, superstitious, and jejune. Philosophy without religion degenerates into inane and dry intellectualism. Reason moves in a circle, creates doubt, and never arrives at finality; it may indicate the possibility, nay the probability, of an Ultimate Reality, but if not animated by faith, it makes its user an agnostic. Religion, in which emotion plays an important part, becomes mere sentimentalism if it is not strengthened by the fibre of philosophy. It is the practical application of philosophy to life, and philosophy supplies it with an unshakable foundation. Religion supplies the aspirant with feeling or passion, and philosophy prevents him from wandering into dark alleys or up dead ends. Therefore the Hindu seers harmonized, in Vedanta, both religion and philosophy, faith and reason; and this fact accounts for its adequacy and universality. A true philosopher has something of the spirit of awe, adoration, and reverence cherished by a religious person; and a truly religious person is not without the intellectual understanding and insight which are the chief characteristics of a philosopher.

It is important to note that whenever religion has emphasized mere forms and dogmas, and thereby clouded men's vision regarding Truth, philosophy has raised its voice in protest and corrected the errors of religion. Thus, the Upanishads and the teachings of Śankara may be regarded as protests of philosophy against the excesses of religion. But the Hindu philosophers recognized the importance of religion and never discarded it altogether.

THE PROOF OF TRUTH

Ultimate Reality is transcendental. It is not perceived by the senses or comprehended by the mind. It is a matter of indubitable experience for the inmost consciousness of man. It is directly and immediately experienced without the instrumentality of the senses and the mind, and does not depend for Its proof upon any external authority. The perception of the external world is neither direct nor immediate, but is dependent upon the senses and the mind and is always coloured by them. On the other hand, the experience of Reality is both immediate and direct, and becomes possible only when the senses and the mind, through the practice of rigid spiritual discipline, have been made absolutely calm. It is the consciousness in man that experiences the Universal Consciousness, the two being, in reality, identical.

But there are infinite possibilities of self-deception. To protect the aspirant from error and delusion the seers of Vedanta lay down three criteria of Truth. These are scriptural authority (*S'ruti*), reasoning (*yukti*), and personal experience (*anubhava*). Any one of these, singly, may enable a man to realize partial truth, but when all three point to the same conclusion, the aspirant may be assured that he has realized the whole of Truth. The meaning of the scriptures, which contain the recorded experiences of knowers of Truth of the past, must be explained by a competent teacher. In order to free reasoning from the pitfalls of rationalisation, rigorous mental disciplines are prescribed so that the aspirant may be grounded in detachment not only from the external world but also from his own pet ideas and exclusive loyalties. The aspirant must be able to view his own thinking objectively and submit it to a searching analysis. Ultimate values must be judged by the standard of eternity and not of time. Lastly, the conclusions of the scriptures, reaffirmed by reasoning, must be experienced by the aspirant himself. Ultimate Truth, the basis of the universe, is self-evident, non-contradictory, and free from fear and friction. The seer perceives Truth everywhere and in everything, and thus becomes completely free from fear, sorrow, and expectation, which characterize the life of falsehood in the relative world.

A spirit of synthesis generally pervades the philosophy of Vedanta. The search is always directed to the discovery of the First Principle, through which the multiplicity of the universe can be known and explained. The Hindu seer insists that the aspirant after knowledge should first, through self-control and meditation, realize Ultimate Reality; only then can he know the nature of the world. As Ramakrishna said, "To know the many, without knowledge of the One, is ignorance, whereas to know the One is knowledge". But it must not be over-looked that some noted Indian philosophers, such as Kapila and Pātanjali, have shown remarkable acumen in their analysis of the mind and the material world.

THE FOUR STAGES OF LIFE

The Hindu view of life, as conceived in the Vedas, is spiritual. It has a spiritual end designated as *mokṣa*, or Liberation. Material enjoyments, which are necessary and legitimate at certain periods of life, should be so regulated that in the end they may lead men to the attainment of the Highest Good. No finite experience can permanently satisfy the craving of the soul, which is of the nature of Infinite Spirit. Nevertheless, in the lower stages of evolution the appetite for material things cannot be ignored. If this appetite is suppressed or inhibited, an unhealthy condition is created affecting both man's body and his mind. The Hindu philosophers want us gradually to transform the inclinations of the senses, will, and mind, so that they may become man's helpers in the attainment of his spiritual end and not remain his enemies. The various divisions of individual and social life as described in the Vedas and the Puranas bear out the ideal of man's spiritual destiny.

Let us state briefly the four stages into which the ancient Hindus divided the lifetime of the individual. The first known as *brahmacarya*, covered the period of the young man's study. He was at that time called a *brahmacāri*, a celibate student who lived with his teacher, practising such disciplines as chastity, obedience, and austerity. He studied the Vedas and particularly participated in sacrifices and ritualistic worship. He was taught orally. Living in a forest retreat away from the complexities of the city, he led a very simple life, looking after the teacher's cattle, chopping wood for his sacrificial fire, and spending a great part of the time closely observing Nature. It was a life of detachment and aloofness from the world. The pupil committed to memory the texts of the Vedas. After completing his education, he took his leave and the teacher said to him: "Do not deviate from truth, do not deviate from the daily recitation of the Vedas."

During the second stage the youth embraced the householder's life, known as *gārhasthya*, and himself was called a *gṛhastha*. In company with his wife he performed various sacrifices and rituals described in Samhita and Brahmana portions of the Vedas. As a citizen he performed his civic duties according to his position in the Hindu-caste system, as priest, military man, or trader.

But secular duties could not keep him bound to the world for ever. As a result of experience and observation he gradually became disillusioned about the glitter of the outer world. He longed for inner peace. As the signs of old age crept in, he entrusted his worldly duties to his children and retired into the forest (*araṇya*) with his wife. He entered upon the *vānaprastha* stage and became known as a *vānaprasthi*, or forest-dweller. He was still, in the technical sense of the term, a householder and, as such, had to perform certain daily sacrifices obligatory for all but the monks. But as it was not possible for him to procure in the forest all the ingredients for such sacrifices, the Vedas laid down for him symbolic worship. He meditated on the symbolic meaning of the various phases of a sacrifice and thus reaped the fruit of its actual performance. To give an illustration: The Vedas enjoined upon all householders the daily performance of the *Agnihotra* sacrifice, which required several material ingredients. But the forest-dweller meditated on the various functions of the *prāṇa*, or life-breath, and regarded these as spiritual counterparts of the different ingredients. The third section of the Vedas, namely *Āraṇyaka*, describes all of these symbolic interpretations of the sacrifices, as well as other forms of such worship. With one or two exceptions all four Vedas have their respective sections of *Samhitā*, *Brāhmana*, *Āraṇyaka*, and *Upaniṣad*.

The last stage of the lifetime of the individual, known as sannyasa, or monastic life, was entered into by those forest-dwellers who totally gave up the world in search of Truth and Freedom. They then became *bhikṣus*, wandering monks, or sannyasis-world-renouncers. The realization of the Supreme Truth has been described as the "flight of the

Alone to the Alone". The last stage of life is to be walked singly. Relinquishing all longing for material happiness both here and hereafter, as well as the desire for self-gratification through progeny, wealth, or heavenly bliss after death, these monks practised total renunciation, both inner and outer. As the ultimate ascent is steep and the lofty air extremely rarefied, they not only left behind material possessions but also stripped themselves of ego and desires. Material objects had no glamour for those who had realized Atman, the Self within, as the source of all bliss and happiness. They were outside all castes and beyond all social conventions. They gave up the sacrifices and ritualistic worship prescribed for the other three stages. They lived a life of freedom, which they had earned through strict observance of religious and moral laws. They were the spiritual teachers of men and were shining examples of peace and detachment. But by no means is a sannyasi a selfish person. His life is dedicated to the service of all, irrespective of caste or creed.

The sannyasis studied the Upanishads, the concluding parts of the Vedas, which describe the Knowledge of Brahman, or the Absolute, and the disciplines for Its attainment. By the spiritually-minded Hindus they were naturally held in the highest esteem for their purity, detachment, unselfishness' and utter devotion to Truth. As the burning tip of the wick shows that a lamp is ablaze, so, likewise, the presence of these free souls at the top of Hindu society demonstrated that its social life was functioning well. Though in general the life of the Indo-Aryans in ancient India followed this pattern and the monastic life was the natural culmination of the three previous stages, yet an aspirant for Truth might become a monk at any stage. An injunction of the Vedas declares: "The day a man is seized with a spirit of dispassion he should forthwith renounce the world." The Vedas speak of young men and women who took the vow of renunciation without going through the stages of the householder's and the forest-dweller's life.

A brahmachari had to read all the Vedas, though the Samhitas really moulded his life. Likewise, the householders followed the injunctions of the *Brahmaṇās*, the forest-dwellers those of the *Āraṇyakas*, and the monks those of the Upanishads.

THE FOUR IDEALS

We have already spoken of the division of the Vedas into *Karmakāṇda*, and *Jñanakāṇda*, dealing with man's natural desire for enjoyment of material happiness and the attainment of the Highest Good. The Vedic seers also speak of the four ideals which serve the ends of human pursuit (*puruṣārtha*). They are the springs of man's action and are known as *dharma*, *artha*, *kāma*, and *mokṣa*. Dharma is righteousness; it is the law of inner growth and the basis of man's actions. It is in harmony with a man's spiritual evolution. Therefore by following dharma one attains success in all actions. By negating dharma one brings confusion into one's life and retards the clock of progress. Dharma is not a sort of duty imposed from outside, but a sense of righteousness, integrity, and honour with which one is born as a result of past actions. So every man has his own dharma, in consequence of which he reacts in his own unique way to the outside world. His education and environment give to this basic life-form only an outer shape. By fulfilling his dharma a man marches along the path of progress until he attains the supreme dharma of all beings, namely, the realization of Truth.

Artha, or wealth, is a legitimate goal of pursuit at a certain stage of man's life. It is, with most people, an effective mode of self-expression and an important means of establishing fellowship with others. But wealth must be acquired according to dharma, righteousness; otherwise, instead of serving a spiritual purpose, it will aggravate greed and lust for power and ultimately be a cause of misery.

Kāma is the fulfilment of sensuous and aesthetic desire. Craving for sense pleasure is present in many sensitive persons to whom the enjoyment of wealth appears gross and therefore inadequate. But *kāma*, too, must be guided by dharma; otherwise it degenerates into voluptuousness.

The satisfaction derived from the pursuit of *dharma, artha* and *kāma* is neither deep nor abiding. There remains a hunger of the soul that can be fulfilled only by the attainment of *mokṣa*, or Freedom. The first three ideals belong to the material world, and the happiness derived from them is therefore ephemeral and illusory. But the ideal of Freedom can be realized only in the realm of Spirit, and the Bliss that follows is everlasting. Therefore the realization of *mokṣa*, freedom, is the coping-stone of human life; and the pursuit of righteousness, wealth, and aesthetic satisfaction only support it.

THE FOUR CASTES

The division of Indo-Āryan society into four castes is described in the Vedas. The caste-system has served to promote the unity and solidarity of Hindu society and to remove the friction inevitable among men born with unequal and dissimilar propensities. It has been the principal support of Hindu civilization up to the present time, sustaining it through many ordeals and dangers. For many thousand years it has preserved the cohesion and vitality of over two hundred million people.

The caste-system in its peculiar form may have originated in India, but its fundamental principles are universal. All human beings, according to the conception of the Vedic seers, form the physical body of the *Puruṣa*, or Cosmic Person. The Spiritual men form, as it were, His head, the warriors His arms, the merchants and traders His thighs, and the labourers His feet. A healthy co-ordination among these four classes of people sustains the strength and the well-being of a society, as a harmony among the four principal physical parts insures the strength and well-being of a body, The Indo-Āryans recognized this natural division of men and delineated it by the caste-system. The brahmins were the custodians of learning and spiritual lore; the *kṣatriyās* were the kings and military protectors; the *vaiśyās* controlled the trade and economic life; and the *śūdrās* supplied the manual labour. The four castes, forming the important parts of society, unified the ancient Hindus. All the castes were indispensable for the preservation of society and their welfare and security were interdependent. No caste, however high or powerful, could prosper at the cost of another. The spiritual ideal in society can be successfully preserved only by a system of caste such as was organised by the Hindus of the Vedic period.

The *Bhagavad-gitā*, much later, defined as follows the duties of the four castes:

"Control of the mind, control of the senses, austerity, cleanliness, forbearance, and uprightness, as also knowledge, realization, and faith—these are the duties of a brahmin, born of his own nature.

"Heroism, high spirit, firmness, resourcefulness, dauntlessness in battle, generosity, and sovereignty—these are the duties of a *kṣatriyā*, born of his own nature.

"Agriculture, cattle-rearing, and trade are the duties

of a *vaiśyā* born of his own nature. And the duty of a *śūdrā*, born of his own nature, is action consisting of service."[5]

From the social standpoint the caste-system admitted an inborn inequality between man and man and assigned to each duties appropriate to his own dharma, or law of inner growth. But these duties, however unequal they might appear, did not stand in the path of any person's attainment of his ultimate spiritual goal. Every duty becomes sacred when performed in the right spirit. "Man attains high perfection by devotion to his own duty. By worshipping Him from whom all beings proceed and by whom the whole universe is pervaded—by worshipping Him through the performance of duty does a man attain perfection. Better is one's own dharma, though imperfect, than the dharma of another well performed. He who does the duty ordained by his own nature incurs no sin. One ought not to give up the work to which one is born, O son of Kunti, though it has its imperfections; for all undertakings are beset with imperfections, as fire with smoke."[6]

According to the Vedic theory of rebirth a member of a lower caste, by faithfully discharging his own duties, will be born into a higher caste in his next life, if he so desires. The hierarchy of the caste-system was determined by spiritual qualities such as renunciation, unselfishness, purity, dedication of life to the acquisition of spiritual knowledge, and the rendering of disinterested service to others. Those endowed with these virtues in their fullest measure belonged to the brahmin caste. As the ancient Indo-Āryans valued spiritual wisdom more than earthly possessions, the brahmins occupied the highest place in Hindu society. The *kṣatriyās* occupied

5 *Bhagavad-gita*, XVIII, 42-44.

6 *Bhagavad-gita*, XVIII, 45-48.

the second place because they staked their lives in righteous war for the protection of the virtuous and the punishment of the wicked. Next in the scale of spiritual qualities stood the *vaiśyās*. And the *śudras* came last. But it must be understood that the four castes formed, as it were, the entire body of Hindu society. Therefore there was no question of one caste being exploited by another. It was on the contrary, the duty and privilege of a member of a higher caste to look to the welfare and interest of those belonging to a lower caste.

Caste was determined by virtue (*guṇa*) and action (*karma*). Naturally, in ancient times, a man could be demoted to a lower caste, if he failed in his duties, or promoted to a higher caste if he qualified for it. The whole system was flexible. Hindu society attained its highest peak of development and excellence when the brahmins and *ksatriyās* worked in harmony for the preservation of the Indo-Āryan spiritual ideal. Though the brahmins were the natural custodians of this ideal, yet they needed the physical support of the warriors to protect society from powerful enemies within and without.

Whenever Hindu society fell into a state of degeneration, the main cause was a lack of coordination between these two castes and their deviation from their respective duties.

As the history of the world abundantly proves, power, when it is wielded too long, corrupts even men of discrimination and ability. The greater the power, the greater the corruption. Hindu society has been no exception to this rule. The brahmins from time to time abused the power accorded them and received their punishment at the hands of the *kṣatriyās*. In the Upanishads we find *kṣatriya* kings sometimes becoming the teachers of the ancient Vedic wisdom. Thus, we read in the *Chāndogya Upaniṣad*, it was the *kṣatriyās* who knew the Secret of the Five Fires and taught it to the brahmins. King Janaka, of the Upanishads, Sri Krishna, the teacher of the *Bhagavad-gitā*, and Buddha, all belonged to the *kṣatriya* caste.

Later on, when the Hindus greatly multipled in number and other complexities arose, the caste-system was no longer based upon the qualities of the individual but became hereditary. As India lost her political freedom and fell a victim to the tide of foreign influence, Hindu society became rigid, the castes inflexible. People belonging to a higher caste claimed privileges without deserving them and exploited the natural helplessness of the lower castes. This corruption infected society as a whole and brought about its general degradation. Instead of acting as a unifying force, the caste-system now divided society into watertight compartments.

KARMA AND REBIRTH

The doctrine of karma and rebirth forms an important part of the Upanishadic teachings and has exerted the greatest practical influence upon Hindu society up to the present time. It is one of the strong pillars on which the Hindu Dharma rests. The doctrine was formulated in response to the question as to what becomes of a man after death. It also explained for the Hindus the inequality between man and man at the time of birth and gave them reasons to believe in a moral foundation of the universe, in which virtue is, in the long run, rewarded and iniquity punished. The doctrine of karma and rebirth is certainly an original contribution of Hinduism to the philosophical thought of the world. It must be clearly understood that this cannot be applied to the Soul, or Ātman, which is in its true nature, beyond birth and death, and unaffected by time, space, and the law of causation. It has reference only to the Jiva, or embodied soul.

It belongs to what is called the "inferior knowledge" (*aparā vidyā*), which one seeks to explain the relative world, and not to the "Superior-Knowledge" (*parā vidyā*), which is the science of Ātman.

Karma, literally meaning action, denotes both action in general and the fruit-producing subtle impressions which remain with the doer even after an action is outwardly accomplished. It is in the latter sense that an action plays an important part in moulding a man's future, not only here on earth, but after death as well. The law of karma is the application of the law of cause and effect in the moral world. No action is exhausted without producing its effect both on the body and on the mind. At the time of death the actions of a man remain in seed form, and the seeds develop when he assumes a new body either on earth or on any other plane of existence. "Every man is born in the world fashioned by himself."[7] '(The good and evil are laid down on the scales in the yonder world; and whichever of the two sinks down, that will he follow, whether it be the good or the evil." "He who does good will be born as good, he who does evil will be born as evil; he becomes holy by holy deeds, evil by evil. Therefore in truth it is said: Man is altogether and throughout composed of desire (*kāma*); in proportion to his desire, so is his discretion (*kratu*); in proportion to his discretion, so he performs acts (*karma*); in proportion to his acts, so does it result to him".[8]

Hinduism teaches that the good and evil tendencies of this life, and a man's happiness and suffering, are the inevitable consequences of the actions of his previous life, and the actions performed in this life determine those of the next.

7 *Satapatha Brahmana*, VII, ii, 2, 27.

8 *Brihadaranyaka Upanishad.* IV, iv, 2-6.

This conviction has taught the Hindus to regard the pain of this life as self-inflicted and to accept it with calmness and resignation. It is also an incentive to right conduct, because if a man sins no more in this life he will be spared grievous suffering in a future existence. Thus a man is free to accelerate or hinder his evolution. Neither his growth nor his action is determined by an outside factor. Through the law of karma the Vedic seers tried to explain the moral foundation of the universe according to which the righteous are rewarded and the wicked punished, in this life or hereafter not by the whim of God but by their own action.

The theory of rebirth is the necessary counterpart of the law of karma and the immortality of the soul. The soul being eternal, cannot be annihilated with the death of the body. The idea of eternal reward or eternal punishment after death did not appeal to the minds of the gentle Hindus. It is disproportionate to the law of cause and effect to imagine that the actions of a short span of life, liable to error, should bear fruit that will last for eternity. The idea that the erring soul should not be given another chance to rectify its mistake seemed both unjust and unmerciful to the seers of the Vedas.

The Vedic mystics often speak of the four courses that men may follow after death. These are determined, as we have seen before, by one's actions and thoughts while on earth. First, the highly developed souls who lead an extremely righteous life, meditate with whole-hearted devotion on Brahman, and practise the various spiritual disciplines, but who do not succeed in attaining complete Self-Knowledge before death, repair to Brahmaloka, or the plane of Brahma (roughly corresponding to the heaven of the Christians), and from there, in due course, attain Liberation. Some, however, return to earth for rebirth. This journey lies through a path known as the *devayāna*, or "way of the gods". Second, the ritualists and philanthropists, who cherish a desire for the fruit of their actions, go after death to Candraloka, or the lunar sphere. This journey lies through a path known as the *pitṛyāna*, or "way of the fathers". After enjoying immense happiness there as the reward for their meritorious action, they come back to earth, since they still cherish desires for worldly happiness. Third, those who perform actions forbidden by religion and ethics assume, after death, subhuman bodies and dwell in what is generally known as hell. After expiating their evil actions, they are reborn on earth as human beings. Fourth, those persons who perform extremely vile actions spend many births as such insignificant creatures as mosquitoes and fleas. They too, in the long run, return to human bodies on earth.[9] These four courses, obviously, do not apply to the fortunate soul who attains the Knowledge of Brahman in the body before or at the time of death. For him no going or coming can be imagined. He is absorbed in Brahman. The sojourn of the soul in a body superior or inferior to a man's is temporary, being of the nature of a reward or punishment. The actions performed

9 From the Vedantic standpoint dying may be compared to falling asleep, and the after-death experiences, to dreams. The actions and thoughts of the waking state determine the nature of dreams. Likewise, the soul reaps, after death, the results of the actions and thoughts which it performed and cherished during its life on earth. These experiences may be described, according to their nature, as those of heaven or of hell. When the soul awakes, after this sleep, it finds itself reborn on earth as a human being. It again takes up the thread of life and continues to progress toward its goal. Thus there is no real break in the upward journey of the soul, though at times it may take a detour. The after-death experiences, though of the nature of dreams, are real and vivid as long as they last. Like ordinary dreams, they may seem to cover ages. It is also admitted that some souls, after death, may be reborn directly as human beings without going through the experiences of heaven or hell.

by creatures through these bodies do not produce any results like those performed in a human body. When the soul again assumes a human body, it takes up the thread of spiritual evolution which was suspended at the time of death. As the attainment of perfection is not possible in one life, the soul assumes many bodies to attain it. According to the Hindus, all souls will ultimately attain perfection.[10]

THE GURU

The purpose of spiritual knowledge is the awakening of the soul and the transformation of life itself. The Hindu tradition emphasizes the point that spiritual knowledge, in order to be effective, must be transmitted from one living soul to another living soul. Even the great Incarnations, such as Christ, Krishna, Buddha, or Ramakrishna, accepted human teachers to guide them in their spiritual practices—

10 The Hindu philosophers divide a man's karma into three portions; *sañcita, āgāmi,* and *prārabdha.* The *sañcita karma* is the vast store of accumulated works done in the past, the fruits of which have not yet been reaped. The *āgāmi karmā* is the action that will be performed by the individual in the future. The *prārabdha karmā* is the action which has begun to fructify, the fruit of which is being reaped in this life. The *prārabdha* is a part of the *sañcita karmā,* since this also is action done in the past. But the difference between the two is that, whereas the sancita karma isnot yet operative, the prarabdha has aleaady begun to yield fruit. The fruit of all karmas must be reaped by the individual himself, the character and circumstances of his life being determined by his prarabdha karma. The prarabdha cannot be avoided in any way. The attainment of Self-Knowledge may enable one to abstain from future fruit-bearing action (agami karma) or to avoid the consequences of the accumulated action that has not yet begun to operate (sancita karma); but the prarabdha, which has begun to bear fruit, must be reaped. The man endowed with Self-Knowledge may not actually suffer from the result, however, because he is detached from the body and the sense-organs.

if for no other reason than to demonstrate that true spiritual wisdom should come down from teacher to disciple. The teacher is known as the guru, and the disciple as the *śiṣyā*. The guru may be compared to a lighted candle that ignites the disciple's soul. Books may give information, but not inspiration. Religion, if it is not transmitted but merely preached, degenerates into intellectual sermons. The ancient spiritual wisdom of India has come down to the present time through an unbroken succession of teachers.

Naturally, a high perfection is expected of the teacher. The ideal guru is, of course, endowed with the direct Knowledge of Brahman; he is established in Brahman. Weversed in the scriptures, he can dispel the disciple's doubts and confusion. He is sinless and free from any worldly motive. Calm and self-controlled, he is like a boundless reservoir of compassion. The apparent limitations of the disciple do not prevent the teacher from showering his grace upon him if the disciple approaches him with true humility and eagerness. The guru is often compared to the season of spring, which, of its own accord and without any selfish motive, covers the winter-withered shrubs and trees with leaves and blossoms.

The teacher is like a father to the disciple. He is accorded even more respect than an earthly father; for he gives the disciple his spiritual birth and shows him the way to eternal life. The disciple serves such a guru with the utmost humility and places at his disposal body, mind, and soul. Afflicted by sense-experiences, confused by the transiency of physical objects, and frightened by the seemingly endless chain of birth and death in the mortal world, he beseeches the teacher to lead him from the unreal to the Real, from darkness to Light, from death, disease, and suffering to Immortality. The *śiṣyā* approaches the benign guru and says to him, in the words of Śankara: "Save me from death, afflicted as I am by the unquenchable fire of the forest of this world, which is shaken violently by the wind of bad deeds done by me in previous lives. Save me, who am terrified and so seek refuge in thee; for I know of no other man with whom to take shelter. How I shall cross the ocean of phenomenal existence, what is to be my fate, and what means I should adopt—as to these I know nothing. Condescend to save me, and describe at length how to put an end to repeated births and deaths, fraught with suffering and frustration."

Complete disillusionment about enjoying true bliss on this earth or in heaven through the experience of finite, material objects is necessary before one seeks Liberation. As long as a man cherishes the slightest hope of perfection in the relative world, he is not yet ready for the highest teaching of Vedanta, namely the Knowledge of the Supreme Brahman. The Upanishad declares that the pupil should relinquish all desires for happiness on earth through wealth and progeny and for felicity in the celestial world.

It is through compassion that the guru most effectively influences the life of the disciple. The disciple is more impressed by the teacher's compassion than by his erudition and spiritual experiences. His distressed mind is soothed by the kind words of the preceptor and feels reassured. "Fear not, O blessed one!" he is told by the guru, to quote again the vivid words of Śankara. "There is no death for you. There is a means of crossing the ocean of apparently interminable births and deaths in this transitory world. The very way the sages have trod before I shall point out to you". Continuing, the teacher says: "It is only through the touch of ignorance that you, who are the Supreme Self, find yourself under the bondage of the non-Self, whence alone proceeds the round of births and deaths. The fire of knowledge, kindled by discrimination between the Self and the non-Self, consumes ignorance with its effects".[11]

THE FOUR QUALIFICATIONS OF THE PUPIL

Vedantic teachers maintain that genuine seekers after Knowledge must practise proper disciplines. True knowledge is always accompanied by a direct personal experience. To know Ātman is to realize that the Self of man is Pure Consciousness. To know Brahman is to become Brahman. Therefore intellectual understanding of Vedanta must be followed by actual transformation of life; otherwise it is of no practical benefit to the aspirant. Further, much of our reasoning is the rationalization of our desires. Most people understand a thing the way they want to understand

11 Vedanta prescribes the total renunciation of illusory names and forms and sets forth the ideal of Freedom through the realization of man's identity with the Absolute only for those rare souls who, in the course of their spiritual evolution, have understood the utter inadequacy and transciency of life—life not only on this earth but on any other plane of time and space governed by the law of causation. On the other hand, for the vast majority of men who still cling to the false idea of individuality, Vedanta assures rebirth on earth or elsewhere through its theory of reincarnation. No religion except Hinduism and Buddhism believes in the existence of the individual soul both before birth and after death. As long as one desires individuality one will be born with I-consciousness. Vedanta also suggests that if one wishes to enjoy material happiness, one should not renounce one's duties, but devote oneself to the cultivation of righteousness (*dharma*), economic security (*artha)*, and sensuous pleasures (*kāma*). After going through all these experiences a man will realize that true Liberation (*mokṣa*) is attained only when he is free from desire, attachment, and ego. The world is full of relative good and evil only to him who is still a victim of ignorance and regards it as existing in time and space and governed by the law of causation. But to the knower of Truth the world is Brahman and therefore the embodiment of Bliss.

it; they prove only what they want to prove. Therefore the attainment of Truth demands complete non-attachment to everything, including our own thoughts and ego.

Seekers of Self-Knowledge are exhorted to practise four disciplines, known in Vedanta philosophy as the *sādhanacatuṣtaya*, or four instruments of spiritual knowledge. They are as follows:

(1) *Viveka or discrimination between the Real and the unreal*: This is an intuitive and unshakable conviction of the mind that Brahman alone is the real Substance and all other things are unreal and illusory. Discrimination is the first and foremost discipline; without it the second one, namely renunciation, is not possible.

(2) *Vairāgya or renunciation*: This is the utter disregard of all pleasures, ranging from the enjoyment of the sensuous objects of this world to the experience of the happiness one expects in heaven after death. From the teachings of the scriptures and personal observation the intelligent aspirant realizes that no pleasure, whether here or hereafter, can have an infinite duration since all pleasures are the results of finite action. Even good actions, such as charity, study, or worship, are finite by nature. Their results, too, are finite. Self-Knowledge, as we shall see later on, is not the direct result of any action. It always exists. The Vedantic discipline merely removes ignorance, the barrier to this Knowledge, and the glory of the Self shines forth. This discipline may be compared to a wind that blows away a dark cloud hiding the radiance of the sun, immediately revealing the solar orb. As the sun is not the product of the wind, so also the Self is not the product of the discipline. But worldly happiness is the direct result of our action.

(3) *S'atsampatti, or the six treasures*: These form the ethical foundation of spiritual life. Their practice prepares

the inner faculties for the cultivation of higher knowledge. They are as follows: (*a*) *S'ama or calmness:* the dwelling of the mind on Brahman after it has detached itself from all sense-objects through firm knowledge of their inherent defects. The concrete effect of this discipline upon the aspirant is that he devotes himself entirely to hearing about Brahman from a teacher or from the scriptures, reasoning about the instruction, and then meditating on its meaning. A student of Vedanta, like all true philosophers, must cultivate inner calmness. He treads a very difficult path, often compared to the sharp edge of a razor. He must have convictions but should never be swaved by passions. A Vedantist is often compared to a fire of blazing charcoal, free from smoke and noise, after the wood is consumed. (*b*) *Dama, or self-control:* restraining the organs of both perception and action from their respective objects, and keeping them under control. The organs of perception are those of tasting, hearing, smelling, seeing, and touching. The organs of action are those of speaking, grasping, moving about, pro-creating, and evacuating. Endowed with this virtue, the aspirant engages only in hearing about Brahman, reasoning about it, and meditating upon it. (*c*) *Uparati, or self-settledness:* a function of the mind which prevents the sense-organs, restrained by *S'ama* and *Dama*, from drifting back to their respective objects. This virtue, according to some Vedantists, means the relinquishment of worldly duties and the acceptance of sannyasa, or monastic life. (*d*) *Titikṣā or forbearance:* the endurance of all afflictions arising from the contact of the senses with their objects. A man practising this discipline does not care to relieve his physical suffering nor does he show any anxiety or grief on its score. By means of this discipline the aspirant remains unagitated by heat and cold, pleasure and pain, love and hate, and the other pairs of opposites. (e) *Samādhāna, or complete concentration:* concentration of the mind (after it has been disciplined by the practice of the above-mentioned virtues) on Brahman as taught by the scriptures and by a competent teacher. (*f*) *śraddhā or faith:* a function of the mind which enables the aspirant to accept as true the words of Vedanta as taught by a competent teacher. This is not a mechanical or unquestioning belief. It is rather an affirmative attitude of mind as opposed to the sceptical and negative. Endowed with this virtue the aspirant intuitively believes in the existence of Ultmate Reality and in the eternity of the Soul. Further, he knows that he is capable of making any sacrifice for the realization of Truth. It is said in the *Kaṭha Upaniṣad* that Naciketa, armed with *śraddha*, went to the abode of the king of death to seek the knowledge of the hereafter. Without this affirmative attitude of the mind no success is possible in spiritual life.

(4) *Mumukṣatvam, or longing for Liberation*: This is the intense longing of the student to free himself, through the Knowledge of the true Self, from all bondages pertaining to the body, the mind, and the ego—bondages created by ignorance. It must be understood that longing is totally different from restlessness, which is an inferior state of mind. A restless mind shows lack of self-control and also a lack of firm belief in the existence of Truth. Restlessness creates confusion; the longing for Freedom is the result of all the virtues mentioned above. It endows the mind with an intense one-pointedness and enables it to pierce through the thick crust of ignorance. Renunciation and the longing for Freedom are the cardinal virtues through which the others bear their fruit. Without these the mere ethical disciplines give only a veneer of spirituality.

The great Śankara lays emphasis on the cultivation of

bhakti or devotion, as supremely necessary to the attainment of Liberation. *Bhakti* is single-minded zeal and unswerving passion for the realization of Truth. Without this emotional urge, the aspirant often becomes lost in the wilderness of dry intellectualism or finds comfort in the ivory tower of a speculative philosophy. He fails to reach the Goal.

THE MEANING OF SELF-CONTROL

Self-control is the very core of the Vedantic discipline; without it no progress is possible in spiritual life, nor any success in meditation. By means of self-control one empties the mind, as it were, of its wordly contents, its transient desires and passions, and then, through contemplation, fills up the void with the spirit of Truth. The attempt to meditate without practising self-control is as futile as to irrigate a field without at first closing the big rat-holes through which the water leaks away.

Self-control should be distinguished from the practice of mortification and meaningless austerities. It is very different from self-torture, which Śri Krishna condemns in the *Bhagavad-gitā*[12]. Self-control really means the development of will-power and also the strengthening of the *buddhi,* or the determinative faculty, which controls all the sense organs. This is illustrated in the *Katha Upaniṣad* by the parable of the chariot.[13] The body is compared to a chariot inside which is seated the Self, the master. The *buddhi* is the charioteer, and the mind, the reins. The senses are the horses, and their objects are the roads along which the vehicle moves. The chariot serves the purpose of taking to the

12 *Bhagavad-gītā* XVII, 5—6.

13 *Kaṭha Upaniṣad* I, iii, 3—9.

destination the master, who is the Supreme Self temporarily identified, through ignorance, with the body, the senses, and the mind. If the *buddhi* (the driver) is weak and the mind (the reins) not held firmly, then the senses (the horses) become uncontrollable, like the vicious horses of a bad charioteer. But if the *buddhi* functions properly and the mind is firmly held, then the senses remain under control, like the trained horses of a good charioteer. If a man is devoid of understanding, unmindful, and impure, he never reaches the Goal, but enters into the round of births in the world of ignorance. But he who is endowed with understanding, purity, and a well controlled mind surely reaches the Goal, from which one does not come back to the world for rebirth. Employing as his charioteer a well developed *buddhi* which holds firmly the reins of the mind, the embodied Self reaches the end of the journey, which is the supreme state of the Godhead.

What is enjoined in this graphic description is not the weakening of the mind and the senses through self-mortification or abstinence from the experience of sense-objects, but the strengthening of the will-power and the determinative faculty. In this manner the mind and the senses can be kept under control and prevented from leading the aspirant astray through the enjoyment of objects inimical to his spiritual progress. This strengthening of the will-power and the *buddhi* is the very core of self-control.

VEDANTA AND WORSHIP

It is often erroneously held that Vedanta, which preaches the reality of Brahman, or the Impersonal Absolute, and the illusoriness of the world, including the gods and other higher beings, is iconoclastic and intolerant of worship. The realization of the illusoriness of the sense-perceived world is, no doubt, the goal of Vedanta philosophy, but a man who is under the spell of ignorance cannot deny the actuality of phenomena. As long as a man remains ignorant, the world is real to him, and so are its pairs of opposites, such as good and evil, righteousness and unrighteousness. Only a highly qualified spiritual aspirant can conceive of the Impersonal Absolute and meditate on it. He alone can seek Brahman and realize it directly by meditation. For the rest the approach to Impersonal Reality lies through the Personal God. Therefore the worship of Īśvara, or the Personal God, is recommended at the beginning of spiritual life. Worship and devotion enable a beginner to fix his mind on God and strengthen his power of concentration. As long as a man regards himself as a psycho-physical being, conscious of his body, mind, and ego, and as long as he is not fully aware of Ātman, or Pure Spirit, as his true Self he cannot effectively meditate on Impersonal Reality. Conscious of his many weaknesses and limitations, he feels the need of prayer and other external supports. He worships the Personal God for protection, guidance, and grace. Though, in the end, the worshipper realizes that both he and the Personal God are non-different, being manifestations of Brahman, yet as long as he remains conscious of his individuality and retains even a trace of his ego, the distinction between himself and the Personal God holds good, and the latter is to be regarded as the highest reality on the relative plane. From the standpoint of name and form, a toy lion and a toy sheep, though both made of clay, cannot be identical; similarly, from the relative standpoint, a man and the Personal God, though both are admitted by the Non-dualist to be manifestations of Brahman, cannot be identical. But the same lion and sheep, reduced to clay, lose their differences;

likewise, a man and the Personal God, reduced to their Ultimate Cause, Brahman, lose their differences. For men, victims of ignorance, there is need of prayer and worship.

But to a Vedantic aspirant the symbolic nature of the Personal God is pointed out from the very beginning. The Reality behind the Divinity is the Impersonal Absolute. The whole relative universe and all material objects are different manifestations of the Absolute; the Personal God is Its highest manifestation. The Personal God is not the creation or imagination of the human mind. He is as real as the universe. When, through self-control and meditation, the aspirant becomes less and less aware of the universe and his ego, he sees more and more of the Absolute. In the end both the worshipper and the Personal God merge in the Absolute. From the realization of the Personal God to the Knowledge of the Impersonal Truth is but a short step.

When not absorbed in communion with the Absolute, Non-dualists show a very exalted spirit of adoration for the personal aspects of the Divine Spirit. Consider, for instance, the following hymn from the *Mahānirvāṇa Tantra:*

I bow to Thee, the Everlasting Cause of the world;
I bow to Thee, Pure Consciousness, the Soul that sustains the whole universe;
I bow to Thee, who art One without duality, who does bestow Liberation;
I bow to Thee, Brahman, the all-pervading Attributeless Reality.
Thou alone art the Refuge, the only object of adoration;
Thou art the only Cause of the universe, the Soul of everything that is;
Thou alone art the world's Creator, Thou its Preserver and Destroyer;
Thou art the immutable Supreme Lord, the Absolute;

Thou art unchanging Consciousness
Dread of the dreadful! Terror of the terrible;
Refuge of all beings! Purity of purifiers!
Thou alone dost rule over those in the high places,
Supreme over the supreme, the Protector of protectors.
Almighty Lord, who art made manifest as the Form of all, yet art Thyself unmanifest and indestructible;
Thou who art imperceptible to the senses, yet art the very Truth:
Incomprehensible, imperishable, all-pervading, hidden and without form;
O Lord! O Light of the universe! Protect us from harm.
On that One alone we meditate; that One is the sole object of our worship!
To That alone, the non-dual Witness of the universe, we bow.
In that One who alone exists and who is our sole eternal Support, we seek refuge,
The self-dependent Lord, the Vessel of Safety in the ocean of this world.

An advanced Non-dualist realizes, however, the inadequacy of the ordinary details of ritualistic worship, as is evidenced in the following hymn:

How can one ever invoke the All-pervading Absolute?
How give a seat to That which is the one Support of all?
How can one bring offerings to That whose nature is Pure Awareness,
Or purify That which is ever pure?
Why should one bathe with water That which is ever free from stain,
Or offer clothes to that which holds the universe is Itself?
Why should one place a sacred thread on Him who needs no support?

What is the use of flowers for One insensitive to smell?
How can perfume be pleasing to Him who is totally unattached,
Or jewels set off the beauty of Him who is all beauty's Source?
Futile are offerings of food to One who is ever satisfied!
How can one circumambulate Him who is boundless in all directions?
How contrive to salute Him who is One without a second?
How can hymns be pleasing to That which the Vedas cannot reveal?
How can one wave lights before the Self-luminous Lord, the All-pervading Reality,
And how, as an image, can He be installed[14] who stands complete within and without?
Therefore it is that perfect knowers of Brahman, always and under all conditions,
Commune with the Lord through contemplating their total identity with Him.

THE METHODS OF VEDANTA

Having described the preliminaries of Vedanta, we shall now proceed to discuss the philosophy itself. The methods by which the Vedantic teachers arrive at Truth are known as *adhyāropa* and *apavāda*. *Adhyāropa* denotes the illusory superimposition, through ignorance, on account of which one thing is perceived as another and the properties of one

14 Such actions as of offering a seat or food and flowers, bathing in water, giving clothes, investing with a sacred thread, waving lights, and installing the deity on a pedestal are the rituals prescribed by the Hindu religion for the worship of the Personal God through an image.

thing are attributed to another. Thus, through *adhyāropa* a rope appears to be a snake and to possess the characteristics of a snake; or the stump of a tree in semi-darkness, to be a man. Vedantists also give the illustrations of the desert, which, in the case of a mirage, appears to contain water, and of shells scattered on a beach, which, on a moonlit night, are mistaken for pieces of silver. In the same manner, Vedanta contends, the attributes of the non-Self (*anātma*) are falsely superimposed upon the Self (Ātman). This is how the Self, which is eternal, immortal, ever pure, beyond time and space, untouched by the law of causation, and of the nature of Pure Consciousness, appears as a *jīva*, or phenomenal being—a physical entity subject to hunger and thirst, disease and death, and the other limitations of the relative world. Through the same inscrutable ignorance the attributes of the Self are superimposed upon the non-Self. Thus Consciousness, Intelligence, Bliss, and such other characteristics, which really belong to the Self, are falsely attributed to the non-Self, comprising the body, the senses, and the mind, all of which are by nature unconscious and inert. Because of this *adhyāropa*, again, one regards the Real as unreal, and the unreal as the Real. Thus Brahman, Pure Consciousness, appears to the ignorant as the universe of multiple names and forms and also as the individual soul. All men, one way or another, are victims of this peculiar and inexplicable illusion. Their thoughts and actions in the relative world are coloured and determined by it.

Apavāda, or negation, is the elimination, through discrimination, of falsely superimposed attributes in order to discover the true nature of a thing. Thus, by negating the attributes of the illusory water in a mirage, one discovers the true nature of the desert; by negating the attributes of the illusory snake, the true nature of the rope; by negating the attributes of the illusory man, the true nature of the stump; by negating the attributes of the illusory silver, the true nature of the shells. In a like manner, by negating, through discrimination, the attributes of the non-Self, one discovers the true nature of the Self, or Ātman, and by negating the attributes of the relative world, the true nature of Brahman.

It is very important to remember that the attributes falsely superimposed upon a thing do not really belong to it and cannot in the least affect its nature. Thus, the illusory water of a mirage cannot soak a single grain of sand in the desert; the illusory snake cannot impart its poison and terror to the harmless rope; the illusory man cannot give the spark of life to the lifeless stump; the illusory silver cannot make a worthless shell valuable. Likewise, such superimposed attributes as birth and death, hunger and thirst, pain and pleasure, cannot change by any means whatsoever the true nature of the Self, which is Existence-Knowledge-Bliss Absolute. Reality is never affected by appearance.

THE "SEER" AND THE "SEEN"

Vedanta philosophy describes at great length the distinction between the "Seer" (*dṛk*) and the "seen" (*dṛśya*), the Subject (*viṣayi*) and the object (*viṣaya*), the "Ego" (*Aham*) and the "non-Ego" (*idam*). The "Seer" is the perceiver, identical with the Subject and the Ego, and is of the nature of Consciousness and Intelligence. The "seen" is the thing perceived, identical with the object and the non-Ego, and is insentient by nature. The "Seer" is all sentiency; therefore the "Seer" and the "seen", the Subject and the object, the "Ego" and the "non-Ego, are mutually opposed and must never be identified with each other. If one associates the attributes of the Subject with the object, or *vice versa,* those of the object with the Subject, one is a victim of an illusory superimposition, the result of one's own ignorance. Yet it is a matter of common experience that in daily practical life people do not distinguish between the Subject and the object, but superimpose the attributes of the one upon the other. Through ignorance they confuse the Subject with the object. This confusion is observable in every action and thought of our daily life, and is expressed in such common statements as "This is I" or "This is mine", whereby we identify the "I", which is of the nature of Pure Consciousness, with such material objects as the body, the mind, the senses, house, or country. On account of the same confusion we associate the Eternal Self with such characteristics of the body as birth, growth, disease, and death; and this confusion is expressed in such statements as "I am born", "I am growing", "I am ill", or "I am dying".

Discrimination between the "Seer" and the "seen" is the road leading to the realization of Truth. The "Seer" is the unchangeable and homogeneous Consciousness, or the knowing principle. It is the perceiver, the Subject, the real "Ego". The "seen" is what is perceived; it is outside the "Seer" and therefore identical with the object. It is matter,non-Self, and "non-Ego". The "seen" is multiple and changeable.

The seer sees an object because the seer is one and unchanging. The various objects of the world, different from one another owing to size, colour, or shape, and changeable by nature, are perceived by the eye; the eye itself, relatively speaking, is one and unchanging. The same is also true of the other senses, namely, the ear, the nose, the tongue, and the skin. Again, the eye, with its changing characteristics of blindness, dullness, or keenness, is the object, and the mind the subject, because the mind relatively speaking, is a unity. Finally, the mind, endowed with such changing characteristics as desire, doubt, determination, constancy, belief, fear and fearlessness, is the object, and it is perceived by the Self, or Consciousness, because the latter is a unity. The Self, unlike the senses and the mind, is the ultimate Subject or Perceiver. The Consciousness belonging to the Self eternally exists. One cannot speak of Its birth, growth, decay, or death. If Consciousness possessed such attributes, then there would have to be a perceiver of these. Who would be that perceiver? Another Self or Consciousness. And who the perceiver of this second Consciousness? The inquiry ends in an infinite regress. The existence of the Self, or Consciousness, cannot finally be doubted, because the doubter himself is the Self, or Conscious Entity. It cannot be denied, because the denier himself is the Self, or Conscious Entity. The presence of an irrefragable Self, or Consciousness, dominates every phase of thinking, and without it no thinking is possible. Vedanta concludes, therefore, that all entities, from the gross, tangible objects in the outside world to the mind, must be of the nature of the "seen", the object. They are by nature insentient (*jada*) and changing. But the Self, or Consciousness, is the true "Seer" or Subject, unchanging Knowledge; It can never be imagined to be insentient or non-intelligent. As the Upanishad declares, the Knower can never be imagined to be bereft of Knowledge. It is Pure Consciousness, which is Ātman in man and Brahman in the universe. The aim of Vedanta is to prove the reality of Ātman and Brahman, and their complete identity.

AJNĀNA, OR IGNORANCE

According to Vedanta philosophy, Brahman, which is One and without a second and is of the nature of Existence, Knowledge, and Bliss, is real and the only Substance; all material objects are unreal and unsubstantial; they are products of ignorance.

How is it that one takes the material universe and its objects to be real? How have unsubstantial names and forms come into existence? If Ultimate Reality is One, why do we see the relative world and its multiplicity? What is the relationship between the One and the many, the Absolute and the relative? These are the most puzzling questions of philosophy, and thinkers from time out of mind have proposed varying replies. Some believe in the creation of the universe by an external power called God, after the manner of the production of a pot by a potter or a piece of furniture by a carpenter. Some believe that God, or the power itself, has become the universe, and that the cause of the universe does not lie outside it. Again, according to some extreme Non-dualists like Gaudapada, there has never been any creation at all. Brahman alone exists and all that is perceived is Brahman. If a man says that he sees the universe of multiplicity, he is the victim of an illusion; for when Truth is known duality does not exist. If names and forms really existed, one should be able to connect them by some such relationship as cause and effect or substance and attribute. But Gaudapada, in his commentary on the *Mańḍukya Upaniṣad,* known as the *Kārika,* admirably refuted all the evidence of relationships and established the view that no real creation ever took place, everything that exists being in reality the non-dual Brahman. The manifold universe has no existence because it is not perceived when Knowledge is attained.

But according to Śankaracarya the universe of names and forms cannot be denied as a fact of everyday experience for people under the spell of ignorance. He is emphatic, however, that from the standpoint of Brahman, it is totally non-existent. The mirage is a fact for people who are victims of the illusion in a desert, even though no moisture inheres in the dry sands. A man sees in semi-darkness only a harmless rope, yet he may firmly believe that it is a snake and nothing else. The snake is real to him. The dream experiences are real to the dreamer. So, likewise, names and forms are real to those who are devoid of true Knowledge. Śankara does not, however, place these three experiences of the relative world, namely, illusions, dreams, and the waking state, in the same category. Waking experiences certainly possess more reality than the other two. But from the standpoint of the Absolute all three are equally unreal. Again, Śankara does not, like some Buddhist philosophers, uphold subjective idealism. He does not believe that the individual soul, or ego, creates the non-ego, or the universe. On account of cosmic illusion the ego and the non-ego come into existence and a fictitious relationship is established.

It must be understood that fundamentally there is no difference between the philosophical views of Gaudapada and Śankara. Gaudapada has written his philosophy from the standpoint of Brahman and has therefore declared the world to be non-existent; whereas Śankara discusses the universe from the standpoint of *māyā*, where it is seen to be real, and shows the way to the realization of Brahman. According to Śankara, a man cannot ignore the universe as long as he sees it; nor can he deny his relationships with other human beings or the various objects of the world as long as they appear to be real. And surely they are real to him if he is conscious of the reality of his own individual ego and of the universe around him. Therefore as long as a man sees multiplicity he must work, pray, worship, reap the results of his action, and experience happiness and unhappiness. In that state he cannot disregard the distinction between morality and immorality. The observance of moral law brings him reward, and the opposite, punishment. According to Śankara the validity of the scriptures, the usefulness of spiritual disciplines, and in short, all the injunctions of religion and morality, are based upon a recognition of the reality of the phenomenal world. From the standpoint of Brahman they are utterly meaningless.

How can the Absolute have become or have produced the relative? How can Ātman, which is nothing but Brahman, identify Itself with the perishable body, the senses, and the ego? With regard to these moot questions Śankara maintains an attitude of enlightened agnosticism. That is to say, he sees the logical impossibility of determining the precise relationship between Brahman and the relative universe for there cannot be any relationship between Reality and appearance. But the ignorant sees the manifold universe, Śankara calls this *māyā*. *Māyā* cannot be known. Even if known, it cannot be explained. In order to determine the relationship of the Absolute to the visible universe, the finite mind would have to know the infinite Absolute. And when the Absolute is known, the finite universe and the finite mind cease to exist. Therefore Śankara does not advance any explanation of creation.

The *Sāṁkhya* philosophers describe the universe as the modification of *Prakṛti*, or Nature. According to them the cause manifests itself as the effect. The effect, before it is produced, exists as the cause. According to another school of philosophers, which includes the Dualists and the Theists, the universe did not exist before it was created. The effect is non-existent before it is produced. Śankara, on the other hand, points out the utter impossibility of the finite mind's ever understanding the nature of the universe in terms of the causal relationship. He speaks of the universe as *māyā* because—as every thoughtful man knows, even while perceiving it with his senses—its nature is impermanence. When Śankara calls the universe *māyā*, he is only stating a fact, namely, the fact, that the One appears inexplicably as many. When a snake is beheld in place of a rope, the phenomenon may be described as *māyā*; this, however, does not imply any explanation of how or why the rope should thus appear. It states only a tangible fact. In the same sense, a mirage is *māyā*, dream objects are *māyā*, the creation is *māyā*.

Vedāntists use such terms as *avidyā*, *ajñāna*, and *Prakṛti* as practically synonymous with *māyā*. The word *māyā* generally signifies the cosmic illusion on account of which Brahman, or Pure Consciousness, appears as the Creator of the universe. Under the influence of *avidyā*, or nescience, Ātman, or pure Consciousness, appears as the *Jīvā*, or individualized self. *Ajñāna* is the ignorance which makes the Absolute appear as the relative or the One as the many. The word *Prakṛti* (matter or Nature) is used to denote *māyā* as the material out of which the universe has been created. But in actual practice these distinctions are not always maintained. The words are often interchanged.

THE MEANING OF MĀYĀ

The word *māyā*[15] was used in the Ṛg-Veda to denote a kind of magical power. There it is said that Indra, through the help of *māyā*, assumed different forms. In the Upanishads

15 It is often contended that the doctrine of *māyā* and the illusoriness of the relative world are in conflict with the affirmative and optimistic view of life described in the Upanishads, and that *māyā* is a later development of the Vedantic school created by Śankara. The Upanishads, no doubt, describe both the universe and the individual soul as manifestations of Brahman, Bliss Absolute, and thereby emphasize the affirmative view of the

the word acquires a philosophical significance. We read in the *S'vetāśvatara Upaniṣad:* "Know *Prakṛti,* or Nature, to be *māyā,* and the Great Lord to be the Master of *māyā*". Krishna says in the *Bhagavad-gītā*: "Verily, this divine *māyā* of Mine, consisting of the three *guṇas,* is hard to overcome. But those who take refuge in Me alone, shall cross over this *māyā*."

Śankara speaks of *māyā* as the Power of the Lord, beginningless, and compounded of the three *guṇas.*[16] Though intangible, it can be inferred from the effect it produces. Sadānanda says that *māyā* is "something positive, though intangible, which cannot be described as either *being* or *non-being,* and which is antagonistic to Knowledge".[17] Let us try to understand the meaning of these definitions.

Māyā cannot be described either as *being* or *non-being;* that is why *māyā* is said to be indefinable. If it were being,

universe. It is also true that the illusoriness of the sense-perceived universe is reiterated in Sankara's philosophy, and the method of negation is emphasized as leading to the realization of Brahman. But there is no conflict between the two views. *Māyā* is both explicit and implicit in the Upanishads. Sankara based his entire philosophy on these sacred scriptures. Furthermore, it is important to remember that the Upanishads contain the truths revealed to the *ṛśis.* These revelations are not presented in the form of a systematic philosophy. Sankara systematized the teachings of the Upanishads through his Non-dualistic Vedanta philosophy. With the aid of unimpeachable reasoning he established the sole reality of Brahman by refuting the arguments of the *Sāṁkhyās*, the Buddhists, and other thinkers. He established the reality of Brahman by proving the illusoriness of names and forms and the transiency of all things existing in time and space and governed by the law of causation. Hence *māyā* forms an important feature of his philosophy. Sankara does not aim at proving the existence or reality of *māyā*; his aim is to prove the reality of Brahman.

16 See discussion of the *guṇas* on p. 54 ff.

17 *Vedāntasāra,* 34.

in the true sense, then its effect, the tangible universe, would be perceived at all times. For being can never become non-being; the Real can never become unreal. But one does not behold the universe in *samādhi* or in communion with Brahman, neither in dreamless sleep. On the other hand, if *māyā* were non-being, a non-existent unreality, like the son of a barren woman, the manifold universe could not be seen. One could not see the world of names and forms as real. Therefore *māyā* is said to be "something positive". The word *something* here denotes its unsubstantiality or worthlessness, because, apart from Brahman, the world, its effect, is both unsubstantial and worthless. The word *positive* denotes its capability of producing the visible universe. It also serves the purpose of removing the erroneous notion that *māyā*, or ignorance, is pure negation because it is the absence of Knowledge. *Māya* is said to be "antagonistic to Knowledge" because both *māyā* and its effect, the material universe, disappear when one attains the Knowledge of Brahman. Brahman and *māyā* cannot co-exist any more than the Absolute and the relative, the One and the many. When one of these is perceived, the other is non-existent. They are not even correlatives. That is why the question often asked as to how the Absolute becomes the relative world is illogical and meaningless.

As long as one sees *māyā* or its effects, one may say that it belongs to Brahman, because nothing exists, ultimately. but Brahman. Thus *māyā* has been described by Vedantists as the inexplicable Power of the Supreme Lord, *Parameśa-śakti*, by which is produced the illusion of the creation, preservation, and dissolution of the universe. But from the standpoint of Brahman, which is all Light and Knowledge, there is no *māyā*. One identified with Brahman does not see even a trace of *māyā*. From the relative standpoint the true nature of Brahman seems to be obscured by an inscrutable power, which lies within Itself and brings into existence the panorama of the phenomenal universe. Thus is produced the illusion of ego and non-ego and their mutual relationship. The infinite Brahman appears as the individual soul endowed with ego, mind, senses, and a physical body. As the mind itself is a product of *māyā*, one cannot, through reasoning, know the cause of *māyā*. It is *māyā*, ignorance, that produces the illusion of *deśa*, *kāla*, and *nimitta*—time, space, and causality—which hides the true nature of Pure Consciousness and projects the multiple universe. Or according to a higher Vedantic concept, *māyā*, through its *nāma* and *rūpa*—names and forms—manifests the multiple objects of the relative world. Brahman, stamped, as it were, by names and forms, appears as the multiple objects.

THE THREE GUNAS

Māyā, or *Prakṛti*, is said to consist of the three *guṇas*, known as *sattva*, *rajas*, and *tamas*. The word *guṇa*, is usually translated into English as "quality", which does not give the precise meaning of the original. *Sattva*, *rajas*. and *tamas* are not qualities of *māyā* in the same sense that hardness is a quality of iron, or softness of butter, or heat of fire. The three *guṇas* are the ingredients of *māyā*; they may be compared to three strands which constitute the rope of *māyā*, the rope by which *māyā* binds man to the illusory world. *Māyā* has no existence independent of the *guṇas*. The three *guṇas* are present, in varying degrees, in all objects, gross or subtle, including the mind, the *buddhi*, and ego. The food which nourishes our body, the thought which is the function of the mind, the duty which elevates a man from the animal level, charity, worship, sacrifice—in short, everything belonging to the universe of *māyā*—contains these three *guṇas*.[18]

At the end of a world cycle, when names and forms go back to the state of non-manifestation or involution, the *guṇas* remain in a state of non-differentiation or equilibrium. This is called the seed state of the universe; it is described as the sleep of the Cosmic Soul. *Māyā*, in association with Brahman, or Pure Consciousness, at that time exists as the Cause, alone, without any of its manifestation. Suddenly this equilibrium is disturbed, by the will of the Lord, and the *guṇas* begin to assert their individual characteristics. Different objects, subtle and gross, come into existence. The tangible universe manifests itself step by step.

Rajas and *tamas* have opposing characteristics, while *sattva* strikes the balance between the two. The principal trait of *rajas* is energy, and from it has emanated the "primal flow of activity". Through its power the phenomenal universe alternates between evolution and involution, manifestation of names and forms and their recession into the seed state. The visible effect of *rajas*, in a human being for instance, is a ceaseless activity through which expression is given to ambition, lust, anger, avarice, arrogance, egotism, envy, pride, jealousy, and so forth. Under its influence a man becomes violently attached to the world. *Rajas* is the source of suffering.

Tamas is the veiling-power that hides the true nature of a thing and makes it appear as other than what it really is. The influence of *tamas* is seen, in man, in his ignorance, lassitude, dullness, inadvertence, and stupidity. When *tamas* predominates over *sattva* and *rajas*, he goes to sleep or remains inactive. It deprives a man of right judgement or definite

18 See *Bhagavad-gita* XVII.

belief and subjects him to doubt and uncertainty. After *tamas* has veiled the true nature of the Self, *rajas* exerts its projecting-power and creates the many fantasies that constitute an unenlightened man's practical life. And alas, even scholars well versed in philosophy cannot escape its hypnotic spell. It is the mother of delusion.

Sattva is the giver of happiness and is the real friend of man in his effort to realize Truth. It manifests itself, in man, as humility, guilelessness, self-control, unselfishness, purity, contentment, truthfulness, fearlessness, faith, devotion, yearning for Liberation, and other similar spiritual attributes. When *sattva* predominates, a man feels detached with respect to the world, lessens his physical activities, intensifies his contemplation, and strives in various ways to attain peace and blessedness. Through the cultivation of *sattva*, both *rajas* and *tamas* are kept under control.

The three *guṇas* always exist together. There cannot be pure *sattva*, without *rajas* and *tamas*; or pure *rajas*, without *sattva* and *tamas*; or pure *tamas*, without *sattva* and *rajas*. The difference between one being and another lies in the varying preponderances of the *guṇas*.

The three *guṇas*, it must not be forgotten, belong to *māyā*, *Prakṛti* or ignorance, which includes everything in Nature—inorganic, organic, or psychic. They are the characteristics of relativity. As long as a man is attached to any of them he is a phenomenal being and not a free soul. Even the gods and angels are under the influence of the *guṇas*. The gods or superhuman beings show a preponderance of *sattva*; men, of *rajas*; and sub-human beings of *tamas*. Brāhman, alone untouched by *māyā*, is beyond the *guṇas*. *Sattva* binds a man with attachment to happiness, *rajas* with attachment to activity, and *tamas* with attachment to delusion.

The three *guṇas* may be compared to three robbers who waylay a man in a forest. *Tamas*, one of the robbers, wants to destroy him; but at the persuasion of *rajas*, the second robber, he is bound hand and foot to a tree and relieved of all his treasures. After some time *sattva*, the third robber, returns, frees the man from his bondage, takes him gently out of the forest, and sets him on the highway leading to his house. Then *sattva* takes leave of him, because he too, being a robber, does not dare accompany the man out of the forest for fear of the police. *Tamas* wants to destroy a man; *rajas* binds him to the world and robs him of his spiritual treasures; *sattva* sets him on the path to Freedom. *Tamas* is to be overcome by *rajas*, and *rajas* by *sattva*. But finally *sattva*, too, is to be given up if the aspirant seeks total Freedom. Truth lies beyond the three *guṇas*.

MĀYĀ A STATEMENT OF FACT

Our daily practical life in the dual world is not possible without *māyā*. We all live, move, and think in *māyā*. Inexplicable in the extreme, *māyā* is described as "*aghaṭana ghaṭanā paṭiyasī*" —making the impossible possible. Under its spell even an Incarnation of God appears to forget his superhuman resplendence and behaves like an ordinary mortal. *Māyā* is responsible for the contradictions in our thinking and actions. Good is inevitably followed by evil, and yet we work to create only good, believing that it will ultimately eliminate evil in this relative world. We believe in the progressive evolution of the universe. This is *māyā*. The cause determines the effect; yet we seek to establish peace through war. This is *māyā*. A man robs his fellow men and then gives away his wealth in philanthropy, expecting eternal happiness hereafter. Attachment, without which no happiness is possible on earth, creates bondage and brings suffering to both lover and beloved. This is all *māyā.* Money creates leisure and builds up culture, and in the end emasculates a nation and brings about its ruin. The performance of duty elevates a man above the animals, and also obstructs his ultimate freedom. We want to conquer Nature through material resources, and in the end we only become slaves of matter. This is *māyā.* As long as we identify ourselves with the relative world, this *māyā* or contradiction broods over our every action and thought. There is no freedom in *māyā.* Freedom lies beyond. "Come unto me, all ye that labour and are heavy laden, and I will give you rest." Souls laden with the burden of relative experience, and weary with journeying hither and thither in the world of ignorance, discover that there is no ultimate happiness in *māyā*, in the desiring of desires or in their fulfilment. Then they see Brahman, the Lord of *māyā*, who is the Embodiment of freedom and Peace. The Lord says in the *Bhagavad-gitā*: "Those who take shelter in Me ultimately go beyond *māyā.*" The Light of Brahman destroys *māyā* as the light of the sun destroys the gloom of night.

It is often contended that the doctrine of *māyā*, which denies the reality of good and evil, is inconsistent with ethics; one can take shelter under *māyā* and trample under foot all moral values. This is a distortion of the concept of *māyā.* As long as a man remains under the spell of *māyā*, good and evil are real to him. As long as one sees a distinction between good and evil, one must shun the evil and follow the good. Śankara admits the reality of the relative world during the state of ignorance, and stresses the fact that in that state both good and evil should be treated as real. Therefore ethical laws must be obeyed. They form the foundation of the Vedantic discipline. Only by pursuing the good and shunning evil one can ultimately go beyond the illusion of the pairs of opposites. Likewise, social service, worship, prayer, and the performance of various duties in the world are not in conflict with man's longing to rid himself of *māyā* and attain Freedom.

THE TWO POWERS OF MĀYĀ

Though *māyā* is indescribable and indefinable, yet its existence can be inferred from its effects, such as the projection or manifestation (*Sṛṣṭi*), the preservation (*sthiti*), and the dissolution (*laya*), of the universe. *Māyā* carries on this work through two powers, known as the power of concealment (*āvaraṇaśakti*) and the power of projection (*vikṣepaśakti*). The former obscures the knowledge of the observer; it conceals, as it were, the true nature of Brahman. Though in itself insignificant and unsubstantial, yet, through an inscrutable power, it hides Existence-Knowledge-Bliss Absolute, as a patch of cloud, which is nothing but water-vapour and no bigger than a man's hand, conceals the effulgent solar disc, which is a million times larger than the earth itself. As the sun, in spite of this concealment, retains its brilliance intact, so also the Self, or Brahman, in spite of Its concealment by *māyā*, retains in full Its nature of Pure Consciousness.

PROJECTION-POWER AND VEILING-POWER

When the true nature of Brahman is hidden by the power of *māyā* there arises the condition of individuation and relative existence; just as when the real nature of a rope is concealed by darkness, there arises the possibility of its being mistaken for a snake or a stick or a fissure in the earth. When the true nature of Ātman becomes concealed by *māyā*, conditions are created for Its appearance as a *jīva*, or finite creature, endowed with the notion of being a doer or agent and the experiencer of pleasure and pain, love and hatred, and the other pairs of opposites; just as when a man's consciousness is obscured by the concealing-power of sleep, there arises the condition in which he sees the fantasies of dreams and takes them to be real.

The concealing-power and the projecting-power of *māyā* function almost simultaneously. Ignorance, which conceals the real nature of the rope, by the very power inherent in it creates the illusion of a snake or stick. The projecting-power of *māyā* creates the entire universe (*Brahmāṇḍa*) and all the objects dwelling therein.

Therefore Brahman, in association with *māyā*, may be called the Projector or Manifester of the universe. But this projection is only an appearance; it is not real. As has been stated above, Brahman, or the Absolute, cannot participate in an act of creation. When one sees the dual universe and seeks its cause, one finds it in Brahman associated with *māyā*. Non-dualists differ with dualists and pantheists, as the latter take the creation to be real. According to the Non-dualists the universe is falsely super-imposed on Brahman through *māyā*; and the superimposition cannot affect the real nature of Brahman.

Māyā is without beginning; that is to say, a man under the spell of *māyā* cannot know its beginning, just as a sleeper, while experiencing a dream, cannot know its beginning. As has already been stated, the very concepts of time, space, and causality, the pillars of the relative world, belong to *māyā*.

TWO MODES OF MĀYĀ

Māyā appears to us in two different modes, or aspects, depending upon our way of looking at it. They are called the collective or cosmic (*samaṣṭi*) aspect and the individual (*vyaṣṭi*) aspect. From the collective standpoint *māyā* is one; but from the individual standpoint it is many. Vedantic philosophers give the following illustrations to explain the two modes of *māyā*. One can look at a number of trees from the collective standpoint and describe them as a wood; one can also regard a wood from the standpoint of the trees and describe it as a number of trees. Or, from the collective standpoint one may describe a body of water as a sea or a lake, and from the individual standpoint one may describe a sea or a lake as quantities of water. In a like manner Vedantists speak of the collective or cosmic aggregate *māyā* and of individual *māyā*.

UPĀDHI

Māyā, both in its cosmic and in its individual aspect, hides the true nature of Brahman. Thus the Infinite and Eternal Absolute appears as a finite being, limited by time and space. In association with the cosmic *māyā*, as we shall see presently, Brahman appears as Īśvara, or the Personal God, and in association with the individual *māyā*, as the *jiva*, or individual soul. Thus *māyā* becomes the *upādhi*, or limiting adjunct, of Brahman. An *upādhi* seems to alter or limit the true nature of an object. The formless sky appears to possess sharp lines when viewed through jagged peaks or sky-scrapers. But this limitation is only apparent, not real. It is the association with the *upādhis* of various material bodies that makes Brahman appear as gods, angels, men, animals, birds, trees, and stones. As Bosanquet remarked, when the Absolute falls into water, It becomes a fish. The water acts as an *upādhi*. But it must not be forgotten that the *upādhi* does not bring about any real change in Brahman. When the *upādhi* is discarded, the object regarded as finite by the ignorant is realized as Brahman.

ĪŚVARA

Brahman associated with the *upādhi* of collective ignorance is designated by Vedantists as Īśvara or *Saguṇa* Brahman, who corresponds roughly to the Personal God of various religions. According to Non-dualistic Vedanta the Personal God is one step lower than Brahman, though He is the highest symbol or manifestation of Brahman in the relative world. Īśvara is endowed with such qualities as omniscience, omnipresence, universal lordship, and unlimited power. Brahman cannot be described by any specific attribute. It is Īśvara, and not Pure Brahman, who in His different aspects, is called the Creator, Preserver, and Destroyer of the universe. Īśvara, or *Saguṇa* Brahman, with the help of *sattva*, creates; with the help of *rajas*, preserves; and with the help of *tamas*, destroys. He is the Inner Controller of the universe. The light of Īśvara that illumines the cosmic ignorance is the Light of Brahman. From the standpoint of Pure Brahman there is no creation; hence none of the attributes ascribed to Īśvara applies to Brahman. As gold without dross cannot be used for ornaments, so pure Brahman, without the dross of *māyā*, cannot create the universe. Īśvara is, as it were, a corruption or deterioration of Brahman.

THE JĪVA

Brahman, or Pure Consciousness, associated with individual ignorance, is called the *jīva*, or individual living soul. The *jīva* dwells in a body. The consciousness of the *jiva*, which is derived from Pure Consciousness, of Brahman, illumines like a lamp the individual ignorance. That is why the mind, the buddhi, the ego, and the senses, which are products of ignorance and material in nature, appear to be

MICROCOSM AND MACROCOSM

The individual maya associated with the *jiva* is not in essence different from the collective or cosmic maya associated with Īśvara. The macrocosm and the microcosm are in reality one. There is no real difference between a wood and the trees that constitute it. There is no real difference between the sea and the quantities of water that form it. The difference lies in the mode of observing them. Likewise, consciousness associated with Īśvara is in reality the same as consciousness associated with the *jīva*. It is all one and the same consciousness. Ā*kāśa* (space or sky) limited by a wood is in reality the same as akasa limited by a tree. Ā*kāśa* reflected in a lake is in reality the same as *ākaśa* reflected in a drop of water. The difference lies in the mode of looking at them.

TURĪYA

But there is another Ā*kāśa*, of which the *ākāśa* limited by the *upādhis* of the wood and the trees, or reflected in the lake and a drop of water, is only a part. That Ā*kāśa* is infinite, eternal and untouched by any limitations. The Ā*kāśa* limited by the *upādhis* cannot exist without the infinite Ā*kāśa*. Likewise, there is an infinite Consciousness, of which the consciousness limited by the collective *māyā*, namely, Ī*śvara*, and the consciousness limited by the individual *māyā*, namely, the *jīva*, are only parts or aspects. This Infinite or Pure Consciousness is eternal and untouched by any limitation of the phenomenal world. The consciousness limited by the *upādhis* of the collective and the individual maya cannot exist without the Infinite Consciousness. This Infinite Consciousness is called *Turīya*, the Fourth. It is Brahman, or Transcendental Consciousness, inexpressible in words and incomprehensible to thought. The unrelated

Substratum of the collective and the individual ignorance and also of Īśvara and *jīva*, It is Ultimate Reality, which Vedanta describes only by its well-known negative method of "*neti, neti*," "not this, not this".

The *Māṇḍūkya Upaniṣad* speaks of *Turīya* in the following manner:

"*Turīya* is not that which is conscious of the inner (subjective) world, nor that which is conscious of the outer (objective) world, nor that which is a mass of consciousness, nor that which is a simple consciousness, nor that which is unconsciousness. It is unperceived (by any sense-organ), incomprehensible (to the mind), unrelated (to any object), uninferable, unthinkable, and indescribable; It is essentially of the nature of Consciousness, constituting the Self alone, and is the negation of all phenomena. It is Peace, Bliss, and the One without a second. This is known as *Turīya*, the Fourth. This is Atman and It has to be realized."[19]

Though the word *Turīya* means, literally, "fourth", yet it has no numerical significance. It is the Absolute. It is called the Fourth in relation to the three states of consciousness, namely, waking, dreaming, and dreamless sleep, which belong to *māyā* and are absent in Brahman. *Turīya* is the unrelated Witness of the three states.

The great Sankara thus invokes *Turīya* at the commencement of his commentary on the *Maṇḍūkya Upaniṣad:*

"I bow to that Brahman, which, after having enjoyed (during the waking state) all gross objects by pervading the entire universe with the omnipresent rays of Its immutable Consciousness, embracing the entire variety of movable and immovable objects; which, again, after having digested, as it were—that is to say, experienced within (in the dream

19 *Mandukya Upanishad* 7.

state)—all the variety of objects produced by desires and brought into existence by the mind, enjoys bliss in deep sleep and makes us experience that bliss through *māyā*; which, further is designated, in terms of *māyā*, as the Fourth (*Turīya*), and which is supreme, immortal, and changeless.

"May that *Turīya*, which, having identified Itself (through *māyā*) with the entire universe, experiences (in the waking state) the manifold gross objects of enjoyment, through ignorance and attachment; which, again, during the dream state, experiences, being illumined by Its own light, the subtle objects of enjoyment, objects that are brought into existence by Its own internal organ; and which, lastly, in dreamless sleep, withdraws all objects (subtle as well as gross) into Itself, and thus becomes free from all distinctions and differences, may that *Turīya*, which is ever devoid of attributes, protect us."

Turīya, or Pure Consciousness, is Ātman, the true Self of man and all living beings. Its nature is Truth (*satyam*,) Knowledge (*jñānam*), and Infinity (*anantam*); Good (*śivam*) and Beauty (*sundaram*); Peace (*śāntam*) and Non-duality (*advitīyam*). It is the indestructible and unchanging Essence in man. It is the immutable Ground of the illusory experiences of waking, dreaming, and deep sleep, as the desert is the changeless ground of the illusion of the mirage, and the rope, of the illusory snake. As waves and bubbles, associated with names and forms, are seen to float on the immeasurable, serene, and homogeneous waters of the ocean, so likewise, the experiences of the three states are seen to subsist in *Turīya*. As, when the illusory names and forms are discarded, the mirage is realized as the desert, the snake as the rope, and the waves and bubbles as the ocean, so likewise, when the names and forms are discarded, every experience is regarded as *Turīya*. or Pure Consciousness. *Turīya* alone is the Reality behind all experiences, the Reality behind the universe. It is the universe in its true essence. As the unmoving and unrelated screen gives connexion and continuity to the disjoined pictures in a cinema, so the attributeless, changeless, and witness-like *Turīya* gives connexion and continuity to the disjoined experiences of the ego, in what we call our phenomenal life. Life is not possible without the substratum of *Turīya,* which is the Reality pervading the universe.

THE THEORY OF THE CYCLE

The Hindu philosophers do not believe in the absolute creation of the world out of nothing at a particular point of time. They speak of the manifestation of the universe, called the beginning of a cycle, and of its non-manifestation which is the termination of the cycle. During the state of manifestation, sometimes poetically described in the Vedas as the "breathing-out" of the *Puruṣa,* or Cosmic Person, names and forms evolve; during the state of non-manifestation, or "breathing-in" of the Cosmic Person, the names and forms go back into the seed, or unmanifested state. At the beginning of each cycle, when names and forms become visible, all the beings of the previous cycle who had not attained Liberation come into existence once again with their desires and latent tendencies. The names and forms repeat themselves in every cycle. The Vedas teach the indestructibility of matter and the conservation of energy. Individual souls attain perfection, but the material forms in which they dwell remain.

COSMOLOGY

The Vedantic cosmology indicates the keen power of observation of the early Indo-Aryans. Their discussion of the subject may appear crude, as far as details are concerned, from the standpoint of modern physical science; yet in principle it is not in conflict with rational thinking. The cosmology of modern science undergoes important changes every now and then. Any interpretation of the relative universe is liable to change; for it depends upon the viewpoint or mode of observation of the interpreter. Thus, solid atoms give place to indefinable electrons. The Ptolemaic interpretation of the universe is modified by the Copernican interpretation, and the Newtonian physics by Einstein's theory of relativity. According to Vedanta all these interpretations are true from their particular standpoints. But in connexion with the Vedantic cosmology it should always be borne in mind that its purpose is not to explain the universe and its origin, but to establish, through it, the ultimate reality of Brahman. Apart from Brahman the universe is unimportant, whether from the standpoint of reality or from the standpoint of value. It is found to be non-existent in the deepest spiritual experience. Its value is transitory. But the reality of Brahman, which exists independent of creation, is self-evident and is revealed in the innermost experience of man. To realize Brahman is infinitely more important to Vedantic philosophers than to analyse the nature of the universe. The interpretation or description of the phenomenal world must not be in conflict with the reality of Brahman. The knowledge of the world must lead to the Knowledge of Brahman; otherwise it is without significance. The real purpose of the Vedantic cosmology is to help the student realize Brahman, and not just to explain the universe of names and forms. Liberation, or Peace, is attained through the Knowledge of Brahman, not through knowledge of the universe.

EFFICIENT AND MATERIAL CAUSE

Vyāsa, the author of the *Vedānta Sūtrās,* describes Brahman as the cause of the creation, preservation, and dissolution of the universe, because Its existence can be inferred through these actions. But as neither action nor attribute can be truly associated with Brahman, or the Absolute, the Vedāntists speak of the *Saguṇa* Brahman as the cause of the universe. No creation is possible without *māyā*. Brahman, through association with *māyā*, as stated before, appears to be endowed with such activities as creation, preservation, and dissolution, and with such attributes as omniscience, omnipresence, and lordship, and becomes known as the *Saguṇa* Brahman. Since *māyā* has no existence independent of Brahman, the *Saguṇa* Brahman and the *Nirguṇa* Brahman (Pure Consciousness) are, in reality, one and the same substance.

Brahman uses *māyā* as the material of creation; that is to say, It creates the universe and its various objects out of *māyā*. Therefore from the standpoint of *māyā*, Brahman is the material cause of the universe. But, as pure Consciousness, It is the efficient cause. Thus Brahman Itself is both the material and the efficient cause of the universe. It is the ultimate Cause. Vedāntist teachers explain this causal relationship by the illustration of the spider and its web. When the spider wants to weave a web, it uses the silk which belongs to it and without which it cannot weave. Therefore the spider, as a conscious entity, is the efficient cause of the web, and from the standpoint of the silk, the material cause. No outside material is needed in the creation of the universe. When, sometimes, *māyā* is described as the cause of the universe, the term "cause" is used to denote the material of creation. Also it must be understood that *māyā* has no existence independent of Brahman. When, at other times, Brahman, or Pure Consciousness, is described as the cause, the term really means the Substratum or unrelated Ground of the universe. No causal relationship, in the usual sense of the term, can exist between Pure Brahman or the Absolute, and the universe of names and forms.

Unlike the *Sāṁkhya* philosophers or the dualists[20] the Non-dualists do not explain the universe through the causal relationship. They hold that Brahman, while creating, preserving, or destroying the universe, does not undergo any change. It remains as Pure Being, or Sat. All changes seen in the sense-perceived world are *māyā.* The creation is a mere appearance. That is to say, Brahman appears, through *māyā*, as the universe with all its living and non-living beings, from the lifeless atom to Īśvara, the exalted Cosmic Soul.

It has already been stated that the three *guṇās,* namely *sattva, rajas,* and *tamas,* constitute *Prakṛti,* and that when there is an equilibrium of the *guṇās,* the universe remains in a state of non-manifestation or dissolution. When that equilibrium is disturbed, on account of the preponderance of one *guṇa* or another, there takes place the creation, or projection, of the material universe.

SUBTLE ELEMENTS

The first element to evolve is *ākāśa,* which is usually translated as "ether", "space" or "sky". The creation, or evolution, of *ākāśa* really means that Brahman, associated with *māyā,* appears as *ākāśa.* It is a well-known fact that the physical world is characterized by grossness, heaviness, and inertness. Hence the Vedantists conclude that at the time of the evolution of *ākāśa,* which is the material out of which the subsequent elements are created, *Prakṛti* has a preponderance of *tamas,* whose chief characteristics are inertness, heaviness and grossness. *Ākaśa* is the intangible material substance that pervades the whole universe.

20 See p. 50.

From *ākāśa* evolves air (*vāyu*); that is to say, Brahman, associated with *māyā*, appearing as *ākāśa*, further appears as air. From air evolves fire (*agni*); from fire, water (*ap*); from water, earth (*pṛthivi*). The principle of illusory superimposition (*vivarta*) must be applied in the evolution of each element, that is to say, Brahman associated with *māyā* appears as each of the five elements, and during the process of evolution there takes place no change in Brahman. As *ākāśa* is prior to air, at the time of evolution, it is figuratively called the cause of the latter. *Sattva*, *rajas*, and *tamas*, which constitute *Pṛakrti* are transmitted, at the time of creation, to the five elements, in accordance with the law that the attributes of the cause determine those of the effect.

The five elements thus evolved are subtle, rudimentary, and unmixed. They are called subtle (*sūkśma*) because at the time of evolution they are unable to participate in any action; rudimentary (*tanmātra*) because each, at that time, possesses its own trait alone; and unmixed (*apaṇcīkrta*) because they are not yet mixed with one another. Out of these subtle elements are produced the subtle bodies and the gross elements. From the gross elements, as will afterwards be seen, is produced the gross universe.

From the standpoint of sense-perception there are only five elementary objects in the universe, namely, sound, touch, form, taste, and smell. That is why Vedānta speaks of five elements only. The unique characteristic of subtle *ākāśa* is sound; of subtle air, touch; of subtle fire, form; of subtle water, taste; and of subtle earth, smell. These traits cannot be grasped by the senses.

SUBTLE BODIES

Out of the subtle elements are formed the subtle bodies of living creatures. The subtle body, which accompanies the soul after death, consists of seventeen parts, namely, the five organs of perception, the five organs of action, the five *prāṇas,* or vital forces, the *manas* (mind), and the *buddhi* (intellect).

The five organs of perception—those of hearing, touching, seeing, tasting, and smelling—are produced, respectively, from the *sattva* elements of *ākāsa,* air, fire, water, and earth. By an organ is meant not the outer instrument, but something subtle, made of finer matter, which functions through the physical instrument. Thus, the organ of seeing does not mean the outer eyes, but an organ made of intangible, finer matter, which is one of the constituents of the subtle body.

The mind, or *manas*, is that function of the inner organ (*antaḥkaraṇa*) which considers the *pros* and *cons* of a situation. The *buddhi,* the intellect or determinative faculty, is a second function of the same organ, by which doubt is resolved and one comes to a conclusion regarding the real nature of an object. There are two other functions of the inner organ, namely, the *citta,* which seeks for pleasurable objects and *ahaṁkāra,* or I-consciousness, which identifies the Self with the body. Sometimes these functions are loosely described as the *manas,* or mind. According to Vedanta the mind is material in nature, because it is produced from the five material elements. *Prakṛti,* or primordial matter, includes everything—inorganic, organic, and psychic. Brahman, or Consciousness, which is self-luminous, is utterly different from it. The five organs of perception and the inner organ are said to be composed of the *sattva* particles of the five elements because they are endowed with luminosity, that is to say, they are capable of illumining or expressing an object. But it must be remembered that this luminosity of *manas*, *buddhi*, *citta,* and *ahaṁkāra* is derived from the self-luminous Ātman, they themselves being material and therefore non-luminous by nature.

THE JĪVA, OR LIVING SOUL

The *buddhi*, or the determinative faculty, together with the five organs of perception, constitutes a unit called the *vijñānmayakośa*, or sheath abounding in intelligence.[21] Pure Consciousness, limited by the *upādhi* of this sheath, appears as a phenomenal being or individualized soul, called the *jīva*. On account of this limitation, the *jīva* forgets its true nature of infinity and blessedness and feels that it is an agent or doer, as enjoyer or experiencer of happiness and misery. Bound by the law of *karma* and subject to transmigration, it assumes a higher or lower body on this earth or on another plane.

It may be stated here that there are two other Vedantic theories regarding the *jīva*. According to one of these, Pure Consciousness appears to be *reflected in* and not *limited by* the *vijñānamayakośa*. The reflection is the *jīva*. A reflection, assumes the characteristics of the medium in which an object is reflected. Thus the reflection of the sun in water appears to be still or moving according to the condition of the water. Likewise, Consciousness reflected in the *vijñānamayakośa* becomes endowed with the characteristics of *buddhi*. According to the third theory, the *jīvā* is like a being seen in a dream. Brahman, or Pure Consciousness, under the influence of *māyā,* dreams, as it were, that It has become a man, an animal, or an inanimate object.

All three theories regarding the nature of the *jīva*, stated above, agree that Brahman appears as a *jīva* on account of *māyā*. The *jīvahood* of the Infinite Ātman is due to the

21 For the important topic of the five sheaths, see pp. 85-90.

upādhi of the *vijṇāmayakośa*; it is apparent and not real. The characteristics of birth and death, disease and decay, happiness and unhappiness, ascribed to the *jīva*, are unreal, from the standpoint of Brahman. The individual soul, after the attainment of Knowledge, realizes that it is the same as Brahman.

The mind (*manas*) and the organs of perception together constitute a unit known as the *manomayakośa* or sheath of the mind. The Self, or Atman, identified with it, assumes the characteristics of the mind and experiences a diversity of names and forms.

The organs of action are the tongue (the organ of speech), the hands, the feet and the organs of evacuation and generation. They are produced from the *rajasic* part of the five subtle elements. The vital force is collectively known as *prāṇa*. It is the primal energy or force, of which all other forces such as gravitation, attraction, repulsion, and the life-breath, are different manifestations. As, at the time of cosmic dissolution, the five elements of matter resolve back into *ākāśa*, so likewise, all forces go back to *prāna*. In the state of involution or non-manifestation, *ākāśa* and *prāṇa* remain in an undifferentiated state, merged in *Prākṛti*. At the time of the next evolution, *prāṇa*, acting upon *ākāśa* manifests, step by step, the different elements and the gross and subtle objects. *Prāṇā* manifesting itself in the individual *jīva*, is called by five names according to its different functions.[22]

The five *praṇās*, together with the five organs of action, constitute a unit known as the *prāṇāmayakośa*, or sheath of the vital force. When the soul is identified with this sheath, it manifests its active nature, because the sheath itself is made of the *rajasic* part of the five subtle elements.

22 See Note on *prāṇa* under sloka 12. Atmabodha.

Intelligence or knowledge, will and activity are the characteristics of the *jīva*, or living being. The *vijṇānamayakośa*, or sheath of intelligence, is endowed with the power of knowledge. The *manomayakośa*, or sheath of the mind, is endowed with the will through which an action is performed. But action is not possible without the vital force, which is the characteristic of the *prāṇamayakośa*. Atman, or Pure Consciousness, limited by the *upādhis* of these three sheaths, is endowed with knowledge, will, and activity. This division is made according to the respective characteristics of the sheaths. These three sheaths together constitute the subtle body, which after death, accompanies the soul in its transmigration.

As in the case of *māyā*, or ignorance, the subtle body may also be viewed either collectively or individually. The collective subtle body, which includes all subtle bodies, is like a wood. The individual subtle bodies are like individual trees that constitute the wood. Consciousness associated with the collective subtle body is called by such epithets as *Hiraṇyagarbha,* Sūtrātmā, and *Praṇā.* All these Sanskrit terms have special meanings, though their general significance may be expressed by the term "Cosmic Soul".[23] The Cosmic Soul is immanent in the universe. It identifies Itself with the five subtle elements and is endowed with the powers of knowledge, will, and activity. The collective subtle body, which consists of the *vijṇānamayakośa, manomayakośa,* and *prāṇamayakośa*, and through which the Cosmic Soul functions, is finer than the gross universe. It is like our dream state.

23 *Sūtrātmā* is That which pervades the universe, like the thread running through the flowers in a garland. *Hiraṇyagarbha,* or th Golden Egg, is the first manifestation of Brahman, in which the future living beings remain in seed form. *Prāṇa* is That which is endowed with the power of activity. Other epithets of the Cosmic Soul are *Prajāpati* and Brahma.

As the waking state merges in the dream state, so, likewise, the gross universe, at the time of involution, merges in the collective subtle body.

Consciousness limited by the individual subtle body is known as taijasa, or the effulgent soul, on account of its being associated with the effulgent inner organ.[24] The individual subtle body, which also consists of three *kośās*, like the collective subtle body, and through which the individual soul functions, is finer than the individual gross body. It corresponds to the dream state, which consists of the impressions of the waking state. At the time of dreaming, the gross body remains in active and the subtle body functions.

The collective subtle body is, in essence, identical with the individual subtle bodies which constitute it, the difference being in the mode of observing them. Likewise, the consciousness associated with the *upādhi* of the collective subtle body, known as the Cosmic Soul, is, in essence, identical with the consciousness associated with the *upādhi* of the individual subtle body, known as the individual soul. The illustration of the wood and the trees, and the *ākāṣa* associated with them, has already been given. All through the relative universe the microcosm and the macrocosm run parallel to each other, whether in respect to gross and subtle object or to the consciousness associated with them. According to Vedanta philosophy the microcosm and the macrocosm are, in essence, identical.

GROSS ELEMENTS

Unlike the subtle elements, the gross elements are compounds. They are produced by combinations of the subtle

24 The inner organ is called effulgent because its experiences consist of ideas, as opposed to gross objects, which are experienced by the organs of perception.

elements in certain proportions. There are five gross elements: ether, air, fire, water, and earth. Each gross element consists of one half portion of its subtle counterpart and one eighth of each of the four remaining subtle elements. Gross *ākāśa*, or ether, for example, consists of one half portion of subtle *ākāśa* and one eighth each of subtle air, fire, water, and earth. Though the one gross element thus contains all five of the subtle, yet its name is derived from the preponderance of its particular counterpart. The attributes of the subtle elements are imperceptible to the senses. They become tangible in the gross elements. Gross ether is endowed with the attribute of sound; gross air, with sound and touch; gross fire, with sound, touch, and form; gross water, with sound, touch, form and taste; and gross earth, with sound, touch, form, taste, and smell. As stated before, the special attributes of air, fire, water, and earth are, respectively, touch, form, taste, and smell. The five elements are, as it were, the bricks of the tangible physical universe.

THE GROSS UNIVERSE

Hindu tradition enumerates fourteen worlds which constitute the universe. Both heaven and hell are included in these. Naturally, the enjoyments of the higher worlds are of a refined nature and those of the nether worlds are gross; nevertheless, all the denizens of the universe are in the realm of *māyā*, and therefore not free. The seven upper worlds are known as *Bhūḥ*, *Bhuvaḥ*, *Swaḥ*, *Mahaḥ*, *Janaḥ*, *Tapaḥ*, and *Satyam;* and the seven nether worlds are *Atala, Vitala*, *Sutala*, *Rasātala*, *Talātala*, *Mahātala*, and *Pātāla*.

The world known as *Bhūḥ* or *Pṛthvi* is this earth on which men dwell. *Swaḥ*, or *Svarga*, is a celestial world where people, after death, enjoy material happiness as a reward for their meritorious action on earth. *Bhuvaḥ* is the intermediary region between these two. *Janaḥ*, *Tapaḥ*, and *Satyam* constitute *Brahmalōka,* or the plane of Brahma, of which Brahma is the controlling deity. It may be said to correspond to the highest heaven of the dualistic religions, where fortunate souls repair after death and enjoy spiritual communion with the Personal God. According to Non-dualistic Vedanta even the inhabitants of this region are not liberated souls. They, too, keep a little trace of *māyā* with *sattva* predominating. At the end of the cycle they merge in the Supreme Brahman and attain Liberation, though a very few return to earth from *Brahmalōka.* The plane of *Mahaḥ* is an intermediary region between *Brahmalōka* and the three other worlds, namely, *Bhūḥ*, *Bhuvaḥ*, and *Swaḥ*.

The seven nether worlds, of which *Pātāla* is the lowest, are regions where wicked souls sojourn after death to reap the results of their unrighteous actions on earth. They too, in due course, are born on earth and take up the thread of spiritual evolution. According to Vedanta no soul can be deprived of ultimate Liberation, which is the birth-right of all.

Besides these fourteen world systems, the five gross elements produce the four kinds of gross bodies dwelling therein and the food and drink appropriate to them. The gross bodies are those that are born of the womb, belonging to men and various animals; those that are born of eggs, belonging to birds and reptiles; those that are born of moisture, belonging to lice and mosquitoes; and those that are born of earth, belonging to trees and creepers. The body that a *jīva* assumes on earth is determined by its past *karma.*

The gross bodies also, in their fourfold variety, may be regarded, like the subtle bodies, collectively or individually. They may be regarded as a whole, like a wood, or as separate entities, like the trees in a wood. Consciousness limited or conditioned by the *upādhi* of the aggregate of gross bodies is called *Virāt* or *Vaiśvānara;* it regards all the gross bodies of the universe as its own body. The body belonging to *Virāt,* through which it functions, is called the *annamayakośa* the gross physical sheath, on account of its being a modification of food. It functions in the waking state and experiences gross objects.

Consciousness limited by the individual gross body—any one of the individual gross bodies belonging to the four classes enumerated above—is called *viśva.* Though it functions through the gross body, yet it does not dissociate itself completely from the subtle body or the mind, which is endowed with the power of thinking and imagining.[25] The gross body belonging to *viśva,* through which it functions, is also called the *annamayakośa.* the gross physical sheath or alimentary sheath, on account of its being a product of food.[26] It functions in the waking state and it experiences, through the organs of perception, objects of sound, touch, form, taste, and smell. It uses the five organs of action for the purpose of speaking, holding, walking, excreting, and procreating. Further, through the inner organ of the mind, it experiences uncertainty, determination, egoism, and remembrance. What is true of *viśva* is also true of *Vaiśvānara*, or Consciousness functioning through the collective gross body in the waking state.

25 The *jīva* or embodied soul, is limited by three kinds of *upādhis* In dreamless sleep it is limited by the *upādhi* of the causal body; in the dream state, by that of the subtle body; and in the waking state, by the *upādhi* of both the gross and the subtle body. Consciousness, as it identifies itself with each of these *upādhis,* is technically known as *prājña, taijasa* and *viśva.*

26 The gross body is created by the sperma and ovum of the parents, which are products of food. After birth the body is sustained by food.

The gross body (including the sense-organs), whether collective or individual, is inert. It is without any consciousness and cannot function by itself. So Vedantists state that different forms of consciousness use the sense-organs as their instruments, control them, and enable them to experience their respective objects. These are but different aspects of Universal Consciousness limited by their respective *upādhis*. Vedantists call them the *devatās*, "shining ones", or the controlling deities. Further, as the macrocosm and the microcosm show the same pattern, the identical deity controls the sense-organs and its counterpart in the universe. Thus, for instance, the sun is the controlling deity or consciousness of the eyes; that is to say, the consciousness that controls the sun is the same as that which controls the eyes. Similarly, *Agni* (Fire) is the controlling deity of the tongue; Indra, of the hands. It seems that the purpose of these thought-patterns is to enable a man to stretch his consciousness so that he may identify himself with the universe and the Consciousness behind it.

The collective gross body and the individual gross body are in essence identical, like a wood and the trees that constitute it. So, likewise are the two forms of consciousness which are limited by them, known as *Vaisvānara* and *viśva*, like the space limited by the wood and the trees.

The sum total of the gross, subtle, and causal world forms a higher aggregate which may be designated as the Vast Universe, just as the sum total of various woods, each consisting of many individual trees, constitutes a vast wood, or the sum total of various bodies of water of many dimensions constitutes a vast lake region. It is one and the same Consciousness that is associated with the *upādhis* of the Vast Universe and the gross, subtle, and causal worlds, as it is one and the same *ākāsa* that is limited by the vast wood and the number of small woods that constitute it. The direct import of the great Vedic dictum "All this is verily Brahman" is the consciousness, associated with the Vast Universe together with, *Turīya* which is the basic and unrelated Consciousness, when these are not differentiated from each other. But *Turīya* Itself, without the consciousness associated with the Vast Universe, is the implied meaning of this Vedic text. This is explained by the illustration of a red-hot iron ball. When such a ball is said to burn an object, the direct meaning of the word *ball* is the iron permeated by fire. But it is really the fire that burns; therefore the implied meaning of the word is fire. The Vedic dictum "All this is verily Brahman" really implies *Turīya*, or Pure Consciousness, without any *upādhi* whatsoever. Therefore when a Non-dualist says that the universe is Brahman, he does not mean, like a pantheist, that Brahman has become the universe with its names and forms. He means that the universe is, in reality, *Turīya* or Pure Consciousness. In the same way Īśvara, that is to say, Brahman associated with the *upādhi* of cosmic *māyā*, together with its substratum, *Turīya*, is the direct meaning of *That* in the Vedic dictum "That thou art"; but its implied meaning is *Turīya* alone. It is only as Pure Consciousness, as will be seen later on, that *That* is identical with thou, or Īśvara with *Jīva*.[27]

SUMMARY OF THE COSMOLOGY

To sum up the cosmology given above; Vedanta philosophy regards the material universe from two standpoints: cosmic or collective and individual or discrete. These divisions may also be described as macrocosmic and microcosmic. Each is again subdivided into three parts: causal, subtle,

27 See p. 92 ff.

and gross. Consciousness limited by the upadhi of maya may likewise be regarded from two different standpoints: cosmic or collective and individual or discrete. Each of these, again may be classified into three parts: causal, subtle and gross. The macrocosm is in essence the same as the microcosm. The cosmos and the individual are made of the same stuff and show the same pattern. Thus it is one Consciousness that appears to be limited by the cosmic as well as by the individual unit, in three different aspects, namely, causal, subtle, and gross. Likewise, it is the one universe alone through which Consciousness functions in Its cosmic and individual forms and in Its causal, subtle, and gross aspects. The subtle is finer than the gross; and the causal, finer than the subtle. Therefore the reflection of Consciousness in the subtle is purer than the reflection of Consciousness in the gross. And the reflection of Consciousness in the causal is purer than the reflection of Consciousness in the subtle; it is closest to Pure Consciousness.

The daily activities of an unillumined person are carried out on the gross physical plane. His experiences are confined mostly to gross physical objects. What he considers to be his soul is Pure Consciousness limited by the *upādhis* of the gross body and the mind. It experiences, through organs of perception, objects of sound, touch, form, taste, and smell. Through the organs of actions it carries on the activities of speaking, holding, walking, and so on. Through the inner organ of the mind it experiences doubt, determination, memory, I-consciousness, and so on. These constitute the daily practical life of the average man in his waking state, and he doubts the reality of anything else beyond. As long as he identifies himself with the outer world he cannot perceive any subtler world. In his daily practical life a man deals only with shadows.

ERRONEOUS IDEAS ABOUT THE SELF

Ignorant men identify the Self with external things, such as their children, house, and wealth. When these are injured or lost they feel that they themselves are injured or lost. Some, who are thorough materialists, consider the body to be the Self and cherish the erroneous notion that the Self is endowed with such characteristics as youth and old age, birth and death. Other materialists consider the sense-organs to be the Self and cherish the erroneous notion that It is blind or deaf. There are, again, others who consider the prana or the mind to be the Self, and believe that the Self is hungry or thirsty, or that the Self is full of doubts and desires. Some Buddhists[28] confuse Ātman with Its reflection in the buddhi, which, as has been stated above, is merely the individualized ego or the doer. The nihilists[29] describe the Self as non-existence and argue that, while searching for the reality of the Self, they see nothing but the pale ivory of the void. But according to the Vedantic seers all these notions of the Self belong really to the category of the non-Self. They are mere objects, like a pot or a cloth, illumined or manifested by Ātman, or Pure Consciousness. Even he who describes Ātman as void or non-existence needs Consciousness to perceive the void. The very Consciousness by which the soul is denied is Ātman. Therefore Vedanta emphatically states that the Self, or Ātman, is Consciousness, which is by nature pure, eternal, and blissful and which is the Witness and Illuminer of all illusory entities, from the external object to the internal ego or the void.

28 These are the Buddhist idealists belonging to the school of Yogacara, according to whom the stream of ideas (*vijnana*) alone is real, and everything else is non-existent.

29 Refers to the Madhyamika school of Buddhism, which maintains that everything is void.

THE FIVE KOSAS

Vedanta analyses the non-Self into five *kośas*, or sheaths, namely the gross physical sheath (*annamayakośa*), the sheath of *prāṇa* or the vital force (*prāṇamayakośa*), the sheath of the mind (*mānomayakośa*), the sheath of the *buddhi* or intelligence (*vijñānamayakośa*), and the sheath of bliss (*ānandamayakośa*). They are called sheaths because, like sheaths, they conceal Ātman. They are figuratively described as one inside the other, the physical sheath being the outermost and the sheath of bliss the innermost. The real meaning is that one sheath is finer than another. As a finer entity permeates a grosser one, so the finer sheath permeates the grosser sheath. Thus, when it is said that the sheath of the vital force is inside the gross physical sheath, it really means that the former is finer than the latter and therefore permeates it. Ātman is the finest substance. It is detached from the sheaths and permeates them all. The effulgence of Ātman shines through all the sheaths, though in varying degrees according to their density. Thus, the sheath of intelligence manifests more of the luminosity of Ātman than the sheath of the mind.

Through ignorance, a man identifies Ātman with one or more of the *kośa*, or sheaths. As this ignorance is stubborn, persistent, and hard to overcome, Vedantic philosophers take considerable pains to describe their illusory nature and exhort the aspirants to negate them. Only when that is done, that is to say, when one cultivates total detachment toward them through discrimination, is the true nature of Ātman revealed.

The annamayakośa, or physical body: This sheath, which constitutes the gross physical body, is produced by the combination of the gross elements and consists of flesh, bones, blood, and other ingredients. Dependent upon food for its existence, it lives as long as it can assimilate food. It is not seen prior to birth or after death; its existence is transitory and its virtues are ephemeral. It is changeable by nature. Therefore the body cannot be the Self. The ignorant identify themselves with the body; the book-learned, with the combination of the body, the mind, and the Self; while the calm man of discrimination regards the Self as distinct from body, mind, and ego. As long as a man does not give up this mistaken identification with the body, he cannot expereince the bliss of Freedom, be he ever so erudite in philosophy or science. The body can be a help to the soul if it is regarded as an instrument, just as a house is a help to its indweller, or a horse to its rider.

The prāṇamayakośa, or sheath of prāṇa, the vital force: This sheath is finer than the gross physical sheath and impels the latter to action. A modification of the vital force, it consists of the five *prāṇas*, enters the body after conception, leaves it at the hour of death, and produces the feelings of hunger and thirst. An insentient and limited object, the sheath of *prāṇa* cannot be Ātman, the omnipresent and all-seeing Witness.

The manomayakośa, or sheath of the mind: This is finer than the sheath of *prāṇa*. The Self identified with the mind feels the diversity of "I" and "you", and also experiences the differences of the names and forms in the outer world. The seed-bed of desires, good and bad, the mind impels the senses to activity for their fulfilment. The phenomenal world has no existence outside the mind, which is a product of ignorance. The mind agitated by desires becomes aware of sense-objects, gross and fine, enjoys them, and also becomes attached to them. The mind alone is responsible for the illusory differences of caste and social position, as also of the notions of action, means, and end. Stained by passion, greed, and lust, it creates bondage, and freed of them, it shows the way to Liberation and Blessedness. The purification of the mind, through the practice of discrimination and dispassion, is the goal of spiritual discipline. In the opinion of Vedantic seers, the mental sheath cannot be Ātman, because it is endowed with a beginning and an end, is subject to change, and is characterized by pain and pleasure. It belongs to the category of the object.

The vijñānamayakośa, or buddhi, the sheath of intelligence: *Buddhi*, the determinative faculty, is, like the mind, a function of the inner organ and therefore a product of *Prakṛti*, or matter. Though insentient by nature, it appears intelligent and conscious because it reflects *Cit* or Pure Intelligence. This reflection of Pure Consciousness in *buddhi* is called the jiva, or individualized soul, whose chief characteristic is I-consciousness. Subject to the law of *karma*, it assumes different bodies, determined by the desires of previous births, and performs good and evil actions. Ātman, identifying Itself with the sheath of intelligence, experiences misery and happiness in the waking and dream states and their absence in dreamless sleep. It is through ignorance that the *upādhi* of *jīvahood* is superimposed on Ātman, the Pure Self; and that is why Ātman appears to be a doer or enjoyer in the relative world.

It may be contended that the superimposition on account of which the Supreme Self appears as the *jīva*, through delusion or otherwise, is without beginning, and hence cannot have an end. Therefore the individuality of the soul, also must have no end. It must go on forever. How, then, can there be Liberation for the soul? In answer the Vedantic philosopher says that the *jīvahood*, or individualization, of Ātman is not real, but is conjured up by ignorance. The unattached, formless, and actionless Ātman cannot be related to the objective world except through delusion. Since the very notion of *jīvahood* is due to delusion, it ceases to exist when the delusion is destroyed by the true Knowledge of the Self. Because of ignorance a rope appears to be a snake; and it continues to be perceived as such so long as the ignorance lasts. But when the true nature of the rope is seen, the idea of the snake disappears. *Avidya* or nescience, and its effects, such as time, space, and causality, are beginningless for those who are subject to it. But when ignorance is destroyed by Right Knowledge all such notions as the *jīva-hood* of Ātman and Its birth and death cease to exist, just as the dream ego functioning in sleep vanishes when the dreamer awakes. Ātman, the only existent Reality, cannot have any connexion with the *buddhi* and thus become a *jīva*, for the *buddhi* does not exist from the standpoint of Ātman. There cannot be any real connexion between Ātman and the sheath of the buddhi, just as there cannot be any point of contact between the desert and the water seen in a mirage. The false superimposition which accounts for the individuality of the *jīva* can be directly destroyed only through the Knowledge of Brahman and not by any other means such as ritualistic worship, study of scripture, or philanthropic activities. This unitive Knowledge—attained through discrimination between the Real and the unreal and relinquishment of the unreal—enables the bound soul to attain Liberation.

The ānandamayakośa, or sheath of bliss: Finer than the sheath of intelligence is the subtle sheath of bliss. This bliss, however, must not be confused with the Supreme Bliss of Brahman. A modification of nescience, or *Prakṛti*, it manifests itself by catching a reflection of the ever blissful Ātman. The chief features of this sheath are pleasure and rest—the pleasure that is experienced when one comes in contact with an agreeable object. The righteous man feels it in a small measure and without the least effort at the time of the fruition of his virtuous deeds. But the fullest manifestation of the sheath of bliss is experienced in deep sleep, when one remains totally unconscious of suffering of any kind. After waking from deep sleep a man remarks that he has slept happily. A partial manifestation is known in the waking state when the senses come in contact with pleasant objects, or in the dream state due to pleasant memory-impressions. The sheath of bliss, though close to Ātman, cannot be Ātman Itself, as it is a product of ignorance; which fact can be known from the experience of unconsciousness in dreamless sleep. Further, this sheath, like the other sheaths, is endowed with changing attributes. But Ātman is omnipresent and self-existent.

The five sheaths are all modifications of *Prakṛti*, or primordial matter. They do not possess absolute reality. Whatever reality they are perceived to possess is due to Ātman's being their Substratum. It must also be remembered that the sheaths are not real coverings of the infinite Ātman. They only appear to be so when the true Knowledge of the Self is forgotten. The Light of Ātman shines in varying measure through the different sheaths, according to their composition. The true glory of Ātman, unobstructed by any sheath, is fully realized by the aspirant when, through discrimination and detachment, self-control and meditation, he no longer identifies himself with the sheaths or with any other modification of *māyā*, such as the sense-organs, the mind, the buddhi, or the ego, but is completely absorbed in the Self. Untouched by the five sheaths, Witness of the three states. Ātman is the unchanging and unsullied Reality, knowledge of which enables one to break the bondage of the relative world and attain Supreme Blessedness.

It may be contended that, after the negation of the five sheaths and the mind and ego as unreal, one finds nothing but a void, the utter absence of everything. What entity then remains with which the illumined soul may realize its identity? In answer it is said by the Vedantist that only after such negation can a man realize Ātman, which is devoid of attributes, is of the nature of Pure Consciousness, and is the Witness of the various modifications of *Prakṛti* seen in the waking and the dream state, such as the mind, the body, and the senses, and also of their absence in profound sleep or in *samādhi*. It may be called "contentless Consciousness", in which both subject and object merge and disappear. It cannot be the void, for one emerging from the experience of Self-Knowledge shows a richer and enchanced personality. Ātman, or Brahman, is according to Vedanta, the real essence of man. After the realization of this all-pervading Consciousness, a man discovers his true Self, just as, after entering the ocean, a river, discarding name and form, finds its real source and ultimate goal.

When the five sheaths are negated, the body, the mind, the *buddhi*, and the other modifications of ignorance and the different reflections of the Self in them, are also negated. And when all these illusory objects disappear, there shines the real Ātman, eternal, omnipresent, and all-powerful, realizing which within himself a man becomes free from sin, fear, grief, taint, and death and becomes the embodiment of Bliss.

APAVĀDA

So far we have dealt with *adhyāropa*, or the superimposition of the unreal upon the Real. Now will be described its refutation or negation, known as *apavāda*, about which Vedanta says: "As a snake perceived in a rope is ultimately found to be nothing but the rope, similarly the world of unreal things, beginning with ignorance, superimposed upon Reality is realized in the end to be nothing but Brahman".[30]

It has already been pointed out that the universe is neither the creation of an external agent nor the modification of its cause. It is a false superimposition (*vivarta*) on Brahman. The cause, namely, Brahman, appears as the effect, the universe, without Itself undergoing any change whatsoever, just as the rope appears as a snake without itself undergoing any change. The effect, being an appearance, is in reality the same as the cause. The *Chandogya Upaniṣad* says that though a jar is a modification of clay, it is in reality non-different from clay. The name given to the jar is only an expression for use in daily practical life. The Vedas state: "All that exists is verily Brahman", "By Brahman alone is everything permeated", "Whatever an ignorant man perceives—maya and all its effects—is really Brahman, and nothing but Brahman", "Whatever is manifested, namely the universe, is the Supreme Brahman Itself, the Real, the One without a second, the Pure, the Essence of Knowledge, the Taintless, the Beginningless, the Actionless, the Essence of Bliss Absolute". In Brahman there exists no differentiation of knower, knowledge, and object of knowledge.

According to the Non-dualists the true nature of Brahman is realized through *apavāda*, the method of negation. It is not the reality of the universe that is negated, which, being Brahman, always exists. What is really negated is the illusory notion of the ignorant that the universe of name and form is real in itself, independent of Brahman.

30 *Vedantasara*, by Sadananda, I, iii, 7.

Since the effect is in reality the cause, the aspirant realizes, through the method of negation, that the gross physical universe consisting of different planes, the various physical bodies, and the different kinds of food and drink suitable for living beings, are in essence nothing but their cause, namely, the five gross elements. The five gross elements, together with such objects as sound and form, and the subtle bodies, are nothing but their cause, namely, the unmixed subtle elements. The five unmixed elements are in essence nothing but their cause, namely, Saguna Brahman, consciousness associated with ignorance, or *māyā.* Cosmic ignorance and the consciousness associated with it are nothing but the transcendental Brahman, or Pure Consciousness. The Brahman is the uncaused Great Cause, the Divine Ground of everything that is perceived, and is identical with all.

"THAT THOU ART"

There are four great Vedic statements through the contemplation of which the mind is led from the world of names and forms to Brahman. They are as follows: "That thou art" (*Tattvamasi*), "I am Brahman" (*Ahaṁ Brahmāsmi*) "This Self is Brahman" (*Ayamātmā Brahma*), "Brahman is Consciousness" (*Prajñānam Brahma*). All of these statements point to the same fact, namely, the ultimate and essential oneness of man, or the individual soul, and God, or the Universal Soul, the reality behind them both being Brahman, or Pure Consciousness. We shall now try to understand the meaning of "That thou art".

The word *That,* in the Vedic statement "That thou art", has two meanings: a direct and an implied. The illustration of a red-hot iron ball has already been given.[31] Iron associated

31 See p. 82.

with fire is the direct agent of burning, but fire unassociated with the iron is the implied, though real, agent. Likewise, collective ignorance (including the cosmic gross and subtle bodies) and the consciousness[32] associated with it, together with Pure Consciousness unassociated with any limiting adjunct, when regarded as one inseparable unit, like the red-hot iron ball, form the direct meaning of the word *That*. In other words, *That* directly conveys the idea of a Personal God associated with the universe as its Creator, Preserver, and Destroyer, and endowed with omniscience, lordship, great power, and similar attributes, together with Pure Consciousness, which underlies both the universe and God. That is to say, the direct meaning of *That* is *Saguṇa* Brahman, or Brahman with attributes. But Pure Consciousness, unassociated with any limiting *māyā*, is the implied meaning of *That*.

Likewise, the word *thou* has two meanings: a direct and an implied. Individual ignorance (including the individual subtle and gross bodies) and the consciousness[33] associated with it together with Pure Consciousness, unassociated with any limiting adjunct, when regarded as one inseparable unit, become the direct meaning of the word *thou*. In other words, *thou* directly conveys the idea of the *jīva*, or individualized soul, associated with an individual body and endowed with little knowledge, little power, dependence, and other similar traits, together with Pure Consciousness, which underlies all this. That is to say, the word signifies a living soul characterized by such limitations as birth and death, hunger and thirst, pain and pleasure. But Pure Consciousness, which is unassociated with any limiting *māyā*, which is

32 Known as Īśvara, or the Personal God.

33 Known as *prajna*, *taijasa*, and *visva*, associated with the individual causal, subtle, and gross bodies respectively.

of the nature of Inmost Bliss, and which also is the substratum of the *jīva*, is the implied meaning of *thou*.

The meaning conveyed by the word *art*, in "That thou art", is the identity of *That* and *thou*.

When the direct meaning of a word in a statement does not agree with actual experience, one interprets it in terms of its implied meaning.[34] It is obvious that *That* and *thou* endowed with contradictory attributes, cannot be identical from the standpoint of the direct meaning of the words, that is to say, in a literal sense. The one, that is to say, the Personal God, differs from the other, the individual soul, as the sun from a glow-worm, the ocean from a well, or Mount Everest from a mustard-seed. But their identity is a fact, realized through the direct and immediate experience of the Vedāntic seers. This identity is explained, therefore, from the standpoint of implied meaning. Vedāntic philosophers reason, as stated above, that the contrasting attributes which distinguish Īśvara from the *jīva* are not ultimately real but are due to superimposition. It is through *māyā* that Brahman, Pure Consciousness, appears to have become the universe and its omnipotent Creator, Preserver, and Destroyer. Through *māyā*, again, the same Brahman appears to have become a limited *jīva*, or individualized soul, possessed of a physical body. The superimpositions are all illusory; their substratum alone is real. It is Brahman that is the substratum of both Īśvara and *jīva*. When, through the Vedāntic discipline of negation, one eliminates the false superimpositions, one realizes by direct experience that the ultimate Reality is Brahman, Pure Consciousness, and not Īśvara or *jīva*.

34 Such a method of interpretation would be followed, for example, in the case of the English sentence, "He spent the night on a *sleepless pillow*".

There are different methods by which the implied meaning of a statement is obtained. The method used by the non-dualistic philosopher consists in the elimination of the conflicting aspects of the two major words and the retention of that which is common to both. To give an illustration: On seeing a man named Devadatta after a long time, one exclaims, "*This is that* Devadatta". Now obviously the Devadatta seen some time ago and at another place, denoted by *that,* cannot be the one seen here and now, denoted by *this.* There is a conflict regarding both time and place. But still there is the fact of recognition; and this is possible because the conflicting elements, namely, the time and place, are disregarded and attention is focused on the man himself. Likewise, in interpreting the sentence "That thou art", the wise man gives up the contradictory elements associated with *That* and *thou,* namely, the notions of Creator and creature, and recognizes their oneness from the standpoint of Brahman, Absolute or Pure Consciousness, which is the essence of both.

The realization of the precise meaning of "That thou art" is a transcendental experience felt only on the spiritual plane. The meaning is lost if the aspirant has the slightest attachment to such material things as body, senses, mind, or ego, or to the pleasure associated with them. The Freedom, Peace, Blessedness, Knowledge, and Immortality which result from the transcendental experience are totally different from their counterparts on the physical plane of time, space, and causality. Through the realization of the ultimate identity of *thou* and *That* one knows the true meaning of religion, which is the realization of the eternal oneness of the eternal God and the eternal Soul. Religion, in its ultimate sense, has nothing to do with devising means to enhance man's material happiness in this transitory world.

Vedantic teachers explain to their pupils the real nature of the Self through the "method of the tenth" (*daśamanyāya*). The following story is told in Vedāntic books: Once ten men forded a swift-flowing river. None of them could swim. Reaching the other side, they wanted to know if they had all safely arrived; so one of them counted the number of men and found only nine—because he had omitted himself. He was sure that one man was drowned. The others did the same thing and came to the same conclusion, because each of them counted all except himself. So they began to bewail the loss of one of their comrades. Another man, passing by, inquired about the cause of their weeping. He was told that while the ten friends were crossing the river, one had been drowned. Of course it took no time for the stranger to detect their mistake. So he asked one of them to count again. The man counted nine and said. "You see, we have lost our tenth friend". Immediately the stranger touched him on the chest and said, "Thou art the tenth". In order to reassure all, he repeated the same thing with each of them; and thus each found out that he was the tenth. So their anguish disappeared and their happiness was restored. Likewise, the disciple comes to the teacher and tells him that he has searched for Truth everywhere—in books, in temples, in images, in heaven—and has not found it. Of course, he has not sought the Truth in the right place, that is to say, in his own self. So the teacher touches him and says, emphatically, "That thou art"

After explaining the meaning of the great Vedic statement "That thou art", the guru exhorts the aspirant to meditate on his real essence:

"That which is beyond caste and creed, family and lineage, which is devoid of name and form, merit and demerit; That which transcends space, time, and sense-objects—that Brahman art thou. Meditate on this in thy mind.

"That Supreme Brahman, which cannot be comprehended by speech, but is accessible to the eye of pure illumination; which is stainless, the Embodiment of Knowledge, the Beginningless Entity—that Brahman art thou. Meditate on this in thy mind.

"That which is untouched by the sixfold wave[35] meditated upon by the yogis in their hearts, but never grasped by any sense-organ; which the *buddhi* cannot know—that unimpeachable Brahman art thou. Meditate on this in thy mind.

"That which is the Ground of the universe and its various parts, which are all creations of *māyā*; which Itself has no other support; which is distinct from the gross and the subtle; which is partless and peerless—that Brahman art thou. Meditate on this in thy mind.

"That which is free from birth and growth, development and decline, disease and death; which is indestructible; which is the cause of the projection, maintenance, and dissolution of the universe—that Brahman art thou. Meditate on this in thy mind.

"That which, though One only, is the cause of the many; which refutes all other causes and is Itself without a cause; distinct from *māyā* and its effect, the universe, and ever free—that Brahman art thou. Meditate on this in thy mind.

"That which is free from duality; which is infinite and indestructible; which is supreme, eternal, and undying; which is taintless—that Brahman art thou. Meditate on this in thy mind.

"That Reality which, though One, appears manifold owing to ignorance, taking on names and forms, attributes and changes, Itself always unchanged, like gold in its

35 Namely, decay and death, hunger and thirst, grief and delusion, which overtake the body and mind.

modifications—that Brahman art thou. Meditate on this in thy mind.

"That, beyond which there is nothing; which shines above *māyā*, and is infinitely greater than the universe; the Inmost Self of all; the One without a second; the true Self; Existence-Knowledge-Bliss Absolute; infinite and immutable—that Brahman art thou. Meditate on this in thy mind."[36]

After hearing these exalted words of the teacher, the aspirant reflects on their meaning. As he realizes, through reason, that the words of the guru are true, he contemplates Brahman with single-minded devotion. Thus he gradually rids himself of all superimpositions, on account of which he had formerly identified himself with transitory objects and cherished the notions of "I" and "mine". He relinquishes the observance of social formalities, the beautifying of the body, and over-engrossment in the scriptures, these being the three strong chains by which a man is bound to the world. He becomes purified by incessant contemplation of Brahman and inhales the fragrance of the Pure Self, which lay covered by the impurities of endless desires. The more the mind is established in the Inner Self, the more it gives up the desire for outer objects. And when all such desires have been totally eliminated, there takes place the uninterrupted realization of Ātman. The discipline of negation must be practised without intermission as long as even a dreamlike perception of the universe and the finite soul remains, and as long as identification with the body is not totally wiped out. Neither sleep nor concern about secular matters nor attachment to sense-objects should be given the slightest opportunity to let one forget the nature of the real Self.

36 *Vivekacudamani*, Sankara, 254-263.

EGO AND DESIRES

The Seeker after Truth must always remember the detached nature of the Self and give up all identification with the ego. It is the ego that brings the Self back again and again to the world of ignorance. It is the ego that aggravates desires. When desires increase, activities also increase. And when there is an increase of activities there is an increase of desires. Thus desires and activities move in a vicious circle and man's imprisonment in the body is never at an end. The destruction of desires has been described as Liberation, and the man free from desires is called a *jīvanmukta*, one liberated in life.

Even after the Truth has been known, there often remains the strong, beginningless, and stubborn notion that one is the doer of action and the experiencer of its results. This notion has to be carefully removed by living in a state of constant communion with the Self. Only thus may one experience the bliss of Liberation even though living in a body. The seeker must not be inadvertent about his steadfastness to Self-Knowledge. Inadvertence is death. Inadvertence, delusion, egoism, bondage, and suffering are the successive links in the chain of worldly life. If the mind ever so slightly strays from the Inner Self and moves into the outer world, it goes down and down, just as a ball carelessly dropped from the top of a staircase bounces from step to step and does not stop until it reaches the bottom. The Truth of the Self is extremely subtle and cannot be reached by a distracted mind. It is realized only by noble souls of pure mind, and even by them only through extraordinary concentration.

"I AM BRAHMAN"

The disciple learns from the teacher the precise meaning of "That thou art". Rejecting the attributes erroneously superimposed on *That* and on *thou,* he understands that the formula refers to the absolute oneness of the individual self and Brahman, or the Supreme Self, experienced on the plane of Pure Consciousness. As he meditates on this oneness, there arises in his mind a state (*vṛtti*) which makes him feel that he is Brahman, pure by nature, eternal, self-illumined, free, infinite, supremely blissful, and One without a second. This mental state, illumined by the reflection of Pure Consciousness, destroys his ignorance and doubts regarding Brahman. Yet even now Brahman is only a state or wave of the mind. As the ignorance is destroyed, its effects, the various mental states, are destroyed too, just as, when a cloth is burnt, the warp and woof are burnt. Hence the mental state coloured by Brahman, which forms part of those effects, is also destroyed. When the mental state is destroyed, there remains only the consciousness reflected in that state, which, unable to illumine the Supreme and Self-effulgent Brahman, becomes overpowered by it. Further, on the destruction of this mental state, the reflection reverts back to the Supreme Brahman, just as the image of a face in a mirror reverts back to the face itself when the mirror is broken or removed. Thus the Subject and the object, Pure Consciousness and the perceiving consciousness, become one. When the duality is removed, there remains only the Supreme Brahman, One without a second. Utterly indescribable in words, this experience is known only to him who has attained it.

THE THREE STEPS

In order that the Knowledge of Brahman may be realized directly and clearly, "like a fruit on the palm of one's hand", and not merely understood intellectually, Vedānta prescribes certain disciplines, known as "hearing" (*śravaṇam*), "reflecting" (*mananam*), "meditating" (*nididhyāsanam*), and "absorption in Brahman" (*samādhi*). "Hearing" means listening to the instruction of a qualified teacher, who explains from the scriptures the oneness of the Individual self and Brahman. "Reflecting" means thinking constantly of Brahman thus taught, and strengthening one's conviction regarding Its reality by means of suitable reasoning. In this way the aspirant's wrong notions and contrary notions regarding the Self are removed. "Meditating" means the constant dwelling of the mind on a stream of ideas identical with the notion of the non-dual Brahman, to the exclusion of such foreign ideas as body, senses, mind, and ego. Meditation, practised uninterruptedly for a long time with intense love for the ideal and with unflagging determination for its realization, leads to *samādhi*, or absorption in Brahman.

THE PRACTICE OF YOGA

The seers of the Upanishads laid down for aspirants endowed with the fourfold Vedāntic disciplines[37] the three steps which lead to the realization of Brahman, mentioned in the preceding paragraph. Later Vedāntic teachers recommend the Yoga system of Patañjali as a practical discipline for the attainment of *samādhi*, in which the Knowledge of Brahman is realized. But it will be noticed that there is not much difference between the Vedāntic disciplines and the Yogic disciplines, the latter being the scientific systematization of the spiritual disciplines prevalent at the time of Patañjali.

The word *yoga* signifies the union of individual soul and Universal Soul and also the practical methods which bring about such union. Patañjali describes the following

37 See pp. 35-37.

eight disciplines necessary for the aspirant after Self-Knowledge.[38]

Yama, or general discipline: This consists of non-injury, truthfulness, non-stealing, continence, and non-acceptance of gifts. Non-injury means not harming anyone by thought, word, or deed, as far as possible. Truthfulness means a perfect concord between thought, wcrd and deed. Acceptance of gifts creates obligations and disturbs the serenity of the mind. The foundation of spiritual life lies in the practice of chastity in word, thought, and action. Continence endows the body, nerves, and mind with the requisite power for fine spiritual perception.

Niyama or particular discipline: This consists of cleanliness, contentment, austerity, study of scripture, and meditation on God. Cleanliness is purity of both body and mind. Contentment is satisfaction with material needs which one obtains without much effort. Study also includes repetition of the sacred word *Om* or the name of the Lord. Meditation includes worship and other devotional exercises.

Āsana, or posture: This consists in placing the arms, legs, and other parts of the body in particular positions and holding the body erect. It is conducive to physical relaxation and inner peace. The aspirant is recommended to assume any posture, with the body erect, in which he feels at ease.

Prāṇāyāma, or control of the vital force: This consists of exhaltion, inhalation, and retention of breath, according to the instructions of the Yoga scriptures, and is to be practised under a qualified teacher. It helps the aspirant to bring both body and mind under control.

Pratyāhāra or self-withdrawal: This is the detachment of the sense-organs from their respective objects.

38 *Raja-Yoga*, by Swami Vivekananda, is recommended for a full study of the subject.

Dhāraṇā, or concentration: The aim of this discipline is to enable the aspirant to fix his mind, after it has become detached from sense-objects, on Brahman, the One without a second.

Dhyāna, or meditation: This is the intermittent resting of the mind on Brahman. At this stage the aspirant does not develop the power of intense and uninterrupted meditation.

Samādhi, or absorption: This is the complete absorption of the mind in Brahman.

Anyone desiring to attain *Samādhi* should live in a retired place. Solitude is helpful for the control of the senses. When the senses are controlled, the mind is controlled. When the mind is controlled the ego is controlled. The control of the ego is followed by an unbroken realization of the Bliss of Brahman. The aspirant must cultivate extreme dispassion for all external objects and detachment toward the body, senses and mind. If he is attached to any one of these, he is bound to it. The thought of the non-Self is evil and productive of misery. Meditation on the Self, Bliss Absolute, is conducive to Liberation.

SAMĀDHI

Samādhi has been described by Non-dualistic Vedāntic seers as of two kinds, depending upon the intensity and the nature of the concentration. They are known respectively as the *savikalpa* and the *nirvikalpa*. In the *savikalpa samādhi* the mental state (*vṛtti*) takes the form of Brahman and rests on It but at the same time retains the distinctions of knower, knowledge, and object of knowledge. The aspirant may still be aware of the relative, though he clearly sees it to be permeated by the Absolute. It is like seeing a clay elephant and also the clay that permeates the elephant. The aspirant still retains I-consciousness, and he says, "I am Brahman, intelligence Absolute, formless as the ether, supreme, eternally luminous, birthless, immutable, unattached, all-pervading ever free, and the One without a second."

But in the *nirvikalpa samādhi*, absorption bereft of I-consciousness, the mind totally merges in Brahman, becomes one with It, and loses all distinction of knower, knowledge, and object of knowledge. Just as a lump of salt, when dissolved in water, is no longer perceived to be distinct from the water and cannot be separated from the water, so, likewise, the mental state, in the *nirvikalpa samādhi*, taking the form of Brahman, is no longer perceived to be distinct from Brahman and cannot be separated from Brahman; it has no existence apart from Brahman. Then Brahman, or the Self, alone exists and shines by Its own radiance. Though the existence of the mind is not felt in dreamless sleep either, yet these two states, namely, the *nirvikalpa samādhi* and dreamless sleep, are totally dissimilar. In dreamless sleep the mind ceases to function, having merged in its cause, *avidyā* or ignorance. It is swallowed, as it were, by the veiling, power of *avidyā*. But in the *nirvikalpa samādhi* the mental state, though not perceived, takes the form of Brahman and exists as Brahman. A man in deep sleep is not aware of any object. Further, after arising from deep sleep he manifests his former characteristics: a thief continues to be a thief, a fool continues to be a fool, a wicked man continues to be a wicked man. But in the *nirvikalpa samādhi*, on account of the mind's taking the form of Brahman, one becomes omniscient. After the experience of this blessed state a person becomes a new being, completely transformed into Brahman.

THE PRACTICE OF MEDITATION[39]

There are two kinds of meditation, namely, the objective and the subjective. In the objective meditation the Ideal is regarded as outside, and in the subjective meditation, inside, the meditator. The objective meditation is, again, of two kinds, according as the Ideal is associated with or conditioned by a sound-symbol (*śabdānuviddha*) or by a form-symbol (*dṛṣyānuviddha*). The meditation associated with a sound-symbol consists in repeating such formulas as "*Om Sacchidanandam Brahma*" or "*Om Sacchidekam Brahma*". The former means " Brahman is Absolute Existence, Absolute Knowledge, and Absolute Bliss". The latter means "Brahman is reality, Consciousness, and the One without a second". As the aspirant repeats the sacred formula he reflects on its meaning. That Brahman is Absolute Reality or Existence does not mean that It exists or is real in the sense that a phenomenal object exists or is real. It is Existence Itself and Reality Itself. It is the essence of Existence, unconditioned by time, space, and perceived causality. The phenomenal world and all things in it are perceived to exist because Brahman, as Reality and Existence, permeates them. They cannot exist apart from Brahman. But Brahman exists even when names and forms disappear, as in the case of *samādhi* or of deep sleep. Likewise, Brahman is Absolute Knowledge or Consciousness. It is not that Brahman knows; Brahman is the essence of Knowledge—Knowledge Itself. All knowledge is possible in the relative world because Brahman, as Consciousness, is the very essence of the knower,

39 The method of meditation described in this section is one of the many recommended by Non-dualistic Vedanta. The meditation pescribed by Dualistic Vedantic teachings may also in the long run lead to the realization of Brahman.

or subject. That Brahman is One means that Brahman is non-dual. It is not one in the sense that the sun is one or the moon is one; for there is also a perceiver of the sun and moon. The idea of one, in the relative world is the correlative of the idea of two and denotes duality. That is why all descriptions of the Absolute comprehended by the intellect really belong to duality. The Oneness of Brahman, on the other hand, means the complete identity of subject and object, an indescribable experience characterized neither by one nor two. Lastly, Brahman is Bliss. Blessedness is not Its attribute but the very stuff of which It is made. The knower of Brahman does not enjoy this Bliss as an object. He becomes one with It. This Blessedness is indistinguishable from Existence, Consciousness, and Oneness. It is not of the nature of the bliss produced by the contact of the sense-organs with their objects. Even the highest bliss of this kind, namely, the bliss experienced in heaven, is only a reflection of the Bliss of Brahman in the mirror of relativity.

In the objective meditation associated with or conditioned by a form-symbol, the aspirant meditates on some external object or form that seems to him closest to Brahman. Every object is a combination of the Absolute and the relative, It contains the characteristics both of Brahman and of the world. In everything one finds not only Existence (*Sat*), Cognizability or knowledge (*Cit*), and Attraction or Bliss (*Ānanda*), which are the different aspects of Brahman, but also a name (*nāma*) and a form (*rūpa*), which are the traits of the phenomenal world created by *avidyā* and therefore illusory. While meditating on a form-symbol, the aspirant should gradually withdraw his mind from the unreal name and form and concentrate on Brahman, which is present in the symbol as Existence-Knowledge-Bliss Absolute. In and through the object he should see Brahman, as one sees the ocean in and through the waves.

The objective meditation has its *savikalpa* and its *nirvikalpa* aspects. In the former the aspirant is conscious of the object of meditation, namely, Brahman associated with a sound or form. But as the meditation deepens he attains to the *nirvikalpa* state, when the entire phenomenal world disappears in Brahman and the aspirant becomes one with it.

In the subjective meditation the Ideal is placed within oneself. Vedāntic seers speak of the heart as an extremely suitable place. For the beginner the heart is the physical organ, shaped like a lotus-bud. Inside there is a subtle, luminous space which is often described as the Brahmapura, the Abode of Brahman. As he makes progress in meditation and becomes capable of subtle perceptions, he realizes that the heart denotes not really the physical organ but the *buddhi*, the determinative faculty, which is the most refined part of the mind and in which one sees best the reflection of Brahman. Thus Brahman is often described in the Upanishad as residing in the "cave of the *buddhi*". At this stage the meditation is raised from the physical to the psychic level. The devotee casts the Absolute, as it were, in the mould of his mind and fashions out of it a mental image of Brahman. Finally he transcends both the heart and the mind and realizes Brahman, the All pervading Consciousness, in his inmost consciousness. The image in the heart and the reflection in the *buddhi* become one with Universal Consciousness. Perhaps the Christian mystics referred to this when they spoke of "deep calling unto deep." This is the direct and immediate realization of the Absolute, without the instrumentality of sense-organs or mind.

As in the objective meditation, so in the subjective meditation, the Ideal may be associated with or conditioned by a sound-symbol or a form-symbol. In the meditation associated with a sound-symbol, the aspirant repeats a Vedic aphorism such as "I am Brahman" (*Aham Brahmāsmi*). While repeating the sacred formula he also reflects on its meaning: he is, in reality, of the nature of Wisdom, Purity, and Eternity; he is beyond time, space, and causation; he is one with the Infinite. In this form of meditation the sound is emphasized. The sound, as we shall see, ultimately leads to silence, as the form leads to the ineffable experience of formlessness.

In the meditation associated with a form-symbol, the aspirant observes that there arise constantly in his mind such forms or ideas as desire, determination, doubt, belief, non-belief, fear and fearlessness. He meditates on the Consciousness which is the Witness of these forms.

The subjective meditation has its *savikalpa* and its *nirvikalpa* aspects. At the outset the aspirant feels that *he* is the unattached Brahman. There is present an element of the cognizer, or I-consciousness. But as the meditation deepens he experiences the *nirvikalpa samādhi*, in which the mind becomes steady, like the unflickering flame of a candle kept in a windless place, and he becomes totally absorbed in the Bliss or Self-realization. There is no more cognition of subject or of object.

By means of meditation, subjective or objective, through gradual steps the aspirant attains to the Knowledge of Brahman in the *nirvikalpa samādhi*. Thus disappears his attachment to the body and the phenomenal world and there arises the Knowledge of the Supreme Self. He sees Brahman everywhere: to his right, to his left, in front, behind, above, below. All verily becomes Brahman. Henceforth in every experience he realizes the Supreme Bliss of *samādhi*. By beholding Brahman with eyes open and with eyes closed, in meditation or while looking at the world, he gets rid of the "fetters of the heart" and resolves "all the doubts of the mind"; he becomes free from the binding effects of his past *karma.*

OBSTACLES TO SAMĀDHI

The need for vigilance is imperative at every step of the spiritual life. Obstacles beset the path until the goal is reached. The higher the aspirant climbs, the subtler are the obstacles. The path has been described in the Upanishad as "sharp as a razor's edge". If he is inadvertent he does not reach the goal and only injures himself. For those practising meditation Vedāntic teachers state four great obstacles. They are torpidity, distraction, attachment, and enjoyment of bliss.

If the mind does not succeed in being established in Brahman after it has been detached from the world, it often lapses into a state of sleep or torpidity (*laya*). A kind of stagnation sets in. The aspirant is reluctant to make fresh efforts. His progress is slowed down.

Or the mind, unable to rest in Brahman after becoming detached from the world, may feel distracted (*vikśepa*) by ideas, for the most part petty, inconsequential and insignificant. These have been described as the "little imbecilities" of the mind. Their number is legion and they are fleeting in nature. They may be the result of the aspirant's futile talk or meaningless actions in the past. They make him restless. Sometimes, unable to reach Brahman, and detached from the world, the aspirant exaggerates a particular emotion or feeling which is inconsequential in itself, and thus creates an obstruction to spiritual life.

Or his mind, unable to rest in Brahman, yet detached from the world, may suddenly be seized by a violent attachment (*kaṣāya*) to a long forgotten experience. The desire, suddenly resurrected from the subconscious mind, agitates him, like a gust of wind tossing a boat lying at anchor on the water.

Or his mind, unable to rest in Brahman, yet detached from the world, may feel quite satisfied with the enjoyment of an inferior bliss (*rasāsvāda*), a foretaste of the Bliss of Brahman, and be then unwilling to make any further effort to reach the Goal. As a result of self-control and meditation he may be rewarded by visions and ecstasies, which are only milestones on his path. The unwary devotee takes these secondary experiences for the real thing and remains absorbed in their enjoyment. Sometimes he may become so engrossed in the bliss of the *savikalpa samādhi* that he refuses to give it up and plunge into the all-annihilating experience of the Great Beyond. It may also happen that the aspirant, in pursuit of his spiritual Ideal, is challenged by the stubborn and importunate craving of a particular sense-organ. He puts up a heroic fight against the enemy. When at last he wins, he feels so happy at his success that he totally gives himself up to the enjoyment of this triumph. He forgets that he had set out to realize Brahman. Vedāntic teachers illustrate this by the story of a man who wanted to lay hold of a treasure buried under a tree and zealously guarded day and night by a powerful dragon. As he came near the tree the dragon challenged him. A vicious and protracted battle ensued. Ultimately the dragon was destroyed. But the man, beside himself with joy at this triumph over his enemy, danced around the tree, forgetting altogether the pot of treasure.

We shall now briefly describe the means of overcoming the above-mentioned obstacles. When the mind feels torpid or sluggish, it should be aroused by means of stimulating spiritual exercises. Study of sacred books, discussion of spiritual topics, singing or pilgrimage are recommended.

When the mind is distracted, the aspirant should pacify it by means of patience and perseverance. Through discrimination the aspirant gets rid of attachment. He should recall the evil results of past attachment to worldly objects. The effective way to *samādhi* is practice and dispassion. Once the mind is controlled it should be protected from further distraction. As regards the last obstacle, namely, the enjoyment of bliss, the aspirant should not permit his mind to dwell long on the experience of any transient happiness. He should constantly remember that happiness based upon the contact of subject and object is transitory. Through discrimination he should detach himself from all forms of reflected bliss, however alluring they may appear.

All these obstacles arise owing to the failure of the mind to rest in Brahman. Once the goal is reached there is no falling back. Therefore the aspirant should not relax his efforts till the Ideal is realized. With sincerity and zeal, earnestness and perseverance, patience and love for the Ideal, he ultimately overcomes all obstacles, great and small, through the grace of God and the blessings of his guru. He enjoys the Bliss of the *nirvikalpa samādhi*.

THE GOAL

The knower of Brahman becomes Brahman. Knowledge is accompanied by realization. The illusion of name, and form is destroyed and the knower is no longer a victim of the false fear and false expectation that plague at every step the life of an unillumined person. For the knower of Truth the seen, the seer, and seeing all merge in the indescribable experience of the Absolute. Consciousness of time and space is obliterated; the fetters of causality are broken for ever. This is the experience of Peace, Knowledge, and

Reality that passes all understanding. In the graphic words of Śankara:[40]

"The illumined person realizes within himself, through *samādhi*, the infinite and indescribable Brahman, which is of the nature of Eternal Knowledge and Absolute Bliss, which is without a peer in the world of relative experience, which transcends all limitations and is ever free and actionless—which is like the limitless sky, indivisible and absolute.

"The illumined person realizes in his heart, through *samādhi*, the Infinite Brahman, which is devoid of the ideas of cause and effect, which is Reality untouched by any imagination, homogeneous, matchless, beyond the range of proofs, established by the pronouncements of the Vedas, and ever familiar through the manifestation of I-consciousness.

"The illumined person realizes in his heart, through *samādhi*, the Infinite Brahman, undecaying and immortal, the positive Substance which precludes all negations, which resembles a serene and waveless ocean and is without a name, in which there are neither merits nor demerits—which is eternal, serene, and One".

The man illumined by the realiztion of Brahman enters the realm of Pure Consciousness. His mind vanishes; his activities associated with the ideas of a doer, instrument, and result come to a stop. Emerging from the experience of *samādhi* and still inebriated with the Bliss of Brahman, he cries out in amazement:

"Where is the universe gone? By whom is it removed? And where is it merged? It was just seen by me; and has it ceased to exist? This is passing strange! I see everywhere the Ocean of Reality filled with the nectar of Absolute Bliss. There is nothing to shun, nothing to accept, nothing to

40 *Vivekacudamani*, 408-410.

despise. I do not see anything; I do not hear anything; I do not know anything. I simply exist as the Self, the Eternal Bliss. Blessed am I; I have attained the Goal of my life. I am free from the clutches of transmigration. I am unattached. I am free from the body, both the gross and the subtle. I am undecaying, immaculate, and eternal. I am neither the doer nor the enjoyer. I am changeless and beyond activity; I am the Essence of Pure Knowledge. I am indeed Brahman, One without a second, without a peer, the Reality that has no beginning, beyond the illusion of 'you' or 'I', 'this' or 'that'. I am the Essence of Eternal Bliss and Truth. I alone reside in all beings as Knowledge and Reality, their internal and external Support. I am the enjoyer and all that is enjoyable. In me, the Ocean of Infinite Bliss, the waves of the universe arise and merge by the playing of the wind of *māyā*. Like the sky, I am beyond contamination; like the sun, I am distinct from things illumined; like a mountain, I am motionless; like the ocean, I am limitless. I have no connexion with the body, as the sky has none with clouds; I am unaffected by waking, dreaming, and deep sleep. I do not engage in work nor desist from it. How can I ever exert myself, since I am all-pervading, like the ether? Merits and demerits cannot affect me, neither heat nor cold, neither good nor evil. I neither work nor make others work; I neither enjoy nor make others enjoy; I neither see nor make others see—I am Ātman, self-effulgent and transcendent. Let this inert body drop away, either in water or on land. I am not touched by what may happen to it. Is the sky inside a jar ever befouled by the properties of the jar? Let there be changes in the body or in the senses, tenfold, a hundredfold, or a thousandfold; I, Pure Consciousness, am ever free. Can the clouds ever touch the dome of the heavens.

"I am verily Brahman, the One without a second, which,

like the sky, is beginningless and endless, in which the whole universe, from the causal to the gross, appears to be a mere shadow. I am verily Brahman, the One without a second, which is the Support of all, which has infinite forms, which is omnipresent, devoid of multiplicity, eternal, pure, unmoved and absolute. I am the Soul of the universe, I am the All, I am transcendent. I am Absolute and Infinite Knowledge".

The illumined person realizes his indebtedness to his guru, through whose grace he has attained the splendour of the sovereignty of Self-effulgence. Prostrating himself before the teacher, he says: "O teacher, out of sheer grace thou hast awakened me from sleep and completely saved me, who was wandering in an interminable dream, in the forest of birth, decay, and death created by illusion, being tormented day after day by countless afflictions and sorely troubled by the ugly beast of egoism. Salutations to thee, O prince of teachers! O thou of indescribable greatness, thee I salute".[41]

41 The state of Liberation cannot be comprehended by our relative minds. The terms *existence* and *non-existence*, as we understand them, cannot be applied to a liberated soul. All that can be said about such a person is that he is for ever freed from the spell of ignorance. He has entered into the realm of Light, compared to which even the highest knowledge of the relative world is sheer darkness. He no longer dreams, but is fully awake. He no longer enjoys the shadows of the phenomenal world. It is often asked how long the embodied soul must practise discipline in the relative world before attaining Liberation. The concept of time cannot be applied to the Knowledge of Brahman. Time is a relative thing, dependent upon the state of the mind. Many years spent in the dream world may be only a few minutes from the waking standpoint. The passage of the soul from the realm of relativity to the Absolute is dependent upon the Knowledge of Reality, and not upon any period of time; it is instantaneous, like lightning.

THE JĪVANMUKTA, OR LIBERATED MAN

Vedāntic seers say that one cannot attain complete Freedom and Knowledge in life by experiencing the *nirvikalpa samādhi* once or twice. Only by repeated practice can one become established in Brahman and rid oneself of all the vestiges of *māyā*. The seed of ignorance must be fully roasted in the fire of *Brahmajñāna*, the Knowledge of the Absolute, so that it may never germinate again. Thus alone does one become a *jīvanmukta*, liberated in this life though still living in a human body. Such a man breaks through the fetters of attachment and rushes out of the prison-house of the world, as a lion rushes out of its cage. This Freedom is achieved when one is rid of ignorance and its paralysing effect.

A *jīvanmukta* demonstrates by his life and action, the reality of Brahman and the illusoriness of the names and forms of the relative world. Having himself crossed the ocean of birth and death, he helps others to the shore of Immortality. Such a man keeps religion alive, not the erudite theologian.

A *jīvanmukta* is freed from the results of action. The stored-up impressions of past actions, which, in the case of an unillumined person, bring about future embodiments, cannot, in his case, produce any fruit. Actions performed by him after his experience of the *nirvikalpa samādhi* do not cling to him, because he is free from desires and ego. Whether he is in *samādhi* or conscious of the outer world, his illumination is steady and his bliss constant. Though he may sometimes seem to others to be like an unillumined person in respect of hunger, thirst, or sleep, yet he himself is never oblivious of his real nature of Immortal Consciousness. Free from desires, worries, and fears, he is not identified with the body though he still possesses one. Though appearing to be active, he is free from the ideas of "I" and "mine". He never forgets that the Spirit within is always at peace, though the *guṇas* may engage his body in various works. He does not dwell on the enjoyments of the past, takes no thought of the future, and is indifferent about the present. Completely free from the illusory notion of the physical individuality he is aware of his identity with all beings. He is conscious that he feels through all hearts, walks with all feet, eats through all mouths, and thinks with all minds. He regards the pain and pleasure of others as his own pain and pleasure. Physical death and birth have no meaning for him, a change of body being to him like a change of garments or like going from one room to another. About such a person it can truly be said that he exists, because he has become one with Existence; knows, because he has become one with Knowledge; and enjoys bliss, because he has become one with Bliss Absolute. He does not have to come back to the world of darkness again; for he has entered into the world of Light. If compassion for mankind moves him to assume again a body, he is born as a free soul always conscious of his divine nature.

Though a *jīvanmukta* lives in a world of diversity, yet he is unruffled by the pairs of opposites. He regards all things with an eye of equality. As he sees no difference between the *jīva* and Brahman, or between Brahman and the universe, he always enjoys inner peace and blessedness whether tormented by the wicked or worshipped by the good he remains undisturbed. His compassion for living being is without bounds. The outside world cannot produce any change in his Self. as the rivers flowing into the ocean cannot disturb its immeasurable and bottomless waters.

A *jīvanmukta* transcends the scriptures and socia

conventions. He is beyond the imperatives of ethics. Yet he cannot do anything that is not good and not conducive to the welfare of others. Long before the attainment of Brahman, when he was an aspirant for the Knowledge of the Absolute, he eradicated all wicked propensities and selfish desires. After the realization of Brahman he becomes free but not whimsical, spontaneous but not given to licence. He is totally unobstructed in his action and thought; yet he never makes a false step or sets a bad example to others. The great ethical virtues, such as humility, unselfishness, purity, kindness, and fellow-feeling, which prior to the attaining of Knowledge, he asiduously practised for the purification of the mind, all now adorn him like so many jewels. He does not seek them; they cling to him.

A *jīvanmukta* alone knows the true meaning of Freedom and enjoys it. He is free from all the bondage imposed on men by the world. He is free from ignorance, ego, desires, and attachment. He may get his food by begging, without anxiety or humiliation, and his drink from the water of a river. He moves about freely and may sleep without fear in forests or in deserted cremation grounds. He may go about naked or wrap himself in bark or in a rag. The earth is his bed and the sky his roof. He roams in the avenue of Vedānta, and his pastime is in the Supreme Brahman. He may wear no outer mark of holiness; he enjoys without attachment, like a child, the sense-objects offered by others. Free from desires, he enjoys material objects but never forgets his omnipotent Divine Self.

Sometimes a fool, sometimes a sage, sometimes possessed of regal splendour; sometimes wandering, sometimes behaving like a motionless python, which waits for its food to come to it; sometimes wearing a benign expression, sometimes honoured, sometimes insulted, sometimes unknown—thus lives the man of realization, ever happy in the Knowledge of Brahman. Though without riches, yet ever content; though helpless, yet endowed with exceeding power; though detached from sense-objects, yet eternally satisfied; though working, yet inactive; though enjoying the fruits of action, yet untouched by them; though possessed of a body yet unidentified with it; though appearing to be a finite soul, yet omnipresent and infinite is he. As a piece of wood is borne by a current to high or low ground, so is his body carried by the momentum of past actions to the varied experiences of their fruits as they present themselves in due course. He neither directs the senses to their objects nor detaches them from these, but looks on as an unconcerned spectator; and he has not the least craving for the fruits of action, his mind being thoroughly intoxicated with drinking the undiluted elixir of the Bliss of Ātman.

A *jīvanmukta* is no longer concerned about bondage or Liberation; for these really do not belong to Ātman, the Spirit ever free. Bondage and freedom are characteristics of the mind, and the mind is falsely superimposed upon the Soul. In his own self-imposed bondage, the ignorant man becomes entangled and then strives for emancipation. But we are told, in the inspiring words of the Upanishad: "There is neither death nor birth, neither a struggling nor a bound soul, neither a seeker after Liberation nor a liberated one—this, indeed, is the ultimate truth."

A liberated soul lives in the body as long as the momentum of the past actions that have produced it endures. The man may remain outwardly inactive, blessing the world with his compassionate thought, or he may engage in various actions for the good of all; but nothing he does can ever be contrary to Truth or Knowledge. He dwells in the physical body and may experience disease, old age, and decay, which are the characteristics of all material forms. Possessed of sense-organs, he may be blind, deaf, or deformed in other ways. He may feel hunger or thirst or may appear to be a victim of grief and sorrow. Nevertheless, though experiencing all of these momentarily—the characteristics of the body, of the senses, and of the mind—he is never overwhelmed by them. Having once realized their nothingness, he never imagines them to be real. Any man who knows that what he is seeing is magic does not consider it to be real, yet he enjoys the performance to his heart's content. Accordingly, it is said: "He who sees nothing in the waking state, even as in dreamless sleep; who, though beholding duality, does not really behold it, since he beholds only the Absolute; who though engaged in work, is really inactive—he, and no other, is the knower of Self. This is the truth."

With the exhaustion of the momentum of his past actions the *jīvanmukta* is ready to depart from the world. His passing away is not like the death of others. The Bhagavad-gita says that he gives up the body as a man gives up his old and worn-out clothes. The Upanishad declares that he comes out of the body purer and brighter, like a snake from its slough. His soul does not go out to be reincarnated again, but is absorbed in the Absolute Brahman, leaving behind no trace of its separate existence. As milk poured into milk becomes one with the milk, as water poured into water becomes one with the water, as oil poured into oil becomes one with the oil, so the illumined soul absorbed in Brahman becomes one with Brahman. A free soul even when dwelling in a body, after discarding that body he attains Supreme Freedom in Brahman and completely merges in Light, Peace, Knowledge, and Reality.

॥ आत्मबोधः ॥

SELF-KNOWLEDGE

॥ आत्मबोधः ॥

SELF-KNOWLEDGE

[1]

तपोभिः क्षीणपापानां शान्तानां वीतरागिणाम् ।
मुमुक्षूणामपेक्ष्योऽयमात्मबोधो विधीयते ॥

I am composing the *Ātmabodha*, or *Self-Knowledge*, to serve the needs of those who have been purified through the practice of austerities. and who are peaceful in heart, free from cravings, and desirous of Liberation.

[*To serve the needs etc.*—Needs conducive to the attainment of Liberation. Only Self-Knowledge can destroy ignorance and free one from repeated rebirths in *samsāra*, the relative world of incessant change and movement, which is characterised by pain and pleasure, weal and woe, love and hate, life and death, and the other pairs of opposites.

Austerities—Various austerities have been prescribed for purification of the mind, such as performance of obligatory duties, practice of daily devotions, worship, and self-control. The Bhagavadgita describes three forms of austerities (XVII, 13-16). The austerity of the body consists in worship of he gods, the brahmins, the religious preceptors, and the twise; in cleanliness, uprightness, continence, and non-violence. The austerity of speech consists in utterance of words that do not give offence and are truthful, pleasant, and beneficial; also in regular study of the Vedās. The austerity of the mind consists in practice of inner serenity, kindliness, silence, self-control, and purity of heart. This threefold austerity should be practised, with supreme faith in the spiritual goal, by men of steady mind without desire for any selfish end.

Peaceful in heart—Unperturbed by attachment and aversion when in contact with agreeable and disagreeable objects.

Cravings—for sensuous happiness in this life or hereafter.

Desirous of Liberation—That is to say, liberation from the sufferings of various kinds which result from selfish desires and actions.

According to Vedānta the study of the scriptures helps in the realization of Truth only when the student is equipped with the necessary disciplines. These are: (1) discrimination between the Real and the unreal, (2) renunciation of the unreal, (3) the six spiritual treasures, such as, self-control, forbearance, faith, etc., and (4) longing for Liberation. (See Introduction, p. 35 ff.)

The word Ātman is generally rendered here as "Soul" or "Self". The Sanskrit word really cannot be translated. Ātman is the deathless, birthless, eternal, and real substance in every individual. It is the unchanging Reality behind the changing body, sense-organs, mind, and ego. It is Spirit, which is Pure Conscioiness and is unaffected by time, space, and causality; therefore It is limitless and One without a second. As the unchanging Reality in the individual is called Ātman, so the unchanging Reality in the universe is called Brahman. Brahman, too, is beyond time, space, and causality and is all-pervading Spirit. Vedānta states that Brahman and Ātman are one and the same. The knowledge of this identity or non-difference is called Self-Knowledge, which confers upon a man the boon of liberation from the bondage and suffering of the world.

Ātman—as the *jīva,* or embodied soul—derives Its

experience in the relative world through three states of consciousness. In the waking state It experiences the gross objects of the outside world; in the dream state It experiences subtle impressions, purely mental in nature and created by the experiences of the waking state; and in deep sleep It enjoys peace and remains as the witness of the absence of the activities of mind and senses. In this last state It is close to Its real nature and the subject-object relationship is absent, yet even here the Knowledge of the Self is obscured by the veiling-power of ignorance. All these three states belong to the realm of relativity or ignorance. There is a fourth state, called *Turīya*, which in reality is not a state; then Ātman is realized as Pure Consciousness without any subject-object relationship. *Turīya* pervades all the three states and forms their substratum. (See Introduction, p. 66 ff.)]

Self-Knowledge alone is the direct cause of Liberation:

[2]

बोधोऽन्यसाधनेभ्यो हि साक्षान्मोक्षैकसाधनम् ।
पाकस्य वह्निवज्ज्ञानं विना मोक्षो न सिध्यति ॥

As fire is the direct cause of cooking, so Knowledge, and not any other form of discipline, is the direct cause of Liberation; for Liberation cannot be attained without Knowledge.

[*Fire etc.*—Though other articles, such as water, pots and pans, are necessary, it is the fire that actually cooks a meal.

Knowledge—Knowledge of the Self.

Any other form of discipline—Such as practice of austerities and of rituals, the bestowing of gifts, and charity. The purpose of these disciplines is purification of the heart and creation of a mental condition that will be conducive to Self-Knowledge.

According to Vedānta the truth about man is that he is Brahman, or Infinite Spirit. The cause of his bondage and suffering is ignorance of his real nature. Knowledge destroys this ignorance, and Self-Realization immediately follows. Spiritual disciplines purify the heart, train the aspirant in concentration, and thus create the necessary condition for the revelation of Knowledge, which always exists. Since the Self is by nature eternal and immortal, It cannot be the result of an antecedent cause. Knowledge, Liberation, Self, and Consciousness all denote the same spiritual experience. Knowledge is stated in the text to be the cause of Liberation only in a figurative sense. The attainment of Knowledge really means the rediscovery of Knowledge, which is never non-existent.]

Why is it not possible for action to destroy ignorance and cause Liberation?

[3]

अविरोधितया कर्म नाविद्यां विनिवर्तयेत् ।
विद्याविद्यां निहन्त्येव तेजस्तिमिरसङ्घवत् ॥

Action cannot destroy ignorance, for it is not in conflict with ignorance. Knowledge alone destroys ignorance, as light destroys dense darkness.

[*Action*—Which is associated with the consciousness of doer, instrument, and result.

Knowledge—of Non-duality.

Ignorance—Which conjures up the multiplicity of the relative world. (See note on verse 5, p. 129). Ignorance must not be confused with illiteracy or absence of book-knowledge. Vedānta declares that the knowledge of the non-duality of Brahman and Ātman is the only true Knowledge; all else is ignorance. Any trace of duality belongs to the state of ignorance. As such, the vision of a god or the experience of happiness in heaven belongs to the realm of ignorance.

According to Non-dualistic Vedānta the Ultimate Reality is Brahman, which is One without a second. It alone exists; names and forms are illusory. One sees multiplicity on account of ignorance. Again, under the influence of ignorance one performs action associated with the multiple factors of doer, instrument, and result. By means of action a man fulfils his various desires. Therefore action is in harmony with ignorance and cannot directly destroy it. But if a man is firmly established in the Knowledge of Non-duality and if he realizes that he is the Absolute, the embodiment of Freedom, Bliss, and Perfection, then the false notion of his self as a finite, physical entity which impels him to various actions disappears. The action performed by a knower of Brahman is free from the notion of duality. The action of an ignorant person is selfish and egocentric. Only a knower of Brahman can perform really unselfish work. According to some Vedāntists even the knower of Brahman retains a trace of ignorance, with the help of which he performs action in the relative world. They contend that *complete* Self-Knowledge is not possible except at the time of death; for, the bare maintenance of the body requires certain activities, such as eating and sleeping, which are not possible without a trace of body-consciousness.]

The notion that the Self is finite and limited to the body is due to ignorance:

[4]

परिच्छिन्न इवाज्ञानात्तन्नाशे सति केवलः ।
स्वयं प्रकाशते ह्यात्मा मेघापायेंऽशुमानिव ॥

It is only because of ignorance that the Self appears to be finite. When ignorance is destroyed, the Self, which does not admit of any multiplicity whatsoever, truly reveals Itself by Itself, like the sun when the cloud is removed.

[*Finite*—As man or animal or god. These illusory notions are superimposed upon the Self by ignorance.

Ignorance is destroyed—By means of contemplation and realization of the truth contained in such Vedic statements as "This Self is Brahman," "I am Brahman", "Brahman is Pure Consciousness," and "All this is verily Brahman."

By Itself—Without the help of any other factor, such as ritual, study, or prayer. Ātman is Pure Consciousness and is self-luminous.

According to Non-dualistic Vedānta, Self-Knowledge which is the goal of man's spiritual endeavour, is not the attainment of something new or foreign; it is a rediscovery of the ever present self, hidden under layers of ignorance. As the true nature of the sun is hidden by a cloud, so the true nature of the eternal Self is hidden by ignorance. On account of this ignorance the all-pervading Spirit *seems* to be a physical and finite being.]

It may be contended that the non-dual Self cannot be revealed by the mere destruction of ignorance. After the destruction of ignorance, Knowledge remains as a modification or state of the mind. Thus there is no escape from duality. The answer follows:

[5]

अज्ञानकलुषं जीवं ज्ञानाभ्यासाद्विनिर्मलम् ।
कृत्वा ज्ञानं स्वयं नश्येज्जलं कतकरेणुवत् ॥

Through repeated practice, Knowledge purifies the embodied soul stained by ignorance, and then itself disappears, as the powder of the kataka-nut disappears after it has cleansed muddy water.

[*Repeated practice*—Long and uninterrupted meditation on Brahman, which firmly stamps a man's consciousness with the knowledge of his true divine nature.

Knowledge—That is to say, Self-knowledge which makes a man realize that he is not a doer or an experiencer but the all-pervading Brahman, Existence-Knowledge-Bliss Absolute.

Purifies—Of such illusory ideas as birth and death, happiness and unhappiness, which are falsely superimposed upon the Self.

Embodied soul—The Self, through ignorance, seems to be embodied.

Stained—As a result of ignorance such finite ideas as "I", "me", and "mine" are superimposed upon the Self.

Ignorance—*Māyā*, *avidyū* and *ajñāna* are terms of Vedānta philosophy usually translated by such words as ignorance, nescience, and illusion. They generally denote the same thing. The Vedāntic philosopher contends that through ignorance, the non-dual Brahman appears to have become the manifold universe; the Absolute and the relative. Ignorance has no absolute existence, for it disappears when one attains the Knowledge of Brahman. But it is not non-existent, like the son of a barren woman, for it is the cause of the names forms of the sense-perceived universe. It cannot be described as either real or unreal, or as both real and unreal; as one with Brahman or other than Brahman; as either corporeal or incorporeal, or as both corporeal and incorporeal. The real nature of ignorance is inscrutable, since the mind through which one tries to understand it is itself a product of ignorance. It is without beginning, for time itself is an effect of ignorance; but it has an end, for it disappears when one attains Knowledge. It cannot be either proved or disproved by reason, since human reasoning is tainted by ignorance. Ignorance manifests itself in the relative world through the three *guṇās*, or attributes, known as *sattva* (harmony), *rajas* (passion or activity), and *tamas* (inertia). (See Introduction, p. 55 ff.).

Itself disappears—Thus there is no possibility of the existence of a second entity besides the Self.

Kataka-nut—A nut used in India to purify water.

Muddy—Mud is a foreign element; it is not a natural ingredient of water. Likewise, all finite ideas associated with the Self are foreign to It.

The knowledge which is the instrument disappears into Knowledge, the Goal, or the Self. (See Introduction, p. 100 ff.)]

It may be contended that the world is directly and tangibly perceived, and hence real. How, then, can the non-duality of the Self be established? The illusoriness of the world is explained by the analogy of a dream:

[6]

संसारः स्वप्नतुल्यो हि रागद्वेषादिसङ्कुलः ।
स्वकाले सत्यवद्भाति प्रबोधे सत्यसद्भवेत् ॥

The world, filled with attachments and aversions, and the rest, is like a dream: it appears to be real as long as one is ignorant, but becomes unreal when one is awake.

[*Attachments and aversions etc.*—These are the pairs of opposites, which support *saṁsāra*, or the relative world. All our sense-experiences involve either attachment or aversion, love or hate, pain or pleasure, and the like.

Appears to be real—Dream experiences appear to be real as long as the dream lasts. In dreams, also are experienced the subject and the object and their mutual relationship. The dream experiences make the dream ego happy or unhappy.

Ignorant—Unillumined or unaware of Reality.

Awake—That is to say, illumined through knowledge of the identity of the Self and Brahman. This knowledge is attained through contemplation of such Vedic statements as "That thou art" and "I am He".

Dream experiences appear to have been illusory when one is awakened from sleep. Likewise, the dual experiences of the sense-perceived world will appear to have been illusory when one attains Self-Knowledge. From the standpoint of Reality only the non-dual Self exists.]

How long does the illusory world appear to be real?

[7]

तावत्सत्यं जगद्भाति शुक्तिकारजतं यथा ।
यावन्न ज्ञायते ब्रह्म सर्वाधिष्ठानमद्वयम् ॥

The world appears to be real as long as the non-dual Brahman, which is the basis of all, is not known. It is like the illusion of silver in an oyster-shell.

[*Basis*—The Sanskrit word *adhiṣṭhāna,* substratum, means that which, itself remaining unperceived and changeless, gives the appearance of reality to an illusion based upon it. In the illusion of a snake in a rope, the rope itself remains unseen and yet is the basis of the illusory snake. The existence and perception of the illusory snake are possible on account of the rope. Stated another way: *adhiṣṭhāna* means that presence through the real knowledge of which one gets rid of the illusion based upon it. When the true nature of the rope is known, the illusory notion of the snake disappears.

All—Names and forms.

Silver etc.—Often, on a moonlit night, the oyster-shells scattered along a beach give an illusion of silver.

Brahman alone exists. Names and forms are superimposed upon It through *māyā*, or ignorance. Brahman, though unperceived, gives an appearance of reality to the names and forms constituting the relative worlds. This illusion of names and forms remains as long as Brahman is not known; but when It is known, the illusion is destroyed. The knowledge of Brahman destroys the existence of names and forms in so far as they are experienced as other than Brahman. To a knower of Brahman everything is Brahman. What appears as the world to an ignorant person, is, to a knower of Reality, nothing but Brahman. The snake, seen by mistake, is in reality the rope itself. Names and forms, as other than Brahman, exist only in the mind of an ignorant person.

Vedānta philosophy admits the reality of the phenomenal world during the state of ignorance. As long as one believes in the existence of relativity, one cannot deny good and evil, pain and pleasure, and the other pairs of opposites. For an unillumined person there is an imperative need of practising ethical disciplines, prayer, and worship. As long as he perceives a distinction between good and evil, he must follow the good and shun the evil; only thus, in the long run, can he go beyond the illusion of good and evil. Good and evil must not be treated as illusory by one who still experiences the sense-perceived world as real. Though a knower of Truth does not consciously strive after good, yet he cannot do evil.]

The phenomenal universe of names and forms is falsely superimposed upon Brahman on account of the ignorance of the perceiver.

[8]

सच्चिदात्मन्यनुस्यूते नित्ये विष्णौ प्रकल्पिताः ।
व्यक्तयो विविधास्सर्वा हाटके कटकादिवत् ॥

All the various forms exist in the imagination of the perceiver, the substratum being the eternal and all-pervading Viṣṇu, whose nature is Existence and Intelligence. Names and forms are like bangles and bracelets, and Viṣṇu is like gold.

[*Various forms*—Seen in the relative universe.

Exist in the imagination etc.—The meaning is that names and forms, apart from their Substratum, Brahman, are unreal, since they are mere fancies of the perceiver, created by ignorance.

Eternal—Unlimited by time.

All-pervading—Brahman interpenetrates all names and forms and endows them with an appearance of reality.

Viṣṇu—The All-pervading Consciousness. The word also signifies a special manifestation of Reality usually designated as the Second Person of the Hindu Trinity.

Names and forms etc.—The names and forms associated with various bangles and bracelets, which appear to distinguish them from gold, are changeable and therefore unreal. Even when the names and forms undergo change, the gold remains as it is. Likewise, the names and forms associated with the different objects of the phenomenal world, which appear to distinguish them from Brahman, are changeable and therefore unreal. Even when the names and forms undergo change, Brahman, the Substratum, remains as It is.

All things in the phenomenal world are endowed with five characteristics: existence, cognizability (that which makes one aware of the existence of a thing), attraction, form, and name. Of these, the first three (corresponding to *Sat*, *Cit*, and *Ānanda*, or Existence, Knowledge, and Bliss) belong to Brahman, which is the basis of everything, and the other two, to the relative world. The characteristics of Existence, Knowledge, and Bliss are equally present in all material elements, animals, men, angels and gods. These constitute their unchanging basis. It is the illusory name and form that make one thing appear to be different from another.

According to Non-dualistic Vedānta a cause is non-different from its effect, nay, the cause *is* the effect. The reality behind the effect is the same as the cause itself. Compare: "And as, my dear, by knowing one nugget of gold all that is made of gold is known, the difference being only in a name arising from speech, but the truth being that all is gold" ... (*Chandogya Upaniṣad* VI. i. 5.) Gold is the cause and bracelet the effect. What differentiates the gold from

Cause is the Effect ---

the bracelet is a name. The name is only a convention of speech. Otherwise there is no essential difference between gold and bracelet. Likewise, there is no essential difference between Brahman, the cause, and the universe, Its effect. Names and forms, which create the difference, exist only in one's mind. Therefore Vedānta says: "All this is verily Brahman".]

It may be contended that there is a real difference between the Lord and the individual soul, and between the different souls themselves; so how can one establish the non-duality of Brahman? The answer is: the difference is not real, but due to illusory superimposition:

[9]

यथाकाशो हृषीकेशो नानोपाधिगतो विभुः ।
तद्भेदाद्भिन्नवद्भाति तन्नाशे केवलो भवेत् ॥

As the all-pervading *ākāśa* appears to be diverse on account of its association with various *upādhis*, which are different from each other, and becomes one on the destruction of the *upādhis*, so also the omnipresent Lord appears to be diverse on account of His association with various *upādhis* and becomes one on the destruction of these *upādhis*.

[*Ākāśa*—The first of the five elements of matter usually translated in English as "sky", "space", or "ether".

Appears to be diverse etc.—Though *ākāśa*, or space is one and indivisible, yet, in association with such objects, as a jar or a tumbler or a cup, it appears to be of diverse forms. The space in a jar takes the form of the jar, in a tumbler the form of the tumbler, in a cup the form of the cup. A similar illusion of different shapes appears in the sky when one looks at it against a line of skyscrapers or against a mountain-range with jagged peaks.

Upādhi—A term of Vedānta philosophy which signifies a limiting or conditioning adjunct. For instance, a cup or a jar limits the all-pervading nature of space; likewise, the mind limits the all-pervading nature of Ātman. (See Introduction, p. 61 ff.)

Lord—The word in the text is *Hṛṣikeśa*, which means "Lord of the senses", that is to say, the omnipotent Spirit.

Appears to be diverse etc.—On account of Its association with various *upādhis* due to *māyā*, Ātman or the all-pervading Consciousness, appears to have become living beings (*jīvas*) and the Creator God (Īśvara). In the case of the *jīva* there is an excess of *tamas* and *rajas* over *sattva*; in the case Īśvara, *māyā* contains predominantly *sattva* and has only a trace of the other two *guṇas*. Furthermore, the *jīva* is under the control of *māyā*, whereas Īśvara is the Lord of *māyā*. The association between Ātman and Its *upādhis* is not a real contact; it is illusory. There cannot be any real contact between the two, which are completely contradictory in nature, like light and darkness. Hence this illusory contact cannot affect, the true nature of Ātman. On the destruction of the illusion the Soul realizes Its oneness with Brahman.

The aim of Non-dualistic Vedānta is to prove the illusory nature of the distinction between living beings and Brahman and between the differing living beings themselves. It teaches the essential oneness of all things. Compare the following passages from the Hindu scriptures: "The one Lord is concealed in all beings". (*Śvetās'vatara Upaniṣad* VI. 11.)

"Though one, He roams in various forms." (*Source unknown.*)

"Though one, He is imagined by people variously". (*Source unknown.*)

"It (Ātman) should be realized as one alone". (*Bṛhadāraṇyaka Upaniṣad* IV, iv, 20.)

"In Brahman there is no diversity whatsoever". (*Bṛhadāraṇyaka Upaniṣad* IV, iv, 19.)

"It is One alone, without a second". (*Chāndogya Upaniṣad* VI, ii. 1.)

"The Soul in all is indeed One; It dwells in every being as his Innermost Guide. The diversity of souls is like the diversity of the reflections of the moon in the waves". (*Brahmabindu Upaniṣad* 12).

"It is indivisible, and yet It is, as it were, divided among beings". (*Bhagavadgītā* XIII, 16.)]

Distinctions of caste, colour, etc., are due to the association of the Soul with upādhis. The upādhis are not real and cannot affect the non-duality and purity of the Soul.

[10]

नानोपाधिवशादेव जातिवर्णाश्रमादयः ।
आत्मन्यारोपितास्तोये रसवर्णादिभेदवत् ॥

Owing to Its association with various *upādhis*, such ideas as caste, colour, and position are superimposed on Ātman, as flavour, colour and so forth, on water.

[*Owing etc.*—On account of ignorance one identifies Ātman with the body, mind, etc., and falsely superimposes on It their attributes.

Upādhis—Such as body and mind.

Position—The word *aśrama* in the text denotes the four stages of life, namely, the stage of a celibate student (*brahmacarya*), the stage of a householder, (*gārhasthya*), the stage of retirement from the world for a contemplative life *vānaprastha*), and the stage of total renunciation (*sannyāsa*). (See Introduction, p. 19 ff.).

As flavour etc.—Such tastes in water as salinity or sweetness, and such colours as red or yellow, are due to the admixture of extraneous things. Water itself is tasteless and colourless.

If caste, colour, etc., were natural characteristics of the Soul, then one would be aware of them in deep sleep, when the Soul approaches most closely the state of Its native purity; or a knower of Truth would be conscious of them in the deepest spiritual experience, when the Soul is revealed to him in Its real nature. But as long as a man is bound by *upādhis*, he cannot neglect the duties pertaining to his caste or position in society. The performance of duties purifies the mind. A pure mind can cultivate devotion to Self-Knowledge.]

There are in men three Upādhis, or limiting adjuncts in association with which Ātman, or the Soul, appears to be different from what It is. Created by ignorance, they are the gross body, the subtle body and the causal body. The aspirant through the power of discrimination, should distinguish them from Ātman. These different bodies are described in the following three verses. First the gross body:

[11]

पञ्चीकृतमहाभूतसम्भवं कर्मसञ्चितम् ।
शरीरं सुखदुःखानां भोगायतनमुच्यते ॥

The gross body, the medium through which the Soul experiences pleasure and pain, is determined by past action and formed out of the five great subtle elements, which become gross when one half portion of one subtle element becomes united with one eighth of each of the other four.

[*Pleasure and pain*—Such as one experiences in the relative world.

Past action—That part of the past action known as *prārabdha karma*, which gives rise to and determines the nature of the present gross body. (See Introduction, p. 31 n.)

Becomes united etc.—Regarding the evolution of the subtle elements, see the Introduction, p. 71 ff. and of the gross elements, p. 77 ff.]

The subtle body:

[12]

पञ्चप्राणमनोबुद्धिदशेन्द्रियसमन्वितम् ।
अपञ्चीकृतभूतोत्थं सूक्ष्माङ्गं भोगसाधनम् ॥

The subtle body, the instrument of the Soul's experience, consists of the five *prāṇas*, the ten organs, the *manas*, and the *buddhi*—all formed from the rudimentary elements before their sub-division and combination with one another.

[*Five prāṇas*—*Prāṇa* or the life-force, though one, is divided into five parts according to its five functions. They are known as (1) *prāṇa*, or the life-force whose presence is felt, as breath, in the nose, (2) *apāna*, which moves downward and expels unassimilated food and drink, (3) *vyāna*, which moves in all directions and pervades the entire body, (4) *udāna* or the ascending life-force, which helps the soul to pass out of the body and also causes vomiting, and (5) *samāna*, which helps in the digestion of food and drink and their conversion into chyle, blood, and other materials of the body. The five *prāṇas* belong to *Prakṛti*, or matter, which consists of the three *guṇas*. They are derived from the combination of the *rājasic* parts of the five rudimentary elements.

Ten organs—These consist of the five organs of perception and the five organs of action. The organs of perception are the ears, the skin, the eyes, the tongue, and the nose. The organs of action are the hands, the feet, and the organs of speech, evacuation, and generation. The five organs of perception are said to be formed from the *sāttvic* parts of the five rudimentary elements, because they are by nature luminous and the characteristic of *sattva* is luminosity. Likewise, the five organs of action are said to be formed from the *rājasic* parts of the five rudimentary elements, because they are by nature active and the characteristic of *rajas* is activity.

Manas -This word, usually translated as "mind", denotes a function of the inner organ (*antaḥkaraṇa*) which considers the *pros* and *cons* of a matter. It is produced from the combined *sāttvic* parts of the five rudimentary elements.

Buddhi—This word, translated as "determinative faculty" or "intellect", denotes a function of the inner organ which determines the true nature of an object. The *buddhi*, like the *manas* is produced from the combined *sāttvic* parts of the five rudimentary elements. There are two other functions of he inner organ, namely, the *citta*, which seeks for pleasurable objects, and *ahaṁkāra* or egoity, characterized by I-consciousness.

The subtle body is an effect of the five elements and therefore material in nature. Accompanied by it, the soul, at the time of death, leaves the gross body. The subtle body is the seat of desires produced by the actions of the *jīva.* It is a beginningless superimposition upon Ātman, brought on by *māyā.* One rids oneself of this superimposition by constantly remembering that the Soul is totally different from the subtle body.]

The causal body, which is the third upādhi, described:

[13]

अनाद्यविद्यानिर्वाच्या कारणोपाधिरुच्यते ।
उपाधित्रितयादन्यमात्मानमवधारयेत् ॥

Avidyā, or nescience, indescribable and beginningless, is called the cause, which is an *upādhi* superimposed on Ātman. Know for certain that Ātman is other than the three *upādhis.*

[*Avidyā*—See note on "ignorance", verse 5; also introduction, p. 48 ff.

Indescribable—Avidyā cannot be described either as *being* or as *non-being*. The mind, through which one understands, is itself a product of *avidyā*, or ignorance.

Beginningless—The beginning of *avidyā* cannot be known by the mind, because the mind, which creates the concepts of time, space, and causality, is a product of *avidyā.* If a boundary be imagined for time or space, it is easy to think of further time or space beyond it.

Cause--It is the cause of both the subtle and the gross body. Brahman, in association with *avidyā*, appears to have become corporeal.

Other than etc.—That is to say, Ātman, or the Soul, is the Witness of the three bodies and never to be identified with them.

The detached and independent nature of Ātman has been described by a Vedāntist teacher named Vidyāraṇya Swāmī with the following illustration: The gross physical body may be compared to a royal court; the individualized soul, which is a reflection of Ātman, to the king; the mind, to the prime minister; the five *prāṇas*, the ten senses, and the five objects, to various officers, courtiers, entertainers, and servants; and Ātman, or self-luminous Consciousness, to a great chandelier. Ātman illumines all the activities of the gross and the subtle body during the waking and the dream state, like the chandelier illumining the activities of the court. When the king and the officers retire, still the chandelier gives its light, illumining the hall and revealing the absence of activities. Likewise, in deep sleep Ātman alone shines, revealing Its immutable reality and the absence of the activities of the body and mind. Thus Ātman is the unrelated Witness of the experiences of the three states, which include a man's diverse activities through his three bodies. It is Itself detached from all the bodies.]

It may be contended that the description of Ātman as independent of the three bodies is not valid, since Ātman is seen to be dependent on food and drink and to be endowed with many physical and mental attributes. In answer it is said that all this is due to the false identification of Ātman through ignorance, with various sheaths. The sheaths are described:

[14]

पञ्चकोशादियोगेन तत्तन्मय इव स्थितः ।
शुद्धात्मा नीलवस्त्रादियोगेन स्फटिको यथा ॥

On account of union with the five sheaths, the pure Ātman appears to be like them, as is the case with a crystal, which appears to be endowed with such colours as blue or red when in contact with a blue or red cloth.

[*Union*—That is to say, false identification. There cannot be any real union between the Self, which is Consciousness, and the sheaths, which are material in nature.

Five sheaths—These consist of gross material particles (*anna*), the vital force (*prāṇa*), the mind (*manas*) knowledge (*vijñāna*), and bliss (*ānanda*). The first sheath is the tangible physical body, the next three constitute the subtle body, and the last is the causal body. Ātman, or the Soul, is beyond them all. These are called sheaths because they are like coverings on Ātman, which manifests Itself through them; or because, like a sheath or scabbard (*kośa*), they contain within them the Soul, which may be compared to a sword. As one studies the nature of the sheaths, from the grossly physical to the blissful, one finds them becoming gradually finer and finer thus reflecting more and more the true nature of the Soul. The realization of the Soul in Its true nature is attained through elimination of all the sheaths by the practice of discrimination and detachment. (See Introduction, p. 85 ff.).

For a fuller description of the five sheaths the reader is referred to the second chapter of the *Taittīriya Upaniṣad*.]

When all the five sheaths are eliminated through discrimination and renunciation, what remains as the non-reducible substratum is Ātman, the self-effulgent Witness, the changeless, Reality, Absolute Knowledge and Everlasting Bliss:

[15]

वपुस्तुषादिभिः कोशैर्युक्तं युक्त्यवघाततः ।
आत्मानमन्तरं शुद्धं विविच्यात्तण्डुलं यथा ॥

One should, through discrimination, separate the pure and inmost Self from the sheaths by which it is covered, as one separates a rice-kernel from the covering husk by striking it with a pestle.

[*Through discrimination*—This is how the aspirant discriminates about the sheaths: The sheaths are material, inert, and changeable by nature; they belong to the category of the object, and Ātman is their Perceiver.

Rice-kernel—It is covered with a husk and appears to be inseparable from the husk.

When a man clearly realizes the Soul to be distinct from the sheaths, he becomes detached from them. This detachment is followed by Knowledge and Freedom.]

Why is it that the all-pervading Ātman is not tangibly manifest through all things?

[16]

सदा सर्वंगतोऽप्यात्मा न सर्वत्रावभासते ।
बुद्धावेवावभासेत स्वच्छेषु प्रतिबिम्बवत् ॥

Though the all-pervading Ātman does not shine in everything, It is manifest only in the *buddhi*, like a reflection in clear water or in a stainless mirror.

[*All-pervading*—Ātman is present in all objects as Existence, Luminosity, and Bliss (See note on verse 8).

Buddhi—A modification of the *antaḥkaraṇa*, or inner organ, which determines the true nature of a thing. Because it has a preponderance of *sattva* and is pellucid by nature, it is the best medium for the reflection of Ātman. This refllection is known as the *jīva*, or embodied soul. (See Introduction, p. 74 ff.)]

Though Ātman is present in the embodied soul endowed with organs, prāṇas etc., yet It is distinct from them:

[17]

देहेन्द्रियमनोबुद्धिप्रकृतिभ्यो विलक्षणम् ।
तद्वृत्तिसाक्षिणं विद्यादात्मानं राजवत्सदा ॥

Realize Ātman to be distinct from the body, sense-organs, mind, *buddhi*, and non-differentiated *Prakṛti*, but the Witness of their functions, comparable to a king.

[*Distinct etc.*—Though the Soul interpenetrates the body, sense-organs, etc., yet It is totally different from them because It is the eternal Subject and unchanging Consciousness.

Prakṛti—Matter.

The king sits in his court on his high throne as the observer of the activities of his ministers and counsellors, and is perceived to be different from all by virtue of his unique majesty. Likewise, the Soul dwells in the body as the Witness of the functions of the body, senses, mind, etc., but is distinct from all these on account of Its being of the nature of Light, Consciousness, and Bliss, which are absent in the matter of material objects.]

It may be objected that Atman *is not a mere witness; Atman also participates in the activities of the body and senses. The objection is answered by means of an illustration:*

[18]

व्यापृतेष्विन्द्रियेष्वात्मा व्यापारीवाविवेकिनाम् ।
दृश्यतेऽभ्रेषु धावत्सु धावन्निव यथा शशी ॥

As the moon appears to be moving when the clouds move in the sky, so also to the non-discriminating. Ātman appears to be active when in reality the senses are active.

[The movement of the clouds on a moonlit night creates the illusion that the moon is moving, and children believe that it is playing hide-and-seek. Likewise, the activity of the mind and the senses creates the illusion that the Soul is active. People who cannot discriminate between the Soul and the body believe in the activity of the Soul.]

If, an opponent may contend, activity belongs to the senses and not to the Soul, then let the senses be called the conscious entity and designated as Ātman. This objection is answered by means of an illustration:

[19]

आत्मचैतन्यमाश्रित्य देहेन्द्रियमनोधियः ।
स्वक्रियार्थेषु वर्तन्ते सूर्यालोकं यथा जनाः ॥

The body, senses, mind, and *buddhi* engage in their respective activities with the help of Consciousness, which is inherent in Ātman, just as men work with the help of the light that is inherent in the sun.

[Another Vedāntic illustration is that of iron filings, which become active in the presence of a magnet. A third illustration is that of the burning of an object by a red-hot iron ball. The power of burning does not belong, in reality, to the iron ball but to the fire by which the ball is heated. The meaning is that neither the body, the senses, the mind, nor the *buddhi*, nor a combination of all of these, is endowed with consciousness; none of these, therefore, nor their combination, can be Ātman.

The illustration of the sun in the text emphasizes the letached nature of Ātman. A man may perform a good or n evil action with the help of the sun's light, and experience od or evil result; but the sun remains unaffected. Likewise, by means of the Intelligence and Light inherent in Ātman, the embodied soul may engage in righteous or in wicked action, and experience the results according to the law of *karma*; but Ātman remains unaffected. Wicked action creates a barrier around Ātman that hides Its resplendence. Good action shatters the barrier and the undimmed Light of Ātman then reveals itself.]

It may be contended that, notwithstanding Ātman's being conscious by nature, It is endowed with such characteristics as birth, growth, and death, because these form the common experience of all. The answer is that these characteristics are falsely superimposed on Ātman:

[20]

देहेन्द्रियगुणान्कर्माण्यमले सच्चिदात्मनि ।
अध्यस्यन्त्यविवेकेन गगने नीलतादिवत् ॥

Fools, through non-discrimination, superimpose on the stainless Ātman, which is Existence and Consciousness Absolute, the characteristics and functions of the body and the senses, just as people attribute such traits as blueness and concavity to the sky.

[*Stainless*—Free from ignorance, or *māyā*, and its effects; such effects as the notion of being a doer or the enjoyer of the fruit of an action.

Characteristics etc.—Birth, growth, old age, death, etc. are attributes of the body; moving about, speaking, etc. are its functions. Sharpness or dullness of vision, deafness, etc. are attributes of the senses; seeing, hearing, touching, etc. are their functions.

An object is not affected by the traits of another object falsely superimposed upon it, as the sands of the desert do not become moist from the water of a mirage. Likewise, the Soul is not affected by the traits of the body and the senses.]

It may be contended that though birth, death, and so forth, may not be characteristics of ātman, yet agency, enjoyment and so forth, belong to it. Such direct experiences as "I am the doer," "I am the enjoyer", "I am happy", and "I am unhappy" are common to all. In answer it is said that these are characteristics of the mind and not of the Soul, though falsely attributed to It:

[21]

अज्ञानान्मानसोपाधेः कर्तृत्वादीनि चात्मनि ।

कल्प्यन्तेऽम्बुगते चन्द्रे चलनादि यथाम्भसः ॥

As the movement that belongs to water is attributed through ignorance, to the moon reflected in it, so also agency, enjoyment, and other limitations, which belong to the mind, are falsely attributed to Ātman.

[*Agency etc.*—Ātman in reality is devoid of I-consciousness and consequently free of the notions of enjoyment, agency, etc. These are experienced by the individualized, or apparent, soul and falsely attributed to the real Soul. The individualized soul is the reflection of Ātman in the mind. In dreams, when the mind alone functions, one sees the ego and its various characteristics, such as happiness and unhappiness, which disappear in deep sleep, when the mind remains actionless.

Kaṇāda, the founder of *Vaiśeṣika* philosophy, states that not only consciousness, but the various functions of *prāṇa*, pleasure and pain, desire, hatred, effort, and so forth, are the proof of the existence of Ātman. According to him Ātman is endowed with activity.]

That attachment, desire, etc., are not characteristics of Ātman but are falsely superimposed upon It is proved by the method of agreement and difference:

[22]

रागेच्छासुखदुःखादि बुद्धौ सत्यां प्रवर्तते ।
सुषुप्तौ नास्ति तन्नाशे तस्माद्बुद्धेस्तु नात्मनः ॥

Attachment, desire, pleasure, pain and the rest, are perceived to exist as long as the *buddhi*, or mind, functions. They are not perceived in deep sleep, when the mind ceases to exist. Therefore they belong to the mind alone and not to Ātman.

[*As long as*—This refers to the waking and the dream states.

Ceases to exist—In deep sleep the mind merges in its cause, *ajñāna*, or ignorance.]

The nature of Ātman:

[23]

प्रकाशोऽर्कस्य तोयस्य शैत्यमग्नेर्यथोष्णता ।
स्वभावः सच्चिदानन्दनित्यनिर्मलतात्मनः ॥

The nature of the Ātman is Eternity, Purity, Reality. Consciousness, and Bliss, just as luminosity is the nature of the sun, coolness of water, and heat of fire.

[*Eternity, Purity etc.,* are not qualities of Ātman,but Its essential nature. They are always present in Ātman, though they may be obscured by *māyā.*]

It may be contended that such characteristics as knowledge and happiness belong to Ātman only when a man feels from experience that he knows or is happy; in that case Ātman by Itself cannot be of the nature of Existence, Knowledge, and Bliss Absolute and free from modification. This contention is denied:

[24]

आत्मनः सच्चिदंशश्च बुद्धेर्वृत्तिरिति द्वयम् ।
संयोज्य चाविवेकेन जानामीति प्रवर्तते ॥

Such a notion as "I know" is produced by the union, due to non-discrimination, of a modification of the mind with two aspects of Ātman, namely, Existence and Consciousness.

[*Due etc.*—The union of Atman, and the mind, which is an effect of ignorance, cannot be real, because no real union is possible between two contradictory things, such as Spirit and matter, or light and darkness. The union is only apparent; it is a case of illusory superimposition. Atman remains for ever unattached to *māyā.*

Modification of the mind—The mind contains three *guṇas*: *sattva*, *rajas*, and *tamas.* Either the memory of a past event or the sight of an object stimulates one of the *guṇas* and creates a wave, or modification (*vṛtti*), in the mind, in which Atman is reflected. Thus the reflection of Atman and the wave in the mind together give rise to such notions as "I know" or "I am happy".

Two aspects—The word two is used in a figurative sense; for Atman in reality is homogeneous, indivisible, and without parts.

Consciousness and Reality, which form the nature of Atman, are reflected in a particular wave of the mind created by a present object or the memory of a past thing. The wave of happiness, unhappiness, or delusion is due to the excessive functioning of sattva, rajas, or tamas. The reflection of Atma in the wave identifies itself with the wave and gives rise to such notions as "I am happy", "I am unhappy", "I know", or "I am ignorant". Happiness, unhappiness, etc., which are characteristics of the mind, are attributed to Atman owing to this identification due to non-discrimination. Atman in reality is always of the nature of Existence, Knowledge, and Bliss. The nature of Ātman does not undergo a real change even when the individual soul, or, *jīva*, thinks itself to be happy, unhappy, or ignorant.]

The unchanging character of Ātman, referred to in the foregoing text, more explicitly stated:

[25]

आत्मनो विक्रिया नास्ति बुद्धेर्बोधो न जात्विति ।
जीवः सर्वमलं ज्ञात्वा ज्ञाता द्रष्टेति मुह्यति ॥

Ātman never undergoes change, and the buddhi is never endowed with consciousness. But man believes Ātman to be identical with the buddhi and falls under such delusions as that he is the seer and the knower.

[*Ātman never etc.*—Changes due to time, space, and causality occur only in material objects. Ātman is all Spirit and has been experienced by the seers as actionless, changeless, stainless, attributeless, partless, unmanifested, incomprehensible, and free from all other traces of matter.

The buddhi is never etc.—Because the *buddhi*, or mind, is a modification of *Prakṛti*, or matter, which is of the nature of inertia and insentiency. The *buddhi* (intellect) and the *manas* (mind), the determinative and the doubting function of the inner organ, are sometimes loosely used synonymously.

The *jīva* or individualized soul, which is the reflection of Consciousness in the mind, falsely identifies Ātman with the body and the mind and superimposes the characteristics of Ātman on the latter; thus one comes by the false notion that Ātman is the knower, doer, etc. In reality Ātman, altogether different from the mind, is Knowledge itself and is not affected by the changes that take place in the mind.]

The results of false and true knowledge described:

[26]

रज्जुसर्पवदात्मानं जीवं ज्ञात्वा भयं वहेत् ।
नाहं जीवः परात्मेति ज्ञातश्चेन्निर्भयो भवेत् ॥

The Soul regarding Itself as a *jīva* is overcome by fear, just like the man who regards a rope as a snake. The Soul regains fearlessness by realising that It is not a *jīva* but the Supreme Soul.

[*Jīva*—A *jīva*, or individualized living being, is conscious of the existence of other beings and their Creator, God. He regards himself as limited by time, space, and the law of causation. He thinks he is a *saṁsārī*, or relative being subject to birth and death. Thus he becomes a prey to fear. According to the *Upaniṣads* consciousness of duality is inevitably accompanied by fear. If a man sees the slightest difference between himself and others, he thereby falls into the clutches of fear. He who thinks of God as separate from himself is overcome by the fear of God. But Ātman never in reality becomes a *jīva*; hence a man's fear is groundless and due to ignorance.

Regards a rope etc.—The fear is groundless and due to ignorance.

Regains etc.—This fearlessness is due to the realization of the non-duality of the Soul, attained through consciousness of the identity of *jīva* and Brahman. "A knower of Brahman verily becomes Brahman." (*Muṇḍaka Upaniṣad* III, ii, 9.)

From the knowledge of the Soul's non-duality comes cessation of the suffering due to ignorance, egoism, love, hatred, and clinging to life. A fearless soul attains abiding peace.

Perception of duality gives rise to fear and expectation, both of which are groundless. The expectation of attaining something in the dual world for happiness of the Soul brings in its train disappointment and suffering; for duality itself is based on illusion. No abiding satisfaction from the fulfilment of desires is ever possible in the dual world. The realization of Non-duality alone brings peace and blessedness.]

The self-luminous Atman manifests all material objects, such as the mind and the outside world, but Itself cannot be manifested by them.

[27]

आत्मावभासयत्येको बुद्ध्यादीनीन्द्रियाण्यपि ।
दीपो घटादिवत्स्वात्मा जडैस्तैर्नावभास्यते ॥

The mind, the sense-organs, and so on, are illumined by Ātman alone, as a jar or pot by a lamp. But these material objects cannot illumine their own Self.

[*The mind etc.*—The apparently luminous nature of the mind, the sense-organs, etc. is in reality due to Atman, their substratum. By themselves they are insentient matter. "That which cannot be seen by the eyes, but by which the eyes see other objects—That alone is Brahman; realize That and not what people worship (through ignorance)".—*Kena Upaniṣad,* I. 6.

Their own Self—The Self, or all-pervading Consciousness, and That alone, is the substratum or real essence of the mind, ego, sense-organs, etc. Ātman reflects itself through *Prakṛti*, or matter, which assumes the forms of the mind, intellect, senses, etc. In reality Brahman, which is One without a second, admits of no differentiation whatsoever. It dwells behind all these illusory forms.]

Ātman, being luminous by nature, illumines Itself. It does not depend on anything else for Its manifestation.

[28]

स्वबोधे नान्यबोधेच्छा बोधरूपतयात्मनः ।
न दीपस्यान्यदीपेच्छा यथा स्वात्मप्रकाशने ॥

As a lighted lamp does not need another lamp to manifest its light, so Ātman, being Consciousness itself, does not need another instrument of consciousness to illumine Itself.

[What is it that illumines Ātman? If another kind of consciousness is assumed for that purpose, then the question may be asked as to what illumines the second consciousness. Thus one faces the difficulty of an infinite regress. On the other hand, if it is said that Ātman is illumined by the light that belongs to Ātman alone, then an objection may be raised that the answer hardly gives any satisfaction. It may be contended that the ignorant man does not know the nature of Ātman at all; therefore his ignorance can hardly be dispelled by the statement that the light of Ātman manifests Ātman. It is like defining fever as a form of illness which has all the symptoms of fever. But this contention cannot apply to Ātman. It is self-luminous. No one can deny or doubt the existence of his own self. Ātman is the Self even of one who denies or doubts Its existence. No thinking is possible without the consciousness of "I am". The real "I" behind "I am" is Ātman.]

The following objection may be raised: If Ātman is self-luminous, and if Its manifestation is natural, spontaneous, and independent of any other agency, then Liberation through Self-Knowledge can be achieved without any effort or discipline, since Knowledge and Consciousness, intrinsic in Ātman, are never absent. In answer it is said that mere intellectual knowledge of the self-luminous nature of Ātman, as is evidenced from every act of cognition is not conducive to Liberation. A man is liberated through the knowledge of the oneness of Ātman and Brahman only by following the instruction of his teacher. What is necessary for the attainment of Liberation is actual realization of the knowledge of the non-duality of Ātman and Brahman:

[29]

निषिध्य निखिलोपाधीन्नेति नेतीति वाक्यतः ।
विद्यादैक्यं महावाक्यैर्जीवात्मपरमात्मनोः ॥

By negating all the *upādhis* through the help of the scriptural statement "It is not this, It is not this," realize the oneness of the individual soul and the Supreme Soul by means of the great Vedic aphorisms.

[*Upādhis*—Such as collective or individual, gross, subtle, or causal. They are extraneous to Ātman and belong to the realm of *ajñāna*, or nescience. On account of association with the collective nescience, Brahman, or Pure Consciousness, is known by such epithets as the Omnipresent Lord;

the Creator, Preserver, and Destroyer of the universe; the all-controlling Isvara. On account of association with the individual nescience, Brahman, or Pure Consciousness, is regarded as endowed with limited power and knowledge and is known as the individual soul. The gross, subtle and causal *upādhis* refer respectively to the gross body (which functions in the waking state), the subtle body (which functions in the dream state) and the causal body (which functions in the state of dreamless sleep).

"It is not this, It is not this", etc.—The well-known injunction of "*Neti, neti*" is taken from *Bṛhadaraṇyaka Upaniṣad* II, iii, 6. It negates in Brahman all such *upādhis* as name, form, action, class, attribute, and division.

Vedic aphorisms—The four great aphorisms of the Vedas are: (1) "That thou art" (*Sāma Veda, Chāndogya Upaniṣad* VI. x. 3); (2) "This Ātman is Brahman" (*Atharva-Veda, Māṇḍūkya Upaniṣad,* 2; *Bṛhadāraṇyaka Upaniṣad* II, v. 19; (3) "Consciousness is Brahman" (*Ṛg-Veda, Aitareya Upaniṣad* V, 3); (4) "I am Brahman" *Yajur Veda, Bṛhadāraṇyaka Upaniṣad* I, iv, 20). All these four aphorisms point out the non-duality of the *jīva*, or the individual soul, and Iśvara, or the Supreme Soul, the Reality behind them both being Brahman, or Pure Consciousness. The knowledge of this non-duality is the Knowledge of Reality (*Tattvajñāna*) and the means for the attainment of Liberation.

Vedāntic scholars derive the meaning of the total identity of Brahman, the Absolute, and the *jīva*, the individual soul, from the four Vedic aphorisms mentioned above, by divesting these terms of their respective *upādhis*, or limitations which are unreal and illusory. (See Introduction, p. 92 ff.)]

Only by elimination of the illusory upādhis can one realize the oneness of jīva and Brahman:

[30]

आविद्यकं शरीरादि दृश्यं बुद्बुदवत्क्षरम् ।
एतद्विलक्षणं विद्यादहं ब्रह्मेति निर्मलम् ॥

The body and so on, created by avidyā and of the nature of an object, are perishable, like bubbles. Realize through discrimination that you are the stainless Brahman, completely different from them.

[*The body etc.*—The body includes the senses, mind, discriminating faculty, ego, and mind-stuff.

Avidyā—All objects are creations of ignorance.

Object—Because the body is perceived by Atman, which is the Subject. (See Introduction, p. 54 ff.)

Stainless—Uncontaminated by *avidyā* and its effects.

The realization of the identity of the individual soul and Brahman enables one to attain the Highest Good.

The following meditation is suggested in order to strengthen the knowledge of the Soul's oneness with Brahman:

[31]

देहान्यत्वान्न मे जन्मजराकार्श्यलयादयः ।
शब्दादिविषयैः सङ्गो निरिन्द्रियतया न च ॥

I am free from changes such as birth, thinness, senility, and death; for I am other than the body. I am unattached to the objects of the senses, such as sound and taste; for I am without sense-organs.

[*Changes*—The inherent characteristics of matter are birth, existence, growth, transformation, decline, and death. They are absent from the Soul, which is Spirit.

Unattached—There cannot be any real contact between two such different entities as matter and Spirit.

Sense-organs—The senses, material in nature, like the body, falsely superimposed on Ātman.]

Ātman is free from the characteristics of the mind:

[32]

अमनस्त्वान्न मे दुःखरागद्वेषभयादयः ।
अप्राणो ह्यमनाः शुभ्र इत्यादिश्रुतिशासनात् ॥

I am free from sorrow, attachment, malice and fear; for I am other than the mind. "He is without breath and without mind, pure, higher than the high, and imperishable."

[*Sorrow etc.*—These are characteristics of the mind, "Desire, deliberation, doubt, faith, want of faith, patience. impatience, shame, intelligence, and fear—all these are but of the mind." (*Bṛhadāraṇyaka Upaniṣad* I, v, 3).

He is etc.—The quotation is from *Muṇḍaka Upaniṣad* II, i, 2.

Breath—Breath, or *prāṇa* is a modification of matter. Hence it does not belong to Ātman.

Higher than the high—That is to say, higher than Brahman, in Its unmanifested form, which is known as *Saguṇa* Brahman, or Brahman with attributes. The Soul, in Its true nature, is the same as the Absolute.]

Atman is other than prāṇa, mind, and senses, because these are transitory and endowed with a beginning and an end:

[33]

एतस्माज्जायते प्राणो मनः सर्वेन्द्रियाणि च ।
खं वायुर्ज्योतिरापः पृथिवी विश्वस्य धारिणी ॥

"From It are born breath, mind and all organs of sense, ether, air, light, water, and earth, which is the support of all."

[*It*—Brahman, which is one with the Soul.

Born—That is to say, projected through the power of *māyā*.

Breath—*Prāṇa*, or the source of action.

Mind—Manas, or the organ of thinking.

The text is a quotation from *Muṇḍaka Upaniṣad* II, i, 3.]

The true nature of the Soul described through a negative method:

[34]

निर्गुणो निष्क्रियो नित्यो निर्विकल्पो निरञ्जनः ।
निर्विकारो निराकारो नित्यमुक्तोऽस्मि निर्मलः ॥

I am without attributes and action, eternal and pure, free from stain and desire, changeless and formless, and always free.

[*Attributes*—Such as *sattva*, *rajas*, and *tamas*, which inhere in *Prakṛti*.

Action—Ātman is free from activity because It is other than the body, the senses, and the mind.

Eternal—Because It is unaffected by time, space, and causality.

Always free—The apparent bondage is falsely superimposed on Ātman.]

The all-pervasive and transcendental nature of the Soul emphasized:

[35]

अहमाकाशवत्सर्वं बहिरन्तर्गतोऽच्युतः ।
सदा सर्वसमस्सिद्धो निस्सङ्गो निर्मलोऽचलः ॥

I fill all things inside and out, like the ether. Changeless and the same in all, I am pure, unattached, stainless, and immutable.

[*Fill all etc.*—The Soul, or Brahman, is present in all things as Existence, Luminosity, and Bliss.

Changeless—Though the Soul is present in all things yet the change in their forms cannot affect It, because forms are perceived to exist on account of *māyā*, like an illusory snake in a rope.

Same in all—As their inmost Spirit.]

Now are described the nature of "That", or Brahman, and Its identity with "thou" or the individual soul:

[36]

नित्यशुद्धविमुक्तैकमखण्डानन्दमद्वयम् ।
सत्यं ज्ञानमनन्तं यत्परं ब्रह्माहमेव तत् ॥

I am verily that Supreme Brahman, which is eternal, stainless, and free; which is One, indivisible and non-dual; and which is of the nature of Bliss, Truth, Knowledge, and Infinity.

[*Stainless*—Free from ignorance and its effects.

Free—From relativity, characterized by birth, death, and other changes.

One—Unlimited by the existence of another entity of Its own kind.

Indivisible—Three kinds of division or distinction are noticed in material objects: the distinction that marks one species from another, such as between a horse and a cow; the distinction between two members of the same species, such as between a red and a white horse; and the distinction between the different parts of one thing, such as between the head, tail, and legs of a horse. No division or distinction of any kind is possible in Ātman, because It is One without a second, partless and homogeneous Consciousness.

Non-dual—Unlimited by the existence of an entity of a different kind.

Truth etc.—A quotation from *Taittirīya Upaniṣad* II, 1.]

The knowledge of the identity of Brahman and Ātman above stated, when intensified by long reflection, destroys ignorance and its effects:

[37]

एवं निरन्तराभ्यस्ता ब्रह्मैवास्मीति वासना ।
हरत्यविद्याविक्षेपाद्रोगानिव रसायनम् ॥

The impression of "I am Brahman", thus created by uninterrupted reflection, destroys ignorance and its distractions, as *rāsayana* medicine destroys diseases.

[*Uninterrupted*—This uninterrupted reflection should be practised for a long time with a loving heart.

Rasāyana medicine—A class of Indian medicine, chiefly prepared from mercury and sulphur and reputed to contain the secret of rejuvenation and longevity.

Through long and uninterrupted reflection a wise man feels as vivid and intense an identity with Ātman as an ignorant person with the body (See Introduction, p. 99 ff.)]

Yogic disciplines for the purpose of creating the impression of identity:

[38]

विविक्तदेश आसीनो विरागो विजितेन्द्रियः ।
भावयेदेकमात्मानं तमनन्तमनन्यधीः ॥

Sitting in a solitary place, freeing the mind from desires, and controlling the senses, meditate with unswerving attention on the Infinite Ātman which is One without a second.

[*One etc.*—That is to say, the Lord and the essence of all that exists are the same as the Self. Ātman, or the Self, is the unchanging Consciousness which is the Witness of the gross experiences of the senses during the waking state, the subtle experiences of the mind during the dream state, and a blissful experience characterized by absence of the subject-object relationship during the state of dreamless sleep.

The Vedāntic teachers recommend the disciplines of Yoga for the actual attainment of Self-Knowledge. Mere study and discussion only indicate the existence of Ātman.]

How is meditation on the unity of jīva and Brahman possible when the manifold phenomena are perceived all around?

[39]

आत्मन्येवाखिलं दृश्यं प्रविलाप्य धिया सुधीः ।
भावयेदेकमात्मानं निर्मलाकाशवत्सदा ॥

The wise one should intelligently merge the entire objective world in Ātman alone and constantly think of that Ātman as the stainless sky.

[*Intelligently*—Through intelligent discrimination.

Merge—The entire sense-perceived world is falsely superimposed on Ātman; it is one with the substratum as the snake is one with the rope in the illusion of the snake seen in the rope. The substratum alone is real, and the thing that is superimposed and seen on account of the association of a name and a form is in essence non-different from it. Through the help of such reasoning the discriminating aspirant should realize the utter non-existence of the world apart from Ātman, and thus merge the universe in Ātman, which is the same as Brahman.

Stainless sky—As is the case with the clear autumn sky, in which the various fantastic forms created by clouds during the rainy season disappear.]

How does the knower of Supreme Reality live?

[40]

रूपवर्णादिकं सर्वं विहाय परमार्थवित् ।
परिपूर्णंचिदानन्दस्वरूपेणावतिष्ठते ॥

He who has attained the Supreme Goal discards all such objects as name and form, and dwells as the embodiment of Infinite Consciousness and Bliss.

[*Discards*—That is to say, merges all these illusory superimpositions in the substratum of Brahman. All that exists is really Brahman. This is, no doubt, true for both the illumined and the ignorant. But the ignorant, owing to illusion, believe in the reality of names and forms and thus see the relative world in place of Brahman. Vedāntic discipline aims at discarding this illusory notion of multiplicity.

Dwells—Compare: " 'As a lamp in a windless place does not flicker'—that is the figure used for the disciplined mind of a yogi practising concentration on the Self." (*Bhagavadgītā* VI, 19.)]

It may be contended that though in samādhi the multiplicity of the objective world may disappear, still there lingers in the mind the triple distinction of the knower, knowledge, and the object of knowledge. This contention is answered:

[41]

ज्ञातृज्ञानज्ञेयभेदः परे नात्मनि विद्यते ।
चिदानन्दैकरूपत्वाद्दीप्यते स्वयमेव तत् ॥

The Supreme Self, on account of Its being of the nature of exceeding Bliss, does not admit of the distinction of the knower, knowledge, and the object of knowledge. It alone shines.

[In the lower *samādhi*, known as *savikalpa samādhi*, the distinction of knower, knowledge, and object is perceived; but this distinction disappears in the higher *samādhi*, called *nirvikalpa samādhi*, in which the individual soul remains completely absorbed in Brahman.]

The direct result of meditation and other spiritual disciplines practised for the purpose of the realization of Oneness is described:

[42]

एवमात्मारणौ ध्यानमथने सततं कृते ।
उदितावगतिर्ज्वाला सर्वाज्ञानेन्धनं दहेत् ॥

By constant meditation (comparable to the rubbing of the fire-wood) is kindled the flame of Knowledge, which completely burns up the fuel of ignorance.

[*Meditation*—The unbroken flow of consciousness toward the object. Meditation should be practised for a long time and with great love for the ideal.

Rubbing etc.—In ancient India the sacrificial fire was kindled by the rubbing of two pieces of wood, one placed upon the other. The mind is compared to the lower piece and *Om* to the upper. Meditation is their friction. That is to say, meditation is intense thinking upon Ātman as Brahman, with the help of the repetition of the symbol *Om*.

Flāme of Knowledge—That is to say, the knowledge of the identity of the Self and Brahman.

Compare: "A sage thinks of his mind as the lower piece of sacrificial wood, and *Om* as the upper piece. Through the practice of constant friction between them, that is to say, through intense thinking, he kindles the fire of Knowledge, which burns up the impurities of the mind." (*Kaivalya Upaniṣad* 13.)

"He...whose works are consumed in the fire of Knowledge—he, by the wise, is called a sage." (*Bhagavadgītā* IV, 19.)]

After ignorance is destroyed, Ātman reveals Itself to the sage:

[43]

अरुणेनेव बोधेन पूर्वं सन्तमसे हृते ।
तत आविर्भवेदात्मा स्वयमेवांशुमानिव ॥

As the sun appears after the destruction of darkness by dawn, so Ātman, appears after the destruction of ignorance by knowledge.

[*Sun*—It is a self-existent, ever luminous orb.

Dawn—In Hindu mythology the dawn is personified as the charioteer of the Sun-god.

Ātman appears etc.—The knowledge produced by the practice of spiritual discipline destroys ignorance. This destruction is at once followed by the revelation of Ātman. No other discipline is required for this purpose. Ātman always exists, but during the state of ignorance remains covered by *māyā*.

Compare: "But for those in whom this ignorance is destroyed by the Knowledge of the Self, that Knowledge like the sun, reveals the Supreme". (*Bhagavadgītā* V, 16.)]

If Ātman is an ever present reality perceived directly and intuitively, then why should one need to destroy ignorance in order to realize It?

[44]

आत्मा तु सततं प्राप्तोऽप्यप्राप्तवदविद्यया ।
तन्नाशे प्राप्तवद्भाति स्वकण्ठाभरणं यथा ॥

Though Ātman is an ever present reality, yet because of ignorance It is unrealized. On the destruction of ignorance, Ātman is realized. It is like the case of the ornament on one's neck.

[*Ever present reality*—To the knower of Ātman, It is perceived at all times. He knows It, as Consciousness and Existence, to be the basis of all perception. Even in the case of an ignorant person Ātman is self-luminous, free, and pure, though It is not realized by him as such.

Ornament etc.—It is a common experience to search for an ornament which all the time is hanging around the neck.

All spiritual disciplines, such as the study of scripture and the practice of austerity, are meant only for the unillumined, to whom Ātman, the ever present Reality, remains as an unknown and unrealized object.]

It may be contended that Brahman alone, and not the jīva, has been described in the scriptures as an ever present reality. The answer is that through ignorance one regards Brahman as the jīva:

[45]

स्थाणौ पुरुषवद्भ्रान्त्या कृता ब्रह्मणि जीवता ।
जीवस्य तात्त्विके रूपे तस्मिन्दृष्टे निवर्तते ॥

Brahman appears to be a jīva through ignorance, as the stump of a tree appears to be a man. This jīva-hood is destroyed when the real nature of the jīva is realized.

[*Jīva*—The individualized soul endowed with the attributes of a doer, enjoyer, and knower.

Stump etc.—In darkness one may mistake the stump of a tree for a man.

Is realized—Through the contemplation of some such Vedic aphorism as "That thou art"

When the true nature of the individualized soul is known, the notion of its individuality disappears. It is then realized as the universal Consciousness, or Brahman.]

The Knowledge of Non-duality destroys at once such mistaken notions as "I" and "mine" which are the effects of ignorance:

[46]

तत्त्वस्वरूपानुभवादुत्पन्नं ज्ञानमञ्जसा ।
अहं ममेति चाज्ञानं बाधते दिग्भ्रमादिवत् ॥

The knowledge produced by the realization of the true nature of Reality destroys immediately the ignorance characterized by notions of ""I" and "mine" as the sun, the mistake regarding one's direction.

[*True nature of Reality*—Described as Existence-Knowledge-Bliss Absolute, which is free from all trace of nescience.

Notions of "I" and "mine"—This is a characteristic of the *Jīva*.

The sun etc.—In darkness one loses one's bearings or mistakes the stump of a tree for a man, and falls a prey to other forms of delusion and confusion. All this is destroyed the moment the sun rises in the sky.

The Knowledge of Non-duality produced by the realization of Brahman destroys, no doubt, ignorance and its effects, such as the relative universe and I-consciousness; yet even a knower is seen to retain the notions of "I" and "mine" and the objective world. This is due to his *prārabdha karma*, the action done in the previous life, which has given rise to his present body and on the termination of which his present life will come to an end. On account of this karma he perceives the relative world, though in reality he is aware of its unreal nature. This *parabdha karma* obstructs his total realization of Non-duality and absorption in Brahman. The obstacle is removed at death, and the knower, who always has been free, realizes his utter freedom in Brahman. But according to some Vedāntists the total realization of Brahman is possible even when one dwells in a physical body.]

How does a knower of Truth, free from ignorance and illusion, view the universe?

[47]

सम्यक् विज्ञानवान् योगी स्वात्मन्येवाखिलं जगत् ।
एकं च सर्वमात्मानमीक्षते ज्ञानचक्षुषा ॥

The yogi endowed with complete enlightenment sees, through the eye of knowledge, the entire universe in his own Self and regards everything as the Self and nothing else.

[*Yogi*—One who has realized the complete identity of the Self and Brahman.

Endowed etc.—Free from doubt and contrary knowledge, because of his experience of Truth.

To a yogi who has attained complete enlightenment the universe of names and forms appears to be mere imagination, like the imaginary existence of the snake in the rope. Further, since an imaginary object is the same as its substratum, the entire universe and its diverse objects are perceived by the yogi to be the same as his Self. Therefore a real sage loves the whole world as his own Self and cannot injure anyone.]

The identity of Ātman and the universe:

[48]

आत्मैवेदं जगत्सर्वमात्मनोऽन्यन्न विद्यते ।
मृदो यद्वद्घटादीनि स्वात्मानं सर्वमीक्षते ॥

The tangible universe is verily Ātman; nothing whatsoever exists that is other than Ātman. As pots and jars are verily clay and cannot be anything but clay, so to the enlightened, all that is perceived is the Self.

[*The tangible universe etc.*—This is because Ātman is the cause and the universe the effect. The illusion of the universe is seen in Ātman as a mirage is seen in the desert.

According to Vedānta a cause is in essence non-different from its effect, jutt as gold is non-different from gold ornaments, or clay from articles made of clay. What differentiates cause from effect is just a name. This realization of the identity of the Self with the universe enables a wise man to cultivate fearlessness, and love for all. (See note on verse, 8.)]

The characteristics of a jīvanmukta, a man enjoying freedom though living in a body, are described:

[49]

जीवन्मुक्तस्तु तद्विद्वान्पूर्वोपाधिगुणांस्त्यजेत् ।
सच्चिदानन्दरूपत्वात् भवेद्भ्रमरकीटवत् ॥

A jīvanmukta, endowed with Self-Knowledge, gives up the traits of his previous upādhis. Because of his realization that he is of the nature of Existence-Knowledge-Bliss Absolute, he verily becomes Brahman, like the cockroach becoming a bhramara insect.

[*Jīvanmukta*—One who has become, through Self-Knowledge, completely free of ignorance while living in the body.

Previous upādhis—Such as the body, senses, and mind, with which a man identifies himself, through *māyā*, prior to his attainment of Self-Knowledge.

Cockroach etc.—According to Indian folklore a cockroach, when approached by a bhramara, is seized with fear. It constantly thinks of its mortal enemy and is thus transformed into a bhramara.

The enlightened sage uninterruptedly meditates on Brahman, Existence-Knowledge-Bliss Absolute, and thus becomes Brahman Itself. A knower of Brahman verily becomes Brahman.]

A jīvanmukta enjoys peace that passes all understanding:

[50]

तीर्त्वा मोहार्णवं हत्वा रागद्वेषादिराक्षसान् ।
योगी शान्तिसमायुक्त आत्मारामो विराजते ॥

A yogi who is a jivanmukta, after crossing the ocean of delusion and killing the monsters of passion and aversion, becomes united with Peace and dwells in the Bliss derived from the realization of the Self alone.

[The above text is an allegory taken from the life of Rama, described in the *Rāmāyana*. In the text Ā*tmārāma*, signifying one who derives satisfaction from the Self-alone, stands for Rama; the ocean stands for the watery expanse that separates India from Ceylon; the monsters for Rāvaṇa and his followers; and Peace for Sīta, the consort of Rama.]

How a jīvanmukta lives in the world:

[51]

बाह्यानित्यसुखासक्तिं हित्वात्मसुखनिर्वृतः ।
घटस्थदीपवत्स्वस्थः स्वान्तरेव प्रकाशते ॥

Relinquishing attachment to illusory external happiness, the Self-abiding jīvanmukta, satisfied with the Bliss derived from Ātman, shines inwardly, like a lamp placed inside a jar.

[*External happiness*—The illusory happiness derived from contact of the sense-organs with external objects.

Self-abiding—Established in the glory of the Self.

Shines inwardly—In the case of an unenlightened person, the mind, through the sense-organs, illumines the external world and its objects. But the *jīvanmukta* withdraws the sense-organs from the outside world and turns the mind inward. His mind perceives the light of the Spirit. The knowledge of the Self shines within him.

Compare: "O Pārtha, when a man completely casts off all the desires of the mind, his Self finding satisfaction in Itself alone, then he is called a man of steady wisdom." (*Bhagavadgītā* II, 55)]

How a jīvanmukta acts toward the world:

[52]

उपाधिस्थोऽपि तद्धर्मैरलिप्तो व्योमवन्मुनिः ।
सर्वविन्मूढवत्तिष्ठेदसक्तो वायुवच्चरेत् ॥

Though associated with *upādhis*, he, the contemplative one, is undefiled by their traits, like the sky, and he remains unaltered under all conditions, like a dumb person. He moves about unattached like the wind.

[*Upādhis*—Such as the body, the mind, and the sense-organs. A *jīvanmuktha*, on account of his living in the body, remains associated with the *upādhis*, but he considers himself as a witness of their activities.

Traits—Such as birth, growth, infirmity, and death.

Like the sky—Sometimes the sky appears to be grey,

on account of dust in the air, but the sky itself remains undefiled by dust.

Like a dumb person—He remains calm and silent while praised or blamed by others. The illumined person sees Brahman within himself and everywhere; he does not engage in actions to fulfil any selfish end.

Moves about—He dwells in the body as long as the momentum of his past *karma* is not exhausted; but he remains unaffected by joy or sorrow, as the wind remains unaffected by the good or bad odours that it carries.]

The death, or Supreme liberation of a jīvanmukta:

[53]

उपाधिविलयाद्विष्णौ निर्विशेषं विशेन्मुनिः ।
जले जलं वियद्व्योम्नि तेजस्तेजसि वा यथा ॥

On the destruction of the upadhis, he, the contemplative one, is totally absorbed in Viṣṇu, the All-pervading Spirit, like water in water, space in space, and light in light.

[*Destruction etc.*—After the momentum of his past karma has exhausted itself, the jivanmukta gives up his body.

Totally—Without retaining the slightest trace of individuality.

Water etc.—When a pot submerged in water is broken, the water inside the pot becomes one with the water outside.

Space etc.—When an empty pot is broken, the space inside the pot merges in the all-pervading space.

Light etc.—When a light is extinguished, the flame merges in the great fire, which is one of the five elements of the material universe. Or when a lamp is extinguished in the daytime, the light merges in the all-pervading light of the sun.

Vedānta describes two kinds of *mukti*, or Liberation: *Jivanmukti*, or Liberation while one still dwells in the body, and *videhamukti*, or Liberation after the body is given up. Some Vedāntists accept *jīvanmukti*, as Supreme Liberation, According to them, Knowledge of Atman attained while one is alive is the only condition of Liberation. Though a liberated soul dwells in the body as long as his past *karma* operates, yet he remains undefiled by the effects of his actions. He never deviates from the Knowledge of Ātman. Though he may behold the relative world, yet he is always aware of its unreality. According to the other school, a *jīvanmukta* retains a trace of ignorance due to his association with the body. The very fact that he lives in the relative world shows that he has come down from the Knowledge of Brahman. Complete absorption in Brahman is possible only when a knower of Brahman becomes free of the body. The following scriptural passages are quoted to support this view:

"As for him, the delay endures only so long as he is not liberated (from the effects of the past *karma* that has given rise to his body); after that (after death) he will reach perfection." (*Chāndogya Upaniṣad* VI. xiv, 2.)

"For him, at the end (after the dissolution of the body), there is cessation of all *māyā* and its effects." (*Svetāśvatara Upaniśad* I. 10.)

"As the following rivers disappear in the ocean, losing their names and forms, so, likewise, an illuminated person, freed from name and form, attains in the Divine Puruṣa, who is greater than the great." (*Muṇḍaka Upanisad* III, ii, 8.)

There is not much real difference between the two views, since, the knower of Brahman, both prior two and after death, enjoys Supreme Bliss freedom, and Peace.]

The nature of Brahman, into which the knower of the Self is absorbed after death, described:

[54]

यल्लाभान्नापरो लाभो यत्सुखान्नापरं सुखम् ।
यज्ज्ञानान्नापरं ज्ञानं तद्ब्रह्मेत्यवधारयेत् ॥

Realize that to be Brahman the attainment of which leaves nothing more to be attained, the blessedness of which leaves no other bliss to be desired, and the knowledge of which leaves nothing more to be known.

[*Attainment etc.*—This is because Brahman is the all-inclusive Reality.

Blessedness etc.—Compare: "This is his highest goal, this is his highest success, this is his highest world, this is his highest bliss. All other creatures live on a small fraction of that bliss." (*Bṛhadāraṇyaka Upaniṣad* IV, iii, 32.)]

Knowledge etc.—Compare: "He who knows that highest Brahman becomes Brahman." (*Muṇḍaka Upaniṣad* III, ii, 9.)

[55]

यद्दृष्ट्वा नापरं दृश्यं यद्भूत्वा न पुनर्भवः ।
यज्ज्ञात्वा नापरं ज्ञेयं तद्ब्रह्मेत्यवधारयेत् ॥

Realize that to be Brahman which, when seen, leaves nothing more to be seen, having become which, one is not born again into the world of becoming, and which, when known, leaves nothing else to be known.

[*Which when seen etc.*—Compare: "Have you ever asked for that instruction by which we hear what is unheard, by which we perceive what is unperceived, by which we know what is unknown?" (*Chāndogya Upaniṣad* VI, i, 3.)

Having become which etc.—Compare: "It is my Supreme Abode, and they who reach it never return." (*Bhagavadgītā* XV, 6.)

Which when known etc.—Brahman is the cause of everything. The reality underlying the effect is non-different from the reality underlying the cause. Compare: "My dear, as by knowing one lump of clay all that is made of clay is known, the difference being only in a name, arising from speech, but the truth being that all is clay..." (*Chāndogya Upaniṣad* VI, i, 4.)]

Brahman is the ultimate goal of man's spiritual aspiration for It is of the nature of Eternity and Bliss:

[56]

तिर्यगूर्ध्वमधः पूर्णं सच्चिदानन्दमद्वयम् ।
अनन्तं नित्यमेकं यत्तद्ब्रह्मेत्यवधारयेत् ॥

Realize that to be Brahman which is Existence, Knowledge-Bliss Absolute, which is non-dual and infinite eternal and One, and which fills all the quarters — all that is above and below and all that exists between.

[That Brahman is the all-pervading Reality is reiterated in the Vedas. Compare: "The immortal Brahman is before, that Brahman is behind, that Brahman is to the right and left. It has gone forth below and above. Brahman alone is all this. It is the Supreme." (*Muṇḍaka Upaniṣad* II, ii, 11.)

"That (invisible Brahman) is full, this (visible Brahman) is full. This full (visible Brahman) proceeds from that full (invisible Brahman). On grasping the fullness of this full (visible Brahman) there is left that full (invisible Brahman)."—(*Bṛhadāraṇyaka Upaniṣad* V, i, 1.)]

Brahman is the goal of Vedānta:

[57]

अतद्व्यावृत्तिरूपेण वेदान्तैर्लक्ष्यतेऽद्वयम् ।
अखण्डानन्दमेकं यत्तद्ब्रह्मेत्यवधारयेत् ॥

Realize that to be Brahman which is non-dual, indivisible, One, and blissful, and which is indicated by Vedānta as the irreducible substratum after the negation of all tangible objects.

[*Non-dual etc.*—Being One without a second, Brahman does not admit of any difference from objects of similar or dissimilar nature. Being of the nature of homogeneous Consciousness, It does not admit of any difference arising from the diversity of Its component parts.

Vedānta—The philosophical system of the Hindus that embodies both the essence and conclusion of the Vedas. Generally speaking, it is represented by the *Upaniṣads*, the *Bhagavadgītā*, and the Brahma-sūtras, with their commentaries.

Negation etc.—A reference to the negative method of Vedānta for arriving at Truth. Compare: "Next follows the description (of Brahman); Not this, not this". (*Bṛhadāraṇyaka Upaniṣad* II, iii, 6).

"There is no diversity whatsoever in It. He goes from death to death who seems to see diversity in It." (*Bṛhadāraṇyaka Upaniṣad* IV, iv, 6.)]

Brahman is the embodiment of Supreme Bliss:

[58]

अखण्डानन्दरूपस्य तस्यानन्दलवाश्रिताः ।
ब्रह्माद्यास्तारतम्येन भवन्त्यानन्दिनो लवाः ॥

Deities like Brahmā and Indra taste only a particle of the unlimited Bliss of Brahman and enjoy, in proportion, their shares of that particle.

[*Deities*—In the Hindu religion and mythology, gods and deities are phenomenal beings subject to the laws of time, space, and causation. Meritorious and righteous men, after death, become gods in order to enjoy the fruit of their good action. Afterwards they come down to the earth in order to resume the thread of their worldly career. Being less gross than men, the gods and deities reflect more of the Consciousness and Bliss of Brahman.

Brahmā—The highest god, the personified Cosmic Soul.

Indra—The king of the gods.

Taste only etc.—This is because only a fragment of Brahman can be manifested through even the highest phenomenal medium.

In proportion—As the gods differ from each other in respect of purity, so their enjoyment of the Bliss of Brahman varies in proportion.

Brahman manifests and sustains the entire universe with only a fragment of Its being. Therefore even the highest bliss of the world is only a particle of the Bliss of Brahman. Compare: "This is his highest goal, this is his highest success, this is his highest world, this is his highest bliss. All other creatures live on a small fraction of that bliss." (*Bṛhadāraṇyaka Upaniṣad* IV, iii, 32.)]

The Bliss of Brahman pervades the whole world and is hidden behind names and forms:

[59]

तद्युक्तमखिलं वस्तु व्यवहारस्तदन्वितः ।
तस्मात्सर्वगतं ब्रह्म क्षीरे सर्पिरिवाखिले ॥

All objects are pervaded by Brahman, all actions are possible because of Brahman; therefore Brahman permeates everything, as butter permeates milk.

[*All objects etc.*—Brahman pervades all objects as existence (*asti*), cognizability (*bhāti*), and attraction (*priyā*). What is real in the phenomenal world is Brahman.

All actions etc.—Such as hearing, seeing, smelling, touching, and tasting. These actions are possible for men because Brahman dwells in them as Consciousness.

Permeates etc.—As Existence-Knowledge-Bliss Absolute.

As butter etc.—As the butter is extracted from milk through churning, so Brahman can be separated from names and forms through intense meditation.

Though Brahman permeates all the objects of the phenomenal world, yet It remains untouched by their attributes.]

Other characteristics of Brahman described:

[60]

अनण्वस्थूलमह्रस्वमदीर्घमजमव्ययम् ।
अरूपगुणवर्णाख्यं तद्ब्रह्मेत्यवधारयेत् ॥

Realize that to be Brahman which is neither subtle

nor gross; neither short nor long; without birth and change; without form, qualities, or colour.

[*Qualities*—Refers to the gunas known as *sattva, rajas,* and *tamas.* (See Introduction, p. 65 ff).

Since Brahman is imperceptible to the senses and incomprehensible to the mind, It is often indicated by the Vedic seers through the negation of all attributes and charac-, teristics. Compare: "O Gargi, the knowers of Brahman say this Immutable (Brahman) is That. It is neither gross nor minute, neither short nor long, neither red nor moist, neither shadow nor darkness, neither air nor ether, neither savour nor odour; unattached, without eyes or ears, without the vocal organ or the mind, non-luminous, without vital force or mouth, without measure, and without exterior or interior. It does not eat anything, nor is It eaten by anything". (*Bṛhadāraṇyaka Upaniṣad,* III, viii, 8.)]

Brahman is the Light of lights:

[61]

यद्भासा भास्यतेऽर्कादि भास्यैर्यत्तु न भास्यते ।
येन सर्वमिदं भाति तद्ब्रह्मेत्यवधारयेत् ॥

Realize that to be Brahman by the light of which luminous orbs like the sun and moon are illumined, but which cannot be illumined by their light, and by which everything is illumined.

[*Compare:* The sun does not shine there, nor the moon and the stars, nor these lightnings, and much less this fire.

When He shines, everything shines after Him; by His light all this is lighted." (*Muṇḍaka Upaniṣad* II, ii, 10.)]

Brahman illumines the world and is self-luminous:

[62]

स्वयमन्तर्बहिर्व्याप्य भासयन्नखिलं जगत् ।
ब्रह्म प्रकाशते वह्निप्रतप्तायसपिण्डवत् ॥

The Supreme Brahman pervades the entire universe outwardly and inwardly and shines of Itself, like the fire that permeates a red-hot iron ball both inwardly and outwardly and shines of itself.

[Brahman, as Existence-Knowledge-Bliss Absolute, interpenetrates the universe and also shines of Itself as the transcendent Reality.]

Brahman is the only Reality that exists. All is Brahman. Anything that is not Brahman is an illusion:

[63]

जगद्विलक्षणं ब्रह्म ब्रह्मणोऽन्यन्न किञ्चन ।
ब्रह्मान्यद्भाति चेन्मिथ्या यथा मरुमरीचिका ॥

Brahman is other than the universe. There exists nothing that is not Brahman. If any object other than Brahman appears to exist, it is unreal like a mirage.

[This text gives the conclusion of Non-dualistic Vedānta

according to which the Real is defined as the entity that is not changed by time or limited by space or affected by the law of causality. The unreal is subject to time, space, and causality. The man endowed with Right Knowledge sees everywhere only Brahman. What appears as the manifold universe to the ignorant is realized by the illumined to be the indivisible and non-dual Brahman. It is ignorance that makes one see multiplicity in place of Brahman. But this multiplicity, being illusory, does not defile Brahman. This is explained by the apt illustration of the desert and the mirage. In reality the desert alone exists. An ignorant person sees the desert as the mirage and is fooled by it. All the time that he believes he is seeing water, he sees in reality, only the dry desert. Again, the ignorance through which Brahman appears as the world, or the desert as the mirage, is itself unreal. Ignorance, which is ultimately destroyed by Knowledge has no objective reality or absolute existence; it is an inexplicable state of the mind of the perceiver.

Compare: "I shall tell you in half a couplet that which has been stated in millions of Vedānta books; Brahman alone is real, and the world illusory; man is none other than Brahman". (*Source unknown.*)

"If the perceived manifold really existed, then certainly it would disappear. This duality is mere illusion; Non-duality alone is the Supreme Reality." (*Māṇdukya Upaniṣad Kārika* I, 17).

Non-dualistic Vedānta does not negate the reality of the universe, because the universe, as Brahman, cannot be negated. All that Vedānta aims at is the destruction of illusion, which projects the universe of name and form and makes it appear as other than Brahman.]

Brahman is all that is perceived to exist:

[64]

दृश्यते श्रूयते यद्यद्ब्रह्मणोऽन्यन्न तद्भवेत् ।
तत्त्वज्ञानाच्च तद्ब्रह्म सच्चिदानन्दमद्वयम् ॥

All that is perceived, all that is heard, is Brahman, and nothing else. Attaining the Knowledge of Reality, one sees the universe as the non-dual Brahman, Existence-Knowledge-Bliss Absolute.

[Attaining Right knowledge one sees Brahman everywhere. From the standpoint of Brahman even ignorance and its products, names and forms, are nothing but Brahman. Whether a man knows it or not, he sees everywhere only Brahman. What appears as other than Brahman, during the state of ignorance, is realized, when Right Knowledge is attained, to be Brahman.]

Though Ātman is the all-pervading Reality, yet it is not perceived by those whose vision is blinded by ignorance:

[65]

सर्वगं सच्चिदात्मानं ज्ञानचक्षुर्निरीक्षते ।
अज्ञानचक्षुर्नेक्षेत भास्वन्तं भानुमन्धवत् ॥

Though Ātman is Reality and Consciousness, and ever present everywhere, yet It is perceived by the eye of Wisdom alone. But one whose vision is obscured by ignorance does not see the radiant Ātman, as the blind do not see the resplendent sun.

[*Is perceived etc.*—Compare: "He is apprehended neither

by the eye nor by speech nor by the other senses, neither through penance nor through good works. When a man's nature has become purified by the serene light of Knowledge, then he sees Him, meditating on Him as without parts", (*Muṇḍaka Upaniṣad.* III, i. 8).

But one etc.—Compare: "Knowledge is veiled in ignorance, and thereby mortals are deluded." (*Bhagavadgītā* V. 15).]

Knowledge is attained through self-purification:

[66]

श्रवणादिभिरुद्दीप्तज्ञानाग्निपरितापितः ।
जीवस्सर्वमलान्मुक्तः स्वर्णवद्द्योतते स्वयम् ॥

The jīva free from impurities, being well heated in the fire of Knowledge kindled by hearing and so on, shines of himself, like gold.

[*Fire of Knowledge*—Knowledge that is utterly free from doubts and errors.

Hearing etc.—The three Vedāntic disciplines namely, hearing of the Truth from the scriptures, as explained by a qualified teacher, reasoning about it, and contemplating its significance.

Of himself—The removal of the impurities of the mind is instantaneously followed by the revelation of Ātman. No intermediary discipline is needed.

Gold—Fire destroys the dross mixed with gold and reveals the genuine metal.

The purpose of spiritual disciplines is the destruction of the impurities of the mind. This is followed by the spontaneous revelation of Ātman.]

Ātman is realized in the heart:

[67]

हृदाकाशोदितो ह्यात्मा बोधभानुस्तमोऽपहृत् ।
सर्वव्यापी सर्वधारी भाति भासयतेऽखिलम् ॥

Ātman, which is the Sun of Knowledge, arises in the firmament of the heart and destroys the darkness. The Pervader of all and the Sustainer of all, It illumines all and also Itself.

[*Sun of Knowledge*—The ultimate Source of light and consciousness.

Firmament of the heart—That is to say, the buddhi. The light of Ātman is reflected clearly through the purified mind. (See Introduction, p. 120).

Darkness—Caused by ignorance. When ignorance is destroyed, the individual soul realizes its identity with Brahman, or Universal Consciousness.

Sustainer of all—Ātman, as Brahman, is the unshakable foundation of the universe and its objects.

The man of Knowledge realizes that Ātman, or the Inmost Soul of the individual, which is vividly felt in the heart and which sustains the body, the senses, and the mind, is one with Brahman, which sustains the universe.]

Self-realization bestows happiness here and Immortality hereafter:

[68]

दिग्देशकालाद्यनपेक्ष्य सर्वगं
शीतादिहृन्नित्यसुखं निरञ्जनम् ।

य: स्वात्मतीर्थं भजते विनिष्क्रियः ।
स सर्ववित्सर्वगतोऽमृतो भवेत् ॥

He who, renouncing all activities, worships in the sacred and stainless shrine of Ātman, which is independent of time, place, and distance; which is present everywhere; which is the destroyer of heat and cold, and the other opposites; and which is the giver of eternal happiness becomes all-knowing and all-pervading and attains, hereafter, Immortality.

[*Renouncing all activities*—The activities refer to the worldly duties of householders.

Independent etc.—Because Ātman is one with Brahman.

Destroyer etc.—The pairs of opposites exist only in the relative world.

Attains etc.—While living in the body he enjoys the Bliss of Freedom, and after death he is absorbed in the infinite Brahman-Consciousness.

The word *shrine* in the text also means a holy place (*tīrtha*). The allusion is to the pilgrimage of pious devotees to a holy place. There are certain disadvantages associated with holy places. As they may be situated at great distances, pilgrimage may entail physical labour and suffering. The merit of a pilgrimage may be slight because of inauspiciousness of the time. The comfort of the pilgrims may be disturbed by the weather. Robbers, thieves, or unscrupulous priests often give them trouble. Further, the merit accruing from a pilgrimage is not everlasting. But the worshipper in the sacred shrine of Ātman is free from all these disadvantages and obstacles. Communion with Ātman bestows upon the soul Immortality and Eternal Bliss.

The *Mahābhārata* describes Ātman as the real sacred river, bathing in which the soul becomes free of impurities:

"The river of Ātman is filled with the water of self-control; truth is its current, righteous conduct its banks, and compassion its waves. O son of Pāndu, bathe in its sacred water; ordinary water does not purify the inmost soul".

By worshipping a holy man who worships in the sacred shrine of Ātman, the seeker obtains the result of pilgrimage:

"A visit to holy men bestows merit, because they may be regarded as moving holy places. The Lord, dwelling in their hearts, renders holy the place where they live."

"A river filled with sacred water is no doubt sacred; an image of stone or clay is no doubt a deity. After worshipping them a long time, the aspirant becomes pure. But by a mere visit to a holy man one attains purity."

Communion with Brahman is the most efficacious form of worship:

"By virtue of even a moment's serenity, attained through knowledge of the identity of Ātman and Brahman, the seeker attains the merit that one may obtain by bathing in the waters of all the holy rivers, by giving away the entire world in an act of charity, by performing a thousand sacrifices, by worshipping the three hundred and thirty millions of gods, and by rescuing, through after-death rites, one's ancestors from the suffering of the nether world."

"By the very birth of a man whose mind is absorbed in the Supreme Brahman—the immeasurable Ocean of Existence-Knowledge-Bliss Absolute—his family becomes sinless, his mother blessed, and the earth sacred."]

॥ इत्यात्मबोधः समाप्तः ॥

THUS ENDS SELF-KNOWLEDGE

APPENDIX

॥ गुर्वष्टकम् ॥

EIGHT STANZAS IN PRAISE OF THE GURU[1]

शरीरं सुरूपं सदा रोगमुक्तं यशश्चारु चित्रं धनं मेरुतुल्यम् ।
मनश्चेन्न लग्नं गुरोरङ्घ्रिपद्मे ततः किं ततः किं ततः किं ततः किम् ॥

Though your body be comely and ever remain in perfect health,
Though your name be unsullied, and mountain-high your hoarded gold,
Yet if the mind be not absorbed in the guru's lotus feet,
What will it all avail you? What, indeed, will it all avail? (1)

कलत्रं धनं पुत्रपौत्रादिसर्वं गृहं बान्धवाः सर्वमेतद्धि जातम् ।
मनश्चेन्न लग्नं गुरोरङ्घ्रिपद्मे ततः किं ततः किं ततः किं ततः किम् ॥

Even if fortune bless you with riches and a virtuous wife,
With children and their children, with friendship and the joys of home,
Yet if the mind be not absorbed in the guru's lotus feet,
What will it all avail you? What, indeed, will it all avail? (2)

1 The preceptor who awakens the disciple's spiritual consciousness. He is venerated as God himself, because God uses his pure body and mind to bring Liberation to the aspirant.

षडङ्गादि वेदो मुखे शास्त्रविद्या कवित्वादि गद्यं सुपद्यं करोति ।
मनश्चेन्न लग्नं गुरोरङ्घ्रिपद्मे ततः किं ततः किं ततः किं ततः किम् ॥

Though the lore of the Vedas take up its dwelling on your tongue,
Though you be learned in scripture, gifted in writing prose and verse,
Yet if the mind be not absorbed in the guru's lotus feet,
What will it all avail you? What, indeed, will it all avail? (3)

विदेशेषु मान्यः स्वदेशेषु धन्यः सदाचारवृत्तेषु मत्तो न चान्यः ।
मनश्चेन्न लग्नं गुरोरङ्घ्रिपद्मे ततः किं ततः किं ततः किं ततः किम् ॥

Even if you be honoured at home and famed in foreign lands,
Given to pious deeds, and ever averse to wickedness, Yet if the mind be not absorbed in the guru's lotus feet,
What will it all avail you? What, indeed, will it all avail? (4)

क्षमामण्डले भूपभूपालवृन्दैः सदासेवितं यस्य पादारविन्दम् ।
मनश्चेन्न लग्नं गुरोरङ्घ्रिपद्मे ततः किं ततः किं ततः किं ततः किम् ॥

Though you become, at last, the emperor of the universe,
Though you possess for servants the mightiest of the kings of earth,
Yet if the mind be not absorbed in the guru's lotus feet,
What will it all avail you? What, indeed, will it all avail? (5)

यशश्चेद् गतं दिक्षु दानप्रतापात् जगद्वस्तु सर्वं करे यत्प्रसादात् ।
मनश्चेन्न लग्नं गुरोरङ्घ्रिपद्मे ततः किं ततः किं ततः किं ततः किम् ॥

Even if every nation resound with your beneficence,
Yet if the mind be not absorbed in the lotus feet of him,
By grace of whom, alone, everything in this world is won,
What will it all avail you? What, indeed, will it all avail? (6)

न भोगे न योगे न वा वाजिमेधे न कान्तासुखे नैव वित्तेषु चित्तम् ॥
मनश्चेन्न लग्नं गुरोरङ्घ्रिपद्मे ततः किं ततः किं ततः किं ततः किम् ॥

Though you pursue no pleasures, derive no joy from wealth or wife,
Reject the powers of Yoga,[1] and scorn the fruits of sacrifice,
Yet if the mind be not absorbed in the guru's lotus feet,
What will it all avail you? What, indeed, will it all avail? (7)

अरण्ये न वा स्वस्य गेहे न कार्ये न देहे मनो वर्तते मे त्वनर्घ्ये ।
मनश्चेन्न लग्नं गुरोरङ्घ्रिपद्मे ततः किं ततः किं ततः किं ततः किम् ॥

Even if you be ready to dwell in the forest as at home,
No more attached to work, untrammelled by an ugly form,
Yet if the mind be not absorbed in the guru's lotus feet,
What will it all avail you? What, indeed, will it all avail? (8)

गुरोरष्टकं यः पठेत्पुण्यदेही यतिर्भूपतिर्ब्रह्मचारी च गेही ।
लभेद्वाञ्छितार्थं पदं ब्रह्मसंज्ञं गुरोरुक्तवाक्ये मनो यस्य लग्नम् ॥

Of novices and monks, of rulers and of worldly men,
That noble soul who ponders these verses in the guru's praise,
And to the guru's teaching applies his mind with constant zeal—
He will attain to Brahman, the treasure coveted by all.

1 i.e., the power to perform miracles.

॥ दक्षिणामूर्तिस्तोत्रम् ॥

HYMN TO SRI DAKSINAMURTI[1]

विश्वं दर्पणदृश्यमाननगरीतुल्यं निजान्तर्गतं
पश्यन्नात्मनि मायया बहिरिवोद्भूतं यथा निद्रया ।
यः साक्षात्कुरुते प्रबोधसमये स्वात्मानमेवाद्वयं
तस्मै श्रीगुरुमूर्तये नम इदं श्रीदक्षिणामूर्तये ॥

I bow to Sri *Dakṣiṇāmūrti* in the form of my guru:
I bow to Him by whose grace the whole of the world
Is found to exist entirely in the mind, like a city's image mirrored in a glass,
Though, like a dream, through maya's power it appears outside;
And by whose grace, again, on the dawn of Knowledge,
It is perceived as the everlasting and non-dual Self. (1)

बीजस्यान्तरिवाङ्कुरो जगदिदं प्राङ्निर्विकल्पं पुनः
मायाकल्पितदेशकालकलनावैचित्र्यचित्रीकृतम्
मायावीव विजृम्भयत्यपि महायोगीव यः स्वेच्छया
तस्मै श्रीगुरुमूर्तये नम इदं श्रीदक्षिणामूर्तये ॥

I bow to Sri *Dakṣiṇāmūrti* in the form of my guru:
I bow to Him who, by the sheer power of His will,
Projects outside, like a magician or a mighty yogi, this infinite universe,
Which, in the beginning, rests without name or form, like the sprout in a seed,

1 An epithet of the guru, or spiritual preceptor, in his benign aspect as the embodiment of grace and compassion.

And after creation, by the power of time and space imagined
through maya,
Appears to be many, possessed of manifold shapes and
hues. (2)

यस्यैव स्फुरणं सदात्मकमसत्कल्पार्थकं भासते
साक्षात्तत्त्वमसीति वेदवचसा यो बोधयत्याश्रितान् ।
यत्साक्षात्करणाद्भवेन्न पुनरावृत्तिर्भवाम्भोनिधौ
तस्मै श्रीगुरुमूर्तये नम इदं श्रीदक्षिणामूर्तये ॥

I bow to Sri *Dakṣiṇāmūrti* in the form of my guru:
To Him whose outward manifestations, though based on the
Real,
Appear as illusory, ever changing objects;
Who grants to those who take refuge in Him through the
Vedic pronouncement "Tattvamasi"[1]
The boon of immediate knowledge of Brahman,
To which attaining, a man returns no more to the realm of
birth and death. (3)

ननाछिद्रघटोदरस्थितमहादीपप्रभाभास्वरं
ज्ञानं यस्य तु चक्षुरादिकरणद्वारा बहिः स्पन्दते ।
जानामीति तमेव भान्तमनुभात्येतत्समस्तं जगत् ।
तस्मै श्रीगुरुमूर्तये नम इदं श्रीदक्षिणामूर्तये ॥

I bow to Sri *Dakṣiṇāmūrti* in the form of my guru:
To him whose knowledge, issuing forth through the organs
of sense,

1 "That thou art".

Like the glow of a powerful lamp placed in a pot with many holes,
Vibrates outside in the shape of the thought "I know";
Whose Light it is that illumines the whole of the universe. (4)

देहं प्राणमपीन्द्रियाण्यपि चलां बुद्धिं च शून्यं विदुः
स्त्रीबालान्धजडोपमास्त्वहमिति भ्रान्त्या भृशंवादिनः ।
मायाशक्तिविलासकल्पितमहाव्यामोहसंहारिणे
तस्मै श्रीगुरुमूर्तये नम इदं श्रीदक्षिणामूर्तये ।

I bow of Sri *Dakṣiṇāmūrti* in the form of my guru:
To Him who dispells the mighty illusion evoked by *māyā's* play,
Impelled by which, unseeing, childish, and misguided men
Continually speak, in error, of body, prana, senses, and even of the fickle mind, as "I",
Though in reality these are all mere emptiness. (5)

राहुग्रस्तदिवाकरेन्दुसदृशो मायासमाच्छादनात्
सन्मात्रः करणोपसंहरणतो योऽभूत्सुषुप्तः पुमान् ।
प्रागस्वाप्समिति प्रबोधसमये यः प्रत्यभिज्ञायते
तस्मै श्रीगुरुमूर्तये नम इदं श्रीदक्षिणामूर्तये ॥

I bow to Sri *Dakṣiṇāmūrti* in the form of my guru:
I bow to Him who, as a man, in deep and dreamless sleep,
Exists as Ultimate Truth Itself,[1]
When outer awareness is obscured, like the sun or moon in Rahu's[2] grasp, and the organs of sense are all withdrawn;
And who, on awakening, tells himself, "It was I who slept"
And sees again the objects he saw before.[3] (6)

बाल्यादिष्वपि जाग्रदादिषु तथा सर्वास्ववस्थास्वपि
व्यावृत्तास्वनुवर्तमानमहमित्यन्तः स्फुरन्तं सदा ।
स्वात्मानं प्रकटीकरोति भजतां यो मुद्रया भद्रया
तस्मै श्रीगुरुमूर्तये नम इदं श्रीदक्षिणामूर्तये ॥

I bow to Sri *Dakṣiṇāmūrti* in the form of my guru:
I bow to Him who, in His loving-kindness reveals to his worshippers,
The eternal Ātman, which—through the changes of waking, dreaming, and dreamless sleep,
Through childhood, youth, maturity, and old age—
Persists as the inexhaustible flow of consciousness.
Revealing Itself in the heart as the ever present sense of "I". (7)

विश्वं पश्यति कार्यकारणतया स्वस्वामिसम्बन्धतः
शिष्याचार्यतया तथैव पितृपुत्राद्यात्मना भेदतः ।
स्वप्ने जाग्रति वा य एष पुरुषो मायापरिभ्रामितः
तस्मै श्रीगुरुमूर्तये नम इदं श्रीदक्षिणामूर्तये ॥

1 According to Non-dualistic Vedānta, Ātman, or the Self of man, exists in dreamless sleep in Its pure Light, free from knowledge of the outer world though covered by the veiling-power of māyā, or ignorance.

2 In Hindu mythology, Rāhu is a monster who now and then swallows, wholly or partly, the sun and the moon, causing their eclipse.

3 Consciousness is present in all the three states, namely, waking, dreaming, and dreamless sleep. The self, which is Pure Consciousness, is the unconcerned Spectator of the experiences of the mind during waking and dreaming, and of their absence during dreamless sleep.

I bow to Sri *Dakṣiṇāmūrti* in the form of my guru seated before me,
Who, as a mortal under the sway of *māyā*, and whether awake or dreaming,
Perceives that the world is composed of multiple entities,
Joined in relation to one another
As cause and effect, owner and owned, teacher and pupil, sire and son. (8)

भूरम्भांस्यनलोऽनिलोऽम्बरमहर्नाथो हिमांशुः पुमान्
इत्याभाति चराचरात्मकमिदं यस्यैव मूर्त्यष्टकम् ।
नान्यत्किञ्चन विद्यते विमृशतां यस्मात्परस्माद्विभोः
तस्मै श्रीगुरुमूर्तये नम इदं श्रीदक्षिणामूर्तये ॥

I bow to Sri *Dakṣiṇāmūrti* in the form of my guru,
Beyond whom, for a wise and discerning man, no being exists superior;
Who has manifested Himself in an eightfold form
As the tangible and insentient earth, water, fire, air, and ether,
As the sun, the lord of day, the moon, of soothing light,
And as living man. (9)

सर्वात्मत्वमिति स्फुटीकृतमिदं यस्मादमुष्मिन्स्तवे
तेनास्य श्रवणात्तदर्थमननाद्ध्यानाच्च सङ्कीर्तनात् ।
सर्वात्मत्वमहाविभूतिसहितं स्यादीश्वरत्व स्वतः
सिध्येत्तत्पुनरष्टधा परिणतं चैश्वर्यमव्याहतम् ॥

This hymn to Sri *Dakṣiṇāmūrti* clearly reveals the Ultimate Truth

As the Soul of everything that has life;
Therefore by hearing it and by pondering on it, by contemplating it and by reciting it,
A man attains unrivalled lordship, acquiring the glory of being the Inmost Self of all,
And effortlessly receives, without interruption, the eight unique powers of the Godhead.[1] (10)

वटविटपिसमीपे भूमिभागे निषण्णं सकलमुनिजनानां
ज्ञानदातारमारात् ।
त्रिभुवनगुरुमीशं दक्षिणामूर्तिदेवं जननमरणदुःखच्छेददक्षं नमामि ॥

I bow to Sri *Dakṣiṇāmūrti* in the form of my guru seated upon the earth by yonder banyan tree;
I bow to Him who bestows on the sages direct knowledge of Ultimate Truth;
I bow to the Teacher of the three worlds,
The Lord Himself, who dispels the misery of birth and death. (11)

चित्रं वटतरोर्मूले वृद्धशिष्या गुरुर्युवा ।
गुरोस्तु मौनं व्याख्यानं शिष्यास्तु छिन्नसंशयाः ॥

Behold, under the banyan are seated the aged disciples about their youthful teacher.
It is strange indeed: the teacher instructs them only through silence,
Which, in itself, is sufficient to scatter the disciples doubts. (12)

1 The Godhead, through these eight unique powers or glories, can make Himself as small as a particle, as huge as a mountain, as heavy as the earth, and as light as the air; He can conquer everything and fulfil all desires.

ओं नमः प्रणवार्थाय शुद्धज्ञानैकमूर्तये ।
निर्मलाय प्रशान्ताय दक्षिणामूर्तये नमः ॥

I bow to Him who is the inner meaning of the sacred syllable *Om*.
To Him whose nature is Pure Awareness;
I bow to Śri *Dakṣiṇāmūrti*, stainless and serene beyond measure. (13)

निधये सर्वविद्यानां भिषजे भवरोगिणाम् :
गुरवे सर्वलोकानां दक्षिणामूर्तये नमः ॥

I bow to Śri *Dakṣiṇāmūrti*, the Mine of Eternal Wisdom,
The Healer of those who suffer from the malady of birth and death,
Who is regarded by all as their own teacher. (14)

मौनव्याख्याप्रकटितपरब्रह्मतत्त्वं युवानं
वर्षिष्ठान्तेवसदृषिगणैरावृतं ब्रह्मनिष्ठैः ।
आचार्येन्द्रं करकलितचिन्मुद्रमानन्दमूर्तिं
स्वात्मारामं मुदितवदनं दक्षिणामूर्तिमीडे ॥

I praise Śri *Dakṣiṇāmūrti*, my youthful teacher.
Who, through silent instruction, reveals the truth of the Parabrahman;[1]
Who is surrounded by aged disciples, mighty sages devoted to Brahman.
I praise the Supreme Teacher, the Essence of Bliss, who revels in His own Self,
The Silent One, whose hand is uplifted in the benediction of knowledge. (15)

1 The Supreme Brahman.

॥ भवान्यष्टकम् ॥

EIGHT STANZAS TO BHAVĀNI[1]

न तातो न माता न बन्धुर्न नप्ता न पुत्रो न पुत्री न भृत्यो न भर्ता ।
न जाया न विद्या न वृत्तिममैव गतिस्त्वं गतिस्त्वं त्वमेका भवा न ॥

No father have I, no mother, no comrade,
No son, no daughter, no wife, and no grandchild,
No servant or master, no wisdom, no calling:
In Thee is my only haven of refuge,
In Thee, my help and my strength, O Bhavāni! (1)

भवाब्धावपारे महादुःखभीरु पपात प्रकामी प्रलोभी प्रमत्तः ।
कुसंसारपाशप्रबद्धः सदाहं गतिस्त्वं गतिस्त्वंत्वमेका भवानि ॥

Immersed as I am in the limitless ocean
Of worldly existence, I tremble to suffer.
Alas! I am lustful and foolish and greedy,
And ever enchained by the fetters of evil:
In Thee is my only haven of refuge,
In Thee is my help and my strength, O Bhavāni! (2)

न जानामि दानं न च ध्यानयोगं न जानामि तन्त्रं न स्तोत्रमन्त्रम् ।
न जानामि पूजां न च न्यासयोग गतिस्त्वं गतिस्त्वं त्वमेका भवाति ॥

To giving of alms and to meditation,
To scriptures and hymns and mantras, a stranger,
I know not of worship, possess no dispassion:
In Thee is my only haven of refuge,
In Thee, my help and my strength, O Bhavāni! (3)

1 The Divine Mother.

न जानामि पुण्यं न जानामि तीर्थं न जानामि मुक्तिं लयं वा कदाचित् ।
न जानामि भक्तिं व्रतं वापि मातर्गतिस्त्वं गतिस्त्वं त्वमेका भवानि ॥

O mother! of pilgrimage or of merit,
Of mental control or the soul's liberation,
Of rigorous vows or devotion, I know not:
In Thee is my only haven of refuge,
In Thee, my help and my strength, O Bhavāni! (4)

कुकर्मी कुसङ्गी कुबुद्धिः कुदासः कुलाचारहीनः कदाचारलीनः ।
कुदृष्टिः कुवाक्यप्रबन्धः सदाहं गतिस्त्वं गतिस्त्वं त्वमेका भवानि ॥

Addicted to sinning and worthless companions,
A slave to ill thoughts and to doers of evil,
Degraded am I, unrighteous, abandoned,
Attached to ill objects, adept in ill-speaking:
In Thee is my only haven of refuge,
In Thee, my help and my strength, O Bhavāni! (5)

प्रजेशं रमेशं सुरेशं दिनेशं निशीथेश्वरं वा कदाचित् ।
न जानामि चान्यं सुराणां शरण्ये गतिस्त्वं गतिस्त्वं त्वमेका भवानि ॥

I know neither Brahma nor Visnu nor Siva,
Nor Indra, sun, moon, or similar being—
Not one of the numberless gods, O Redeemer!
In Thee is my only haven of refuge,
In Thee, my help and my strength, O Bhavāni! (6)

विवादे विषादे प्रमादे प्रवासे जले चानले पर्वते शत्रुमध्ये ।
अरण्ये शरण्ये सदा मां प्रपाहि गतिस्त्वं गतिस्त्वं त्वमेका भवानि ॥

In strife or in sadness, abroad or in danger,
In water, in fire, in the wilds, on the mountains,
Surrounded by foes, my Saviour! protect me:
In thee is my only haven of refuge,
In Thee, my help and my strength, O Bhavāni! (7)

अनाथो दरिद्रो जरारोगयुक्तो महाक्षीणदीनः सदा जाड्यवक्त्रः ।
विपत्तौ प्रविष्टः प्रनष्टः सदाहं गतिस्त्वं गतिस्त्वं त्वमेका भवानि ॥

Defenceless am I—ill, again, and helpless,
Enfeebled, exhausted, and dumbly despairing,
Afflicted with sorrow, and utterly ruined:
In Thee is my only haven of refuge,
In Thee, my help and my strength, O Bhavāni! (8)

॥ अन्नपूर्णास्तोत्रम् ॥

HYMN TO ANNAPURNĀ[1]

नित्यानन्दकरी वराभयकरी सौन्दर्यरत्नाकरी
निर्धूताखिलघोरपावनकरी प्रत्यक्षमाहेश्वरी ।
प्रालेयाचलवंशपावनकरी काशीपुराधीश्वरी
भिक्षां देहि कृपावलम्बनकरी मातान्नपूर्णेश्वरी ।

O benign Mother, who pourest out upon us Everlasting Bliss!
Thou, the Ocean of Beauty! Bestower of boons and of fearlessness!
O Supreme Purifier, who washest away all sins!

1 Lit., One overflowing with food. The Divine Mother, under the name of Annapūrṇā, is worshipped in Benares as the Giver of food, both spiritual and material.

Thou, the visible Ruler of the world, the sanctifier of King Himālaya's[1] line!
O Thou, the Queen Empress of holy Kāsi[2]! Divine Annapūrṇā!
Be gracious unto me and grant me alms[3]. (1)

नानारत्नविचित्रभूषणकरी हेमाम्बराडम्बरी
मुक्ताहारविलम्बमानविलसद्वक्षोजकुम्भान्तरी ।
काश्मीरागुरुवासिता रुचिकरी काशीपुराधीश्वरी
भिक्षां देहि कृपावलम्बनकरी मातान्नपूर्णेश्वरी ॥

Thou whose apparel sparkles, sewn with innumerable gems;
Who wearest a golden sari to heighten Thine unsurpassable loveliness!
Thou on whose comely bosom reposes a necklace of many pearls;
Who dost breathe forth a fragrance, being anointed with saffron and sandal-paste!
O benign Mother! Thou whose form is soothing to the eyes!
O Thou, the Queen Empress of holy Kāsi! Divine Annapūrṇā!
Be gracious unto me and grant me alms. (2)

योगानन्दकरी रिपुक्षयकरी धर्मार्थनिष्ठाकरी
चन्द्रार्कानलभासमानलहरी त्रैलोक्यरक्षाकरी ।
सर्वैश्वर्यसमस्तवाञ्छितकरी काशीपुराधीश्वरी
भिक्षां देहि कृपावलम्बनकरी मातान्नपूर्णेश्वरी ॥

1 According to Hindu mythology the Divine Mother in one of Her incarnations, was born as the daughter of King Himālaya.

2 The modern Benares.

3 i.e., spiritual or material food according to the inclination of the devotees.

Bestower of yoga's bliss! Destroyer of the foe!
Fulfiller of wealth and of righteousness!
Thou who appearest like waves of light, or the radiance of sun and moon and fire!
Protectress of the three worlds! Giver of wealth and of all things wished for!
O Thou, the Queen Empress of holy Kāsi! Divine Annapūrṇā!
Be gracious unto me and grant me alms. (3)

कैलासाचलकन्दरालयकरी गौरी उमा शङ्करी
कौमारी निगमार्थगोचरकरी ओङ्कारबीजाक्षरी ।
मोक्षद्वारकपाटपाटनकरी काशीपुराधीश्वरी
भिक्षां देहि कृपावलम्बनकरी मातान्नपूर्णेश्वरी ॥

O Gauri[1]! O Uma! O Śankari[2]! O Kaumāri[3]
Thou who hast Thy dwelling in the cave of sacred Mount Kailās!
Thou who dost reveal the meaning of the holy Vedas;
Who art the very Embodiment of the mystic syllable *Om*;
Who openest the gates of Liberation!
O Thou. the Queen Empress of holy Kāsi! Divine Annapūrṇā!
Be gracious unto me and grant me alms. (4)

दृश्यादृश्यप्रभूतवाहनकरी ब्रह्माण्डभाण्डोदरी
लीलानाटकसूत्रभेदनकरी विज्ञानदीपाङ्कुरी ।
श्रीविश्वेशमनःप्रसादनकरी काशीपुराधीश्वरी
भिक्षां देहि कृपावलम्बनकरी मातान्नपूर्णेश्वरी ॥

1 Lit., One with complexion of Gold.
2 Lit., Consort of Sankara, or Siva, the Benign Lord.
3 Lit., Virgin.

Thou who bearest the manifold world of the visible and the invisible;
Who holdest the universe in Thy womb!
Thou who severest the thread of the play we play upon this earth!
Who lightest the lamp of wisdom; who bringest joy to the heart of Siva, Thy Lord!
O Thou, the Queen Empress of holy, Kāsi! Divine Annapūrṇā!
Be gracious unto me and grant me alms. (5)

उर्वीसर्वजनेश्वरी भगवती मातान्नपूर्णेश्वरी
वेणीनीलसमानकुन्तलहरी नित्यान्नदानेश्वरी ।
सर्वानन्दकरी दशाशुभकरी काशीपुराधीश्वरी
भिक्षां देहि कृपावलम्बनकरी मातान्नपूर्णेश्वरी ॥

O Bhagavati[1]! Thou who art the Sovereign of the world!
O Mother Annapūrṇā! O Supreme Deity! Ocean of mercy!
Thou whose long tresses, falling to Thy knees,
Ripple restlessly like a river's current and sparkle like a blue gem!
Mother, ever eager to give us food and bliss and all good fortune!
O Thou, the Queen Empress of holy Kasi! Divine Annapurna!
Be gracious unto me and grant me alms. (6)

आदिक्षान्तसमस्तवर्णनकरी शम्भोस्त्रिभावाकरी
काश्मीरा त्रिजनेश्वरी त्रिलहरी नित्याङ्कुरा शर्वरी ।
कामाकाङ्क्षकरी जनोदयकरी काशीपुराधीश्वरी
भिक्षां देहि कृपावलम्बनकरी मातान्नपूर्णेश्वरी ॥

1 Lit., One endowed with lordly powers.

Thou who revealest all the letters, from the first to the last!
Mother of the cosmos, gross and subtle, and of its Lord as well!
Ruler of earth and heaven and the nether world,
Who dost embody in Thyself the waves of creation, sustenance, and dissolution!
Eternal, uncaused Cause, who art the thick darkness of the cosmic dissolution!
Thou who bringest desire to the heart of man; who dost bestow on him well-being in this world!
O Thou, the Queen Empress of holy Kāsi! Divine Annapūrṇā!
Be gracious unto me and grant me alms. (7)

दर्वी स्वर्णविचित्ररत्नरचिता दक्षे करे संस्थिता
वामे स्वादुपयोधरी प्रियकरी सौभाग्यमाहेश्वरी ।
भक्ताभीष्टकरी दशा शुभकरी काशीपुराधीश्वरी
भिक्षां देहि कृपावलम्बनकरी मातान्नपूर्णेश्वरी ॥

Thou who holdest in Thy right hand a ladle of gold studded with jewels,
And in Thy left hand holdest a cup of delicious food!
Thou Giver of good fortune, who dost fulfil the wishes of Thy worshippers.
And bringest about their welfare with a mere wink of Thine eye!
O Thou, the Queen Empress of holy Kāsi! Divine Annapūrṇā!
Be gracious unto me and grant me alms. (8)

चन्द्रार्कानलकोटिकोटिसदृशा चन्द्रांशुबिम्बाधरी
चन्द्रार्काग्निसमानकुण्डलधरी चन्द्रार्कवर्णेश्वरी ।

मालापुस्तकपाशसाङ्कुशधरी काशीपुराधीश्वरी
भिक्षां देहि कृपावलम्बनकरी मातान्नपूर्णेश्वरी ॥

Thou whose radiance burns a million times more bright than sun and moon and fire:
For whom the light of the moon is but the shadow of Thy lips;
Whose ear-rings sparkle like the sun and moon and fire; who shinest like the sun and moon!
Thou, the Supreme Empress, who in Thy four hands holdest rosary and book and goad and dice!
O Thou, the Queen Empress of holy Kāśi! Divine Annapūrṇa!
Be gracious unto me and grant me alms. (9)

क्षत्रत्राणकरी महाभयकरी माता कृपासागरी
साक्षान्मोक्षकरी सदा शिवकरी विश्वेश्वरश्रीधरी ।
दक्षाक्रन्दकरी निरामयकरी काशीपुराधीश्वरी
भिक्षां देहि कृपावलम्बनकरी मातान्नपूर्णेश्वरी ॥

Protectress of the ksatriya[1] line! Giver of utter fearlessness!
Benign Mother of all! Ocean of infinite mercy!
Thou, the Bestower of instantaneous Liberation, the Giver of Eternal Good!
Provider of Siva's welfare! Destroyer of every bodily ill!
O Thou, the Queen Empress of holy Kāśi! Divine Annapūrṇa!
Be gracious unto me and grant me alms. (10)

1 The military caste in Hindu society.

अन्नपूर्णे सदापूर्णे शङ्करप्राणवल्लभे ।
ज्ञानवैराग्यसिद्ध्यर्थं भिक्षां देहि च पार्वति ॥

O Annapūrṇā! Thou who never lackest for anything, who holdest Sankara's heart in thrall!
O Pārvati[1]! Grant me alms: I supplicate Thee for the boon of wisdom and renunciation above all. (11)

माता मे पार्वती देवी पिता देवो महेश्वरः ।
बान्धवाः शिवभक्ताश्च स्वदेशो भुवनत्रयम् ॥

My Mother is the Goddess Pārvati; my Father is Siva, the Lord whose power none can withstand.
Their worshippers I own as my kith and kin; and the three worlds are my native land. (12)

॥ विष्णुषट्पदी ॥

SIX STANZAS TO VIṢNU

अविनयमपनय विष्णो दमय मनः शमय विषयमृगतृष्णाम् ।
भूतदयां विस्तारय तारय संसारसागरतः ॥

Save me from pride, O Viṣṇu! Curb my restless mind.
Still my thirst for the waters of this world's mirage.
Be gracious, Lord! to this Thy humble creature
And rescue him from the ocean of the world. (1)

1 Daughter of King Himālaya and Consort of Siva; a name of the Divine Mother.

दिव्यधुनीमकरन्दे परिमलपरिभोगसच्चिदानन्दे ।
श्रीपतिपदारविन्दे भवभयखेदच्छिदे वन्दे ॥

I worship the lotus of Thy feet, whose honey is the sacred
Ganges,
Whose fragrance is Knowledge, Truth, and Bliss;
I worship the feet of Laksmī's[1] Consort,
Who overcomes the fear and misery of the world. (2)

सत्यपि भेदापगमे नाथ तवाहं न मामकीनस्त्वम् ।
सामुद्रो हि तरङ्गः क्वचन समुद्रो न तारङ्गः ॥

Even when I am not duality's slave, O Lord,
The Truth is that I am Thine, and not that Thou art mine;
The waves may belong to the ocean,
But the ocean never belongs to the waves. (3)

उद्धृतनग नगभिदनुज दनुजकुलामित्र मित्रशशिदृष्टे ।
दृष्टे भवति प्रभवति न भवति किं भवतिरस्कारः ॥

Bearer of Govardhana![2] Slayer of the demon hosts!
Almighty One, whose eyes are the sun and moon:
Can anyone doubt, O Lord of the universe!
That the vision of Thy form dispels this world's mirage? (4)

मत्स्यादिभिरवतारैरवतारवताऽवता सदा वसुधाम् ।
परमेश्वर परिपाल्यो भवता भवतापभीतोऽहम् ॥

1 The Goddess of fortune and Consort of Viṣṇu.

2 A hill near Mathurā which Srī Kṛṣṇa lifted in his hands to protect the inhabitants of the surrounding countryside from a deluge of rain.

Sovereign Lord! with Thy manifold Incarnations
Ever hast Thou protected the universe from harm!
Come to my rescue, then, O Lord!
Save me, who am afflicted by the fire of the world. (5)

दामोदर गुणमन्दिर सुन्दरवदनारविन्द गोविन्द ।
भवजलधिमथनमन्दर परमं दरमपनय त्वं मे ॥

Govinda! Dāmodara! Thou who art possessed
Of infinite virtues and surpassing charm!
Thou Churner of the sea of worldliness!
Be gracious unto me and destroy my extreme fear. (6)

नारायण करुणामय शरणं करवाणि तावकौ चरणौ ।
इति षट्पदी मदीये वदनसरोजे सदा वसतु ॥

Nārāyana! Thou who art ever compassionate!
I have taken refuge in Thy two feet:
May these six stanzas, even as a honey bee,
Ever remain on the lotus of my lips! (7)

॥ गङ्गास्तोत्रम् ॥

HYMN TO GANGĀ[1]

देवि सुरेश्वरि भगवति गङ्गे त्रिभुवनतारिणि तरलतरङ्गे ।
शङ्करमौलिविहारिणि विमले मम मतिरास्तां तव पदकमले ॥

1 The sacred river Ganges.

Heaven-born river! Bhagavati Gangā!
Goddess, Redeemer of all the world!
In ripples Thy waters playfully are flowing;
Thou wanderest in Siva's matted hair,
Grant that my mind, O Thou who art stainless!
Ever may dwell at the lotus of Thy feet. (1)

भागीरथि सुखदायिनि मातस्तवजलमहिमा निगमे ख्यातः ।
नाहं जाने तव महिमानं त्राहि कृपामयि मामज्ञानम् ॥

Bhāgīrathi![1] Mother! Giver of gladness!
The scriptures celebrate the glory of Thy stream;
But I, alas! know nothing of Thy glories.
Foolish as I am, do Thou redeem me,
Thou, the embodiment of merciful love! (2)

हरिपदपाद्यतरङ्गिणि गङ्गे हिमविधुमुक्ताधवलतरङ्गे ।
दूरीकुरु मम दुष्कृतिभारं, कुरु कृपया भवसागरपारम् ॥

Rippling, Thou flowest from the feet of Hari,[2]
Whiter than frost or diamonds or the moon.
O Mother Gangā! take away the burden
Of wicked deeds that weighs upon me:
Bear me across the ocean of the world. (3)

तव जलममलं येन निपीतं परमपदं खलु तेन गृहीतम् ।
मातर्गङ्गे त्वयि यो भक्तः किल तं द्रष्टुं न यमः शक्तः ॥

1 A name given to the Ganges because of its having been brought down from heaven to earth by King Bhagīratha for the redeeming of his forefathers.

2 Viṣṇu

He who has drunk Thy refreshing waters
Verily has tasted of the Highest;
He, Thy worshipper, O Mother Gangā!
Never will be seized by the King of Death. (4)

पतितोद्धारिणि जाह्नवि गङ्गे खण्डितगिरिवरमंण्डितभङ्गे ।
भीष्मजननि खलु मुनिवरकन्ये पतितनिवारिणि त्रिभुवनधन्ये ॥

Gangā! Jāhnavi![1] Saviour of sinners!
Murmuring, Thou flowest on Thy broken stones.
Mother of Bhisma![2] Daughter of Jahnu!
Thou, the almighty Conqueror of evil!
Truly Thou art blest in all the worlds. (5)

कल्पलतामिव फलदां लोके प्रणमति यस्त्वां न पतति शोके ।
पारावारविहारिणि गङ्गे सुरवनिताकृततरलापाङ्गे ॥

Like the celestial Tree of Wishes,
Thou grantest the boons of men's desiring;
He who salutes Thee will not grieve again.
Thou sportest, O Gangā, with the limitless ocean:
Wondering, the damsels of heaven regard Thee,
Watching with restless, sidelong glances. (6)

तव कृपया चेत् स्रोतः स्नातः पुनरपि जठरे सोऽपि न जातः ।
नरकनिवारिणि जाह्नवि गङ्गे कलुषविनाशिनि महिमोत्तुङ्गे ॥

If, by Thy grace, one bathes in Thy waters
Never again need one enter a mother's womb:

1 Lit., Daughter of the sage Jahnu. An epithet of the Ganges.
2 A great warrior, one of the heroes of *Mahabharata*.

The sins of a lifetime for all annulling,
The claims of destiny at death dispelling.
Jāhnavi! Gangā! the worlds accord Thee
Honour and renown for the glory that is Thine. (7)

परिलसदङ्गे पुण्यतरङ्गे जय जय जाह्नवि करुणापाङ्गे ।
इन्द्रमुकुटमणिराजितचरणे सुखदे शुभदे सेवकशरणे ॥

Brightly, O Jāhnavi, Thy waters sparkle;
Thou lookest on Thy worshippers with loving glance.
Indra himself, the ruler of the devas,[1]
Bows at Thy feet with his jewelled crown.
Giver of happiness! Bringer of good fortune!
Help of Thy bondslaves, hail to Thee! (8)

रोगं शोकं तापं पापं हर मे भगवति कुमतिकलापम् ।
त्रिभुवनसारे वसुधाहारे त्वमसि गतिर्मम खलु संसारे ॥

Banish, O Bhagavathi! all my illness;
Take away my troubles, my sins and my grief;
Utterly crush my wanton cravings,
Goddess, supreme in all the world!
Thou, Mother Earth's most precious necklace!
Thou art my refuge here in this world! (9)

अलकानन्दे परमानन्दे कुरु मयि करुणां कातरवन्द्ये ।
तव तटनिकटे यस्य हि वासः खलु वैकुण्ठे तस्य निवासः ॥

Giver of delight to the gods in heaven!
Essence of Bliss, adored by the afflicted!

1 The gods of Hindu mythology.

On me shower Thy compassionate love.
He who has made Thy bank his dwelling
Verily abides in Viṣṇu's realm. (10)

वरमिह नीरे कमठो मीनः किं वा तीरे सरटः क्षीणः ।
अथवा श्वपचो गव्युतिदीनः न च तव दूरे नृपतिकुलीनः ॥

Rather a fish or a turtle in Thy waters,
A tiny lizard on Thy bank, would I be,
Or even a shunned and hated outcaste
Living but a mile from Thy sacred stream,
Than the proudest emperor afar from Thee. (11)

भो भुवनेश्वरि पुण्ये धन्ये देवि द्रवमयि मुनिवरकन्ये ।
गङ्गास्तवमिदममलं नित्यं पठति नरो यः स जयति सत्यम् ॥

Thou, the auspicious Ruler of creation!
Daughter of a sage and Mother benign!
Flowing Deity! Veritable Goddess!
He who repeats this hymn to Gangā
Surely will succeed in everything. (12)

येषां हृदये गङ्गाभक्तिस्तेषां भवति सदा सुखमुक्तिः ।
मधुरमनोहरपज्झटिकाभिः परमानन्दाकरललिताभिः ॥
गङ्गास्तोत्रमिदं भवसारं वाञ्छितफलदं विगलितभारम् ।
शङ्करसेवकशङ्कररचितं पठतु च विषयी तद्गतचित्तम् ॥

He who cherishes his Mother Gangā
Wins salvation with the greatest of ease.
This, Her hymn, felicitous in rhythm,
Pleasant to the ear, to the tongue like nectar,

Never surpassed, the wish-fulfiller,
Noble and exalted in mood, was written
In the mind-bewitching Pajjhaṭikā metre[1]
By Sankara, servant of Sankara[2] Himself,
Foolish mortal, given to enjoyment,
Read it daily for your lasting good. (13)

॥ देव्यपराधक्षमापणस्तोत्रम् ॥

HYMN TO THE DIVINE MOTHER FOR FORGIVENESS OF TRANSGRESSIONS

न मन्त्रं नो यन्त्रं तदपि च न जाने स्तुतिमहो
न चाह्वानं तदपि च न जाने स्तुतिकथाः ।
न जाने मुद्रास्ते तदपि च न जाने विलपनं
परं जाने मातस्त्वदनुसरणं क्लेशहरणम् ॥

I know, alas! no hymn, no mantra,
Neither prayer nor meditation;
Not even how to give Thee praise.
The proper ritual of the worship,
The placement of the hands, I know not,
Nor how to make Thee supplication.
But Mother, this at least I know:
Whoever comes to Thee for shelter
Reaches the end of all his woe. (1)

1 A metre suggestive of the rippling water of a stream.
2 Siva, the Great God, is known also as Sankara.

विधेरज्ञानेन द्रविणविरहेणालसतया
विधेयाशक्यत्वात् तव चरणयोर्या च्युतिरभूत् ।
तदेतत्क्षन्तव्यं जननि सकलोद्धारिणि शिवे
कुपुत्रो जायेत क्वचिदपि कुमाता न भवति ॥

Ignorant of the commands of scripture,
Utterly devoid of wealth,
Shiftless, indolent, am I,
Unable to do as I ought to do.
Numerous, therefore, are the offences
I have committed at Thy feet.
Mother! Saviour of all mankind!
Auspicious One! forgive my sins.
A wicked son is sometimes born,
But an unkind mother there cannot be. (2)

पृथिव्यां पुत्रास्ते जननि बहवः सन्ति सरलाः
परं तेषां मध्ये विरलतरलोऽहं तव सुतः ।
मदीयोऽयं त्यागः समुचितमिदं नो तव शिवे
कुपुत्रो जायेत क्वचिदपि कुमाता न भवति ॥

Here in this world of Thine, O Mother!
Many are Thy guileless children;
But restless am I among them all,
And so it is nothing very strange
That I should turn myself from Thee.
Yet surely it were impossible
That Thou shouldst ever turn from me:
A wicked son is sometimes born,
But an unkind mother there cannot be. (3)

जगन्मातर्मातस्तव चरणसेवा न रचिता
न वा दत्तं देवि द्रविणमपि भूयस्तव मया ।
तथापित्वं स्नेहं मयि निरुपमं यत्प्रकुरुषे
कुपुत्रो जायेत क्वचिदपि कुमाता न भवति ॥

Mother of the world! Thou, my own Mother!
Never have I served Thee, never yet
Offered Thee gold or precious gems;
And still Thy love is beyond compare.
A wicked son is sometimes born,
But an unkind mother there cannot be. (4

परित्यक्ता देवाः विविधविधिसेवाकुलतया
मया पञ्चाशीतेरधिकमपनीते तु वयसि ।
इदानीं चेन्मातस्तव यदि कृपा नापि भविता
निरालम्बो लम्बोदरजननि कं यामि शरणम् ॥

Bewildered by the rules of conduct,
By the injunctions of the scriptures,
I have abandoned, one by one,
The shining gods; and now my life
Has passed beyond the meridian.
Mother, shouldst Thou withhold Thy mercy,
Where, then, shall I fly for shelter,
Weak and helpless as I am? (5

श्वपाको जल्पाको भवति मधुपाकोपमगिरा
निरातङ्को रङ्को विहरति चिरं कोटिकनकैः ।
तवापर्णे कर्णे विशति मनुवर्णे फलमिदं
जनः को जानीते जननि जपनीयं जपविधौ ॥

If one who feeds on the flesh of dogs
Can learn to speak with honeyed words,
A beggar gain uncounted wealth
And so live long and fearlessly,
Simply hearing Thy magic name—
Who can describe what must befall
One who repeats it night and day? (6)

चिताभस्मालेपो गरलमशनं दिक्पटधरो
जटाधारी कण्ठे भुजगपतिहारी पशुपतिः ।
कपाली भूतेशो भजति जगदीशैकपदवीं
भवानि त्वत्पाणिग्रहणपरिपाटीफलमिदम् ।

Only by taking Thee for Spouse
Did Siva become the unrivalled Lord—
He who is naked and uncouth,
Besmeared with ash from the funeral pyre;
Whose hair is matted on his head,
About whose neck are venomous snakes—
The Lord of every living thing. (7)

न मोक्षस्याकाङ्क्षा न च विभववाञ्छापि च न मे
न विज्ञानापेक्षा शशिमुखि सुखेच्छापि न पुनः ।
अतस्त्वां संयाचे जननि जननं यातु मम वै
मृडानी रुद्राणी शिवशिवभवानीति जपतः ॥

I do not ask of Thee, O Mother!
Riches, good fortune, or salvation;
I seek no happiness, no knowledge.
This is my only prayer to Thee:
That, as the breath of life forsakes me,
Still I may chant Thy holy name. (8)

नाराधितासि विधिना विविधोपचारैः
किं रूक्षचिन्तनपरैर्न कृतं वचोभिः ।
श्यामे त्वमेव यदि किञ्चन मय्यनाथे
धत्से कृपामुचितमम्ब परं तवैव ॥

Mother, I have not worshipped Thee
With proper rituals and the prescribed
Ingredients of sacrifice.
Many are my sinful deeds!
Day and night I have spent myself
In idle talk, forgetting Thee.
O Divine Mother, if Thou canst show
The slightest mercy to one so frail,
It will befit Thy majesty. (9)

आपत्सु मग्नः स्मरणं त्वदीयं करोमि दुर्गे करुणार्णवेशि ।
नैतच्छठत्वं मम भावयेथाः क्षुधातृषार्ता जननीं स्मरन्ति ॥

Durgā! Goddess of Mercy's Ocean!
Stricken with grief, to Thee I pray:
Do not believe me insincere;
A child who is seized with thirst or hunger
Thinks of his mother constantly. (10)

जगदम्ब विचित्रमत्र किं परिपूर्णा करुणास्ति चेन्मयि ।
अपराधपरम्परावृतं न हि माता समुपेक्षते सुतम् ॥

Mother of all the universe!
If Thou shouldst show Thy fullest mercy,
Would even that be a cause for wonder?
A mother cannot refuse her son,
Though he has done a million wrongs. (11)

मत्समः पातकी नास्ति पापघ्नी त्वत्समा न हि ।
एवं ज्ञात्वा महादेवि यथा योग्यं तथा कुरु ॥

Nowhere exists, in all the world,
Another sinner to equal me,
Nowhere, a Power like Thyself
For overcoming sinfulness:
O Goddess! keeping this in mind,
Do Thou as it pleases Thee. (12)

॥ वेदसारशिवस्तोत्रम् ॥

HYMN TO SIVA

पशूनां पतिं पापनाशं परेशं गजेन्द्रस्य कृत्तिं वसानं वरेण्यम् ।
जटाजूटमध्ये स्फुरद्गाङ्गवारिं महादेवमेकं स्मरामि स्मरारिम् ॥

Him do I cherish, the Lord of living creatures, the Almighty One, the Slayer of sin,
Who is adored by all,
Within whose matted locks the Ganges wanders murmuring:
Him do I cherish—Siva, the Great God, the One without a second, the Destroyer of lust. (1)

महेशं सुरेशं सुरारातिनाशं विभुं विश्वनाथं विभूत्यङ्गभूषम् ।
विरूपाक्षमिन्द्वर्कवह्नित्रिनेत्रं सदानन्दमीडे प्रभुं पञ्चवक्त्रम् ॥

Him do I praise, the Lord Supreme, the God of gods, the Demon-slayer,

Who is the Spirit pervading all,
The Lord of the world, whose body is ash-besmeared,
whose three eyes are the sun, the moon, and fire:
Him do I praise--Siva, the Ever Blessed, the Five-faced One. (2)

गिरीशं गणेशं गले नीलवर्णं गवेन्द्राधिरूढं गुणातीतरूपम् ।
भवं भास्वरं भस्मना भूषिताङ्गं भवानीकलत्रं भजे पञ्चवक्त्रम् ॥

Him do I worship, the King of the holy mountains, the Lord of hosts, the Blue-throated God[1]
Who dwells beyond the three gunas[2],
The Primal Cause, the Shining One, whose body is white with ashes, who rides on the sacred bull:
Him do I worship—Siva, the Five-faced One, whose Consort is Bhavāni. (3)

शिवाकान्त शम्भो शशाङ्कार्धमौले महेशान शूलिन् जटाजूटधारिन् ।
त्वमेको जगद्व्यापको विश्वरूप प्रसीद प्रसीद प्रभो पूर्णरूप ॥

O Lord of Uma! Sambhu,[3] whose brow is adorned with the crescent moon!
O Mahādeva,[4] Wielder of the trident, Wearer of matted locks!

1 According to Hindu mythology, when the ocean was churned by the gods and the demons to obtain the nectar of immortality. Siva drank the deadly poison that first came out. The poison remained in His throat and made it blue.

2 Sattva, rajas, and tamas.

3 An epithet of Siva.

4 Lit., the Great God.

O Thou who alone pervadest the universe! O Thou of cosmic form!
O Lord, eternally complete! Be Thou propitious unto us! Be gracious unto us, O Lord! (4)

परात्मानमेकं जगद्बीजमाद्यं निरीहं निराकारमोङ्कारवेद्यम् ।
यतो जायते पाल्यते येन विश्वं तमीशं भजे लीयते यत्र विश्वम् ॥

Him do I Worship, the Paramātman,[1] One and without a second,
Who is the cause of the universe,
The Primal Being, Spirit formless and actionless, who is attained through the syllable *Om:*
Him do I worship—Siva, of whom the universe is born, by whom it is sustained, in whom it merges. (5)

न भूमिर्नं चापो न वह्निर्न वायुर्न चाकाशमास्ते न तन्द्रा न निद्रा ।
न चोष्णं न शीतं न देशो न वेशो न यस्यास्ति मूर्तिस्त्रिमूर्तिं तमीडे ॥

Him do I worship, who is neither earth nor water, who is neither fire nor air nor ether,
Who is unvisited by sleep, yet evermore unwearied,
Beyond both heat and cold, without a country and without a home;
Him do I worship—Siva, the Formless One, the Trimūrti.[2] (6)

1 The Supreme Self.

2 Refers to an aspect of Siva in which are conjoined the forms of Brahmā, the Creator, Viṣṇu, the Preserver, and Siva, the Destroyer.

अजं शाश्वतं कारणं कारणानां शिवं केवलं भासकं भासकानाम् ।
तुरीयं तमः पारमाद्यन्तहीनं प्रपद्ये परं पावनं द्वैतहीनम् ॥

In Him do I take refuge, the Birthless, the Everlasting, the Cause of all causes,
The transcendental, who is beyond all darkness,
The Auspicious One, the Self-existent, the light of lights, who is without beginning or end:
In Him do I take refuge—Siva, the Supreme Purifier, the One without a second. (7)

नमस्ते नमस्ते विभो विश्वमूर्ते नमस्ते नमस्ते चिदानन्दमूर्ते ।
नमस्ते नमस्ते तपोयोगगम्य नमस्ते नमस्ते श्रुतिज्ञानगम्य ॥

O All-pervasive Spirit! Thou whose visible form is the universe! Thee I salute again and again;
O Thou who art the Embodiment of Consciousness and Bliss! Again and again do I salute Thee.
Thee I salute again and again, who art attainable through yoga and self-control;
Again and again do I salute Thee, who art only to be known through knowledge of the Vedas. (8)

प्रभो शूलपाणे विभो विश्वनाथ महादेव शम्भो महेश त्रिनेत्र ।
शिवाकान्त शान्त स्मरारे पुरारे त्वदन्यो वरेण्यो न मान्यो न गण्यः ॥

O Lord! O Omnipresent Spirit! Wielder of the trident! Ruler of the universe!
O Mahādeva, Giver of happiness! O Supreme Lord! O Three-eyed Siva!

Serene One! Consort of Uma! Slayer of demons! Destroyer of lust!
None but Thee should we cherish and honour and adore, O Lord! (9)

शम्भो महेश करुणामय शूलपाणे गौरीपते पशुपते पशुपाशनाशिन् ।
काशीपते करुणया जगदेतदेकस्त्वं हंसि पासि विदधासि महेश्वरोऽसि ॥

O Sambhu, Giver of joy! Merciful One! Almighty Lord!
Consort of Gaurī! Lord of all living creatures! Thou who destroyest the fetters of the world!
O King of Kāsī! Thou who art alone supreme!
Moved by compassion, Thou dost create, sustain, and destroy this world. (10)

त्वत्तो जगद्भवति देव भव स्मरारे त्वय्येव तिष्ठति जगन्मृड विश्वनाथ ।
त्वय्येव गच्छति लयं जगदेतदीश लिङ्गात्मके हर चराचरविश्वरूपिन् ॥

Lord and Primeval Cause! Slayer of Madana[1]! From Thee alone the world has sprung.
Compassionate One! Thou who art Lord of all! In Thee alone does the world endure.
Lord Siva, who does reveal Thyself through all things living and all without life!
To Thee alone does the world at last return. (11)

1 The god of earthly love.

॥ शिवनामावल्यष्टकम् ॥

HYMN TO MAHADEVA

हे चन्द्रचूड मदनान्तक शूलपाणे स्थाणो गिरीश गिरिजेश
महेश शम्भो ।
भूतेश भीतभयसूदन मामनाथं संसारदुःखगहनाज्जगदीश
रक्ष ॥

O Mahādeva! O Thou Auspicious One, with the moon shining in Thy crest!
Slayer of Madana! Wielder of the trident! Unmoving One! Lord of the Himālayas!
O Consort of Durga! Lord of all creatures! Thou who scatterest the distress of the fearful!
Rescue me, helpless as I am, from the trackless forest of this miserable world. (1)

हे पार्वतीहृदयवल्लभ चन्द्रमौले भूताधिप प्रमथनाथ
गिरीशजाप ।
हे वामदेव भवरुद्र पिनाकपाणे संसारदुःखगहनाज्जगदीश
रक्ष ॥

O Beloved of Pārvatī's heart! O Thou moon-crested Deity!
Master of every being! Lord of hosts! O Thou, the Lord of Pārvatī!
O Vāmadeva, Self-existent One! O Rudra, Wielder of the bow!
Rescue me, helpless as I am, from the trackless forest of this miserable world. (2)

हे नीलकण्ठ वृषभध्वज पञ्चवक्त्र लोकेश शेषवलय
प्रमथेश शर्व ।
हे धूर्जटे पशुपते गिरिजापते मां संसारदुःख
गहनाज्जगदीश रक्ष ॥

O Blue-throated God! Siva, whose emblem is the bull!
O Five-faced One!
Lord of the worlds, who wearest snakes about Thy wrists!
O Thou Auspicious One!
O Siva! O Pasupati![1] O Thou, the Lord of Pārvatī!
Rescue me, helpless as I am, from the trackless forest of this miserable world. (3)

हे विश्वनाथ शिव शङ्कर देवदेव गङ्गाधर प्रमथनायक
नन्दिकेश ।
बाणेश्वरान्धकरिपो हर लोकनाथ संसारदुःखगहनाज्ज-
गदीश रक्ष ॥

O Lord of the universe! O Siva Sankara! O God of gods!
Thou who dost bear the river Ganges in Thy matted locks!
Thou, the Master of Pramatha and Nandika![2] O Hara, Lord of the world!
Rescue me, helpless as I am, from the trackless forest of this miserable world. (4)

वाराणसीपुरपते मणिकर्णिकेश वीरेश दक्षमखकाल
विभो गणेश ।
सर्वज्ञ सर्वहृदयैकनिवास नाथ संसारदुःखगहनाज्जगदीश
रक्ष ॥

1 Lord of beings.

2 Attendants of Siva.

O King of Kāsī! Lord of the cremation ground of Maṇikarṇikā!
O mighty Hero! Thou, the Destroyer of Dakṣa's[1] sacrifice! O All-pervasive One!
O Lord of hosts! Omniscient One, who art the sole Indweller in every heart! O God!
Rescue me, helpless as I am, from the trackless forest of this miserable world. (5)

श्रीमन्महेश्वर कृपामय हे दयालो हे व्योमकेश शितिकण्ठ गणाधिनाथ ।
भस्माङ्गराग नृकपालकलापमाल संसारदुःखगहनाज्जगदीश रक्ष ॥

O Mahādeva! Compassionate One! Benign Deity!
O Vyomakesa![2] Blue-throated One! O Lord of hosts!
Thou whose body is besmeared with ashes! Thou who art garlanded with human skulls!
Rescue me, helpless as I am, from the trackless forest of this miserable world. (6)

कैलासशैलविनिवास वृषाकपे हे मृत्युञ्जय त्रिनयन त्रिजगन्निवास ।
नारायणप्रिय मदापह शक्तिनाथ संसारदुःखगहनाज्जगदीश रक्ष ॥

O Thou who dwellest on Mount Kailās! Thou whose carrier is the bull!

1 Siva's father-in-law.
2 Lit., the One whose hair is the sky; a name of Siva.

O Conqueror of death! O Three-eyed One! Lord of the three worlds!
Beloved of Nārāyaṇa! Slayer of lust! Thou, Sakti's Lord!
Rescue me, helpless as I am, from the trackless forest of this miserable world. (7)

विश्वेश विश्वभवनाशित विश्वरूप विश्वात्मक
त्रिभुवनैकगुणाभिवेश ।
हे विश्ववन्द्य करुणामय दीनबन्धो संसारदुःख
गहनाज्जगदीश रक्ष ॥

Lord of the universe! Refuge of the whole world! O Thou of infinite forms!
Soul of the universe! O Thou in whom repose the infinite virtues of the world!
O Thou adored by all! Compassionate One! O Friend of the poor!
Rescue me, helpless as I am, from the trackless forest of this miserable world. (8)

॥ शिवापराधक्षमापणस्तोत्रम् ॥

HYMN FOR FORGIVENESS

आदौ कर्मप्रसङ्गात्कलयति कलुषं मातृकुक्षौ स्थितं मां
विण्मूत्रामेध्यमध्ये कथयति नितरां जाठरो जातवेदाः ।
यद्यद्वै तत्र दुःखं व्यथयति नितरां शक्यते केन वक्तुं
क्षन्तव्यो मेऽपराधः शिव शिव शिव भो श्रीमहादेव शम्भो ॥

Even before I saw the light of this world, my sins from previous births,
Through which I passed because of desire for the fruit of my deeds,
Punished me as I lay in my mother's womb.
There I was boiled in the midst of unclean things.
Who can describe the pain that afflicts the child in its mother's womb?
Therefore, O Siva! O Māhādeva! O Sambhu! Forgive me, I pray, for my transgressions. (1)

बाल्ये दुःखातिरेको मललुलितवपुः स्तन्यपाने पिपासा
नो शक्तश्चेन्द्रियेभ्यो भवगुणजनिता जन्तवो मां तुदन्ति ।
नानारोगादिदुःखाद्रुदनपरवशः शङ्करं न स्मरामि
क्षन्तव्यो मेऽपराधः शिव शिव शिव भो श्रीमहादेव शम्भो ॥

In childhood my suffering never came to an end;
My body was covered with filth and I craved for my mother's breasts.
Over my body and limbs I had no control;
I was pursued by troublesome flies and mosquitoes;
Day and night I cried with the pain of many an ailment, forgetting Thee, O Sankara!
Therefore, O Siva! O Māhadeva! O Sambhu! Forgive me, I pray, for my transgressions. (2)

प्रौढोऽहं यौवनस्थो विषयविषधरैः पञ्चभिर्मर्मसन्धौ
दष्टो नष्टोऽविवेकः सुतधनयुवतिस्वादुसौख्ये निषण्णः ।
शैवीचिन्ताविहीनं मम हृदयमहो मानगर्वाधिरूढं
क्षन्तव्यो मेऽपराधः शिव शिव शिव भो श्रीमहादेव शम्भो ॥

In youth the venomous snakes of sound and sight, of taste and touch and smell,
Fastened upon my vitals and slew my discrimination;
I was engrossed in the pleasures of wealth and sons and a youthful wife,
Alas! my heart, bereft of the thought of Siva,
Swelled with arrogance and pride.
Therefore, O Siva! O Mahādeva! O S'ambhu! Forgive me, I pray, for my transgressions. (3)

वार्धक्ये चेन्द्रियाणां विगतगतिमतिश्चाधिदैवादितापैः
पापै रोगैर्वियोगैस्त्वनवसितवपुः प्रौढिहीनं च दीनम् ।
मिथ्यामोहाभिलाषैर्भ्रमति मम मनो धूर्जटेर्ध्यानशून्यं
क्षन्तव्यो मेऽपराधः शिव शिव शिव भो श्रीमहादेव शम्भो ॥

Now in old age my senses have lost the power of proper judging and acting;
My body, though still not wholly bereft of life,
Is weak and senile from many afflictions, from sins and illnesses and bereavements;
But even now my mind, instead of meditating on Siva
Runs after vain desires and hollow delusions.
Therefore, O Siva! O Mahādeva! O Sambhu!
Forgive me, I pray, for my transgressions. (4)

नो शक्यं स्मार्तकर्मप्रतिपदगहनप्रत्यवायाकुलाख्यं
श्रौते वार्ता कथं मे द्विजकुलविहिते ब्रह्ममार्गे सुसारे
नास्था धर्मे विचारः श्रवणमननयोः किं निदिध्यासितव्यं
क्षन्तव्यो मेऽपराधः शिव शिव शिव भो श्रीमहादेव शम्भो ॥

The duties laid down in the Smṛti—perilous and abstruse—are now beyond me;

How can I speak of the Vedic injunctions for brahmins, as means for attaining Brahman?
Never yet have I rightly grasped, through discrimination,
The meaning of hearing the scriptures from the guru and reasoning on his instruction;
How, then, speak of reflecting on Truth without interruption?
Therefore, O Siva! O Mahādeva! O Sambhu! Forgive me, I pray, for my transgressions. (5)

स्नात्वा प्रत्यूषकाले स्नपनविधिविधौ नाहृतं गाङ्गतोयं
पूजार्थं वा कदाचिद्बहुतरगहनात्खण्डबिल्वीदलानि ।
नानीता पद्ममाला सरसि विकसिता गन्धधूपौ त्वदर्थं
क्षन्तव्यो मेऽपराधः शिव शिव शिव भो श्रीमहादेव शम्भो ॥

Not even once have I finished my bath before sunrise and brought from the Ganges
Water to bathe Thy holy image;
Never, from the deep woods, have I brought the sacred bel-leaves for Thy worship;
Nor have I gathered full-blown lotuses from the lakes,
Nor ever arranged the lights and the incense for worshipping Thee.
Therefore, O Siva! O Mahādeva! O Sambhu!
Forgive me, I pray, for my transgressions. (6)

दुग्धैर्मध्वाज्ययुक्तैर्दधिसितसहितैः स्नापितं नैव लिङ्गं
नो लिप्तं चन्दनाद्यैः कनकविरचितैः पूजितं न प्रसूनैः ।
धूपैः कर्पूरदीपैर्विविधरसयुतैर्नैव भक्ष्योपहारैः
क्षन्तव्यो मेऽपराधः शिव शिव शिव भो श्रीमहादेव शम्भो ॥

I have not bathed Thine image with milk and honey, with butter and other oblations;

I have not decked it with fragrant sandal-paste:
I have not worshipped Thee with golden flowers, with incense, with camphor flame and savoury offerings.
Therefore, O Siva! O Mahādeva! O Sambhu! forgive me, I pray, for my transgressions. (7)

ध्यात्वा चित्ते शिवाख्यं प्रचुरतरधनं नैव दत्तं द्विजेभ्यो
हव्यं ते लक्षसंख्यैर्हुतवहवदने नार्पितं बीजमन्त्रैः ।
नो तप्तं गाङ्गतीरे व्रतजपनियमैः रुद्रजाप्यैर्न वेदैः
क्षन्तव्यो मेऽपराधः शिव शिव शिव भो श्रीमहादेव शम्भो ॥

I have not made rich gifts to the brahmins, cherishing in my heart,
O Mahādeva! Thy hallowed form;
I have not made, in the sacred fire, million oblations of butter,
Repeating the holy mantra given me by the guru;
Never have I done penance along the Ganges with japa and study of the Vedas.
Therefore, O Siva! O Mahādeva! O Sambhu! forgive me, I pray, for my transgressions. (8)

स्थित्वा स्थाने सरोजे प्रणवमयमरुत्कुम्भके सूक्ष्ममार्गे
शान्ते स्वान्ते प्रलीने प्रकटितविभवे ज्योतिरूपे पराख्ये ।
लिङ्गज्ञे ब्रह्मवाक्ये सकलतनुगतं शङ्करं न स्मरामि
क्षन्तव्यो मेऽपराधः शिव शिव शिव भो श्रीमहादेव शम्भो ॥

I have not sat in the lotus posture, nor have I ever controlled
The prāṇa along the Susumna, repeating the syllable *Om*;
Never have I suppressed the turbulent waves of my mind, nor merged the self-effulgent *Om*

In the ever shining Witness-Consciousness, whose nature is that of the highest Brahman;
Nor have I, in samādhi, meditated on Sankara, dwelling in every form as the Inner Guide.
Therefore, O Siva! O Mahādeva! O Sambhu! Forgive me. I pray, for my transgressions. (9)

नग्नो निःसङ्गशुद्धस्त्रिगुणविरहितो ध्वस्तमोहान्धकारो
नासाग्रे न्यस्तदृष्टिर्विदितभवगुणो नैव दृष्टः कदाचित् ।
उन्मन्यावस्थया त्वां विगतकलिमलं शङ्करं न स्मरामि
क्षन्तव्यो मेऽपराधः शिव शिव शिव भो श्रीमहादेव शम्भो ॥

Never, O Siva! have I seen Thee, the Pure, the Unattached, the Naked One,
Beyond the three guṇas, free from delusion and darkness absorbed in meditation,
And ever aware of the true nature of the world;
Nor, with a longing heart, have I meditated on Thine auspicious and sin-destroying form.
Therefore, O S'iva! O Mahādeva! O Sambhu! Forgive me, I pray, for my transgressions. (10)

चन्द्रोद्भासितशेखरे स्मरहरे गंगाधरे शङ्करे
सर्पैर्भूषितकण्ठकर्णयुगले नेत्रोत्थवैश्वानरे ।
दन्तित्वक्कृतसुन्दराम्बरधरे त्रैलोक्यसारे हरे
मोक्षार्थं कुरु चित्तवृत्तिमचलामन्यैस्तु किं कर्मभिः ॥

O Mind, to gain Liberation, concentrate wholly on Siva,
The sole Reality underlying the worlds, the Giver of good
Whose head is illumined by the crescent moon and in whose hair the Ganges is hidden;

Whose fire-darting eyes consumed the god of earthly love;
whose throat and ears are decked with snakes;
Whose upper garment is a comely elephant skin.
Of what avail are all other rituals? (11)

किं वानेन धनेन वाजिकरिभिः प्राप्तेन राज्येन किं
किं वा पुत्रकलत्रमित्रपशुभिर्देहेन गेहेन किम् ।
ज्ञात्वैतत्क्षणभङ्गुरं सपदि रे त्याज्यं मनो दूरतः
स्वात्मार्थं गुरुवाक्यतो भज मन श्रीपार्वतीवल्लभम् ॥

O Mind, of what avail are wealth or horses, elephants or a kingdom?
Of what avail is a son, the wife, a friend, cattle the body and the home?
Know all these to be transitory, and quickly shun them:
Worship Siva, as your guru instructs you, for the attaining of Self-Knowledge. (12)

आयुर्नश्यति पश्यतां प्रतिदिनं याति क्षयं यौवनं
प्रत्यायान्ति गताः पुनर्न दिवसाः कालो जगद्भक्षकः ।
लक्ष्मीस्तोयतरङ्गभङ्गचपला विद्युच्चलं जीवितं
तस्मात्त्वां शरणागतं शरणद त्वं रक्ष रक्षाधुना ॥

Day by day, a man comes nearer to death;
His youth wears away; the day that is gone never returns;
Time, the almighty, swallows up everything;
Transient as the ripples on a stream is the goddess of fortune;
Fickle as lightning is life itself.
O Siva! O Giver of shelter to those that come to Thee for refuge!
Protect me, who has taken refuge at thy feet. (13)

वन्दे देवमुमापतिं सुरगुरुं वन्दे जगत्कारणं
वन्दे पन्नगभूषणं मृगधरं वन्दे पशूनां पतिम् ।
वन्दे सूर्यशशाङ्कवह्निनयनं वन्दे मुकुन्दप्रियं
वन्दे भक्तजनाश्रयं च वरदं वन्दे शिव शङ्करम् ॥

I salute the self-effulgent Guru of the gods, the Lord of Uma;
I salute the Cause of the universe;
I salute the Lord of beasts, adorned with snakes;
I salute Siva, whose three eyes shine like the sun, the moon, and fire;
I salute the Beloved of Kṛṣṇa; I salute Sankara, He who bestows boons on His devotees and gives them shelter;
I salute the auspicious Siva (14)

गात्रं भस्मसितं च हसितं हस्ते कपालं सितं
खट्वाङ्गं च सितं सितश्च वृषभः कर्णे सिते कुण्डले ।
गङ्गाफेनसिता जटा पशुपतेश्चन्द्रः सितो मूर्धनि
सोऽयं सर्वसितो ददातु विभवं पापक्षयं सर्वदा ॥

O Siva! white is Thy body, covered with ashes; white gleam Thy teeth when Thou smilest!
White is the skull Thou holdest in Thy hand; white is Thy club, which threatens the wicked!
White are the rings that hang from Thine ears; white is the bull on which Thou ridest!
White appear Thy matted locks, flecked with the foam of the Ganges!
White shines the moon on Thy forehead!
May He, who is all white, all pure, bestow on me the treasure of forgiveness for my transgressions! (15)

करचरणकृतं वाक्कायजं कर्मजं वा श्रवणनयनजं वा मानसं
वाऽपराधम् ।
विहितमविहितं वा सर्वमेतत्क्षमस्व जय जय करुणाब्धे
श्रीमहादेवशंभो ॥

O Siva! forgive all the sins that I have committed
With hands or feet, with ears or eyes, with words or body, with mind or heart;
Forgive my sins, those past and those that are yet to come.
Victory unto Siva, the Ocean of Compassion, the Great God, the Abode of Blessedness! (16)

॥ कौपीनपञ्चकम् ॥

FIVE STANZAS ON THE KAUPINA[1]

वेदान्तवाक्येषु सदा रमन्तो भिक्षान्नमात्रेण च तुष्टिमन्तः ।
विशोकमन्तःकरणे चरन्तः कौपीनवन्त खलु भाग्यवन्तः ॥

Roaming ever in the grove of Vedānta
Ever pleased with his beggar's morsel,
Wandering onward, his heart free from sorrow,
Blest indeed is the wearer of the loin-cloth. (1)

मूलं तरोः केवलमाश्रयन्तः पाणिद्वयं भोक्तुममन्त्रयन्तः ॥
कन्थामिव श्रीमपि कुत्सयन्तः कौपीनवन्तः खलु भाग्यवन्तः ॥

Sitting at the foot of a tree for shelter.
Eating from his hands his meagre portion,

1 The loin-cloth of the sannyasi, which is an emblem of renunciation.

Spurning wealth like a patched-up garment,
Blest indeed is the wearer of the loin-cloth. (2)

स्वानन्दभावे परितुष्टिमन्तः सुशान्तसर्वेन्द्रियवृत्तिमन्तः ।
अहर्निशं ब्रह्मसुखे रमन्तः कौपीनवन्तः खलु भाग्यवन्तः ॥

Satisfied fully by the Bliss within him,
Curbing wholly the cravings of his senses,
Delighting day and night in the bliss of Brahman,
Blest indeed is the wearer of the loin-cloth. (3)

देहादिभावं परिवर्तयन्तः स्वात्मानमात्मन्यवलोकयन्तः ।
नान्तं न मध्यं न बहिः स्मरन्तः कौपीनवन्तः खलु भाग्यवन्तः ॥

Witnessing the changes of mind and body,
Naught but the Self within him beholding,
Heedless of outer, of inner, of middle,
Blest indeed is the wearer of the loin-cloth. (4)

ब्रह्माक्षरं पावनमुच्चरन्तो ब्रह्माहमस्मीति विभावयन्तः ।
भिक्षाशिनो दिक्षु परिभ्रमन्तः कौपीनवन्तः खलु भाग्यवन्तः ॥

Chanting Brahman, the Word of redemption,
Meditating only on "I am Brahman",
Living on alms and wandering freely,
Blest indeed is the wearer of the loin-cloth. (5)

॥ चर्पटपञ्जरिकास्तोत्रम् ॥

HYMN OF RENUNCIATION[1]

दिनयामिन्यौ सायं प्रातश्शिशिरवसन्तौ पुनरायातः ।
कालः क्रीडति गच्छत्यायुस्तदपि न मुञ्चत्याशावायुः ॥

भज गोविन्दं भज गोविन्दं भज गोविन्दं मूढमते ।
संप्राप्ते सन्निहिते काले न हि न हि रक्षति डुकृञ्करणे ॥

Sunrise and sunset, daylight and darkness,
Winter and springtime, come and go;
Even the course of time is playful;
Life itself soon ebbs away;
But man's vain hope, alas! goes onward,
Tirelessly onward evermore.
Worship Govinda,[2] worship Govinda,
Worship Govinda, foolish one!
Rules of grammar profit nothing
Once the hour of death draws nigh. (1)

अग्रे वह्निः पृष्ठे भानुः रात्रौ चुबुकसमर्पितजानुः ।
करतलभिक्षस्तरुतलवासस्तदपि न मुञ्चत्याशापाशः ॥

1 Early one morning Śankaracārya was going to the Ganges for his daily ablutions, when he heard a student loudly repeating one of the rules of grammar in order to memorize it. The sage thought that this morning hour should have been devoted to the contemplation of God. Feeling sad at the waste of time he composed the "Hymn of Renunciation."

2 An epithet of Śrī Kṛṣṇa.

भज गोविन्दं भज गोविन्दं भज गोविन्दं मूढमते ।
संप्राप्ते सन्निहिते काले न हि न हि रक्षति डुकृञ्करणे ॥

Seeking for warmth, the penniless beggar
Closely crouches before his fire,
Or sits with only the sun to warm him;
Nightly he lays him down to slumber,
Curling up to keep out the cold;
Hungrily eats his beggar's portion
Out of the bowl his hands provide him;
Takes up his dwelling under a tree:
Still is his heart a helpless prisoner
Bound with the chains of empty hope.
Worship Govinda, worship Govinda,
Worship Govinda, foolish one!
Rules of grammar profit nothing
Once the hour of death draws nigh. (2)

यावद्वित्तोपार्जनसक्तस्तावन्निजपरिवारो रक्तः ।
पश्चाज्जीवति जर्जरदेहे वार्तां कोऽपि न पृच्छति गेहे ॥

भज गोविन्दं भज गोविन्दं भज गोविन्दं मूढमते ।
संप्राप्ते सन्निहिते काले न हि न हि रक्षति डुकृञ्करणे ॥

While a man supports his family,
See what loving care they show!
But when his aging body falters,
Nearing the time of dissolution,
None, not even his nearest kin,
Will think to ask him how he fares.
Worship Govinda, worship Govinda,

Worship Govinda, foolish one!
Rules of grammar profit nothing
Once the hour of death draws nigh. (3)

जटिलो मुण्डी लुञ्छितकेशः काषांयाम्बरबहुकृतवेषः ।
पश्यन्नपि च न पश्यति मूढो उदरनिमित्तं बहुकृतवेषः ॥

भज गोविन्दं भज गोविन्दं भज गोविन्दं मूढमते ।
संप्राप्ते सन्निहिते काले न हि न हि रक्षति डुकृञ्करणे ॥

Many are those whose locks are matted,
Many whose heads are closely shaved,
Many who pluck out all their hair;
Some of them wearing robes of ochre,
Some of them clad in other colours—
All these things for their stomachs' sake[1].
Seeing Truth revealed before them,
Still the deluded see It not.
Worship Govinda, worship Govinda,
Worship Govinda, foolish one!
Rules of grammar profit nothing
Once the hour of death draws nigh.

(4)

भगवद्गीता किञ्चिदधीता गङ्गाजललवकणिका पीता ।
सकृदपि यस्य मुरारिसमर्चा तस्य यमः किं कुरुते चर्चाम् ।

भज गोविन्दं भज गोविन्दं भज गोविन्दं मूढमते ।
संप्राप्ते सन्निहिते काले न हि न हि रक्षति डुकृञ्करणे ॥

1 A reference to the various kinds of false world-renouncers, who put on the outer marks of holiness to earn their livelihood.

Let a man but read from the Gītā,
Drink of the Ganges but a drop,
Worship but once the Lord Almighty,
And he will set at rest for ever
All his fear of the King of Death.
Worship Govinda, worship Govinda,
Worship Govinda, foolish one!
Rules of grammar profit nothing
Once the hour of death draws nigh. (5)

अङ्गं गलितं पलितं मुण्डं दशनविहीनं जातं तुण्डम् ।
वृद्धो याति गृहीत्वा दण्डं तदपि न मुञ्चत्याशापिण्डम् ॥

भज गोविन्दं भज गोविन्दं भज गोविन्दं मूढमते ।
संप्राप्ते सन्निहिते काले न हि न हि रक्षति डुकृञ्करणे ॥

Feeble has grown the old man's body,
Toothless his gums and bald his head;
But there he goes, upon his crutches,
Clinging firmly to fruitless hope!
Worship Govinda, worship Govinda,
Worship Govinda, foolish one!
Rules of grammar profit nothing
Once the hour of death draws nigh. (6)

बालस्तावत्क्रीडासक्तः तरुणस्तावत्तरुणीरक्तः ।
वृद्धस्तावच्चिन्तामग्नः परे ब्रह्मणि कोऽपि न लग्नः ॥

भज गोविन्दं भज गोविन्दं भज गोविन्दं मूढमते ।
संप्राप्ते सन्निहिते काले न हि न हि रक्षति डुकृञ्करणे ॥

Lost in play is the carefree stripling,
Lost in his sweetheart's charms, the youth;

The old man broods upon his sorrows;
None there is, alas! whose spirit
Yearns to be lost in the Parabrahman.
Worship Govinda, worship Govinda,
Worship Govinda, foolish one!
Rules of grammar profit nothing
Once the hour of death draws nigh. (7)

पुनरपि जननं पुनरपि मरणं पुनरपि जननीजठरे शयनम् ।
इह संसारे बहुदुस्तारे कृपयापारे पाहि मुरारे ॥

भज गोविन्दं भज गोविन्दं भज गोविन्दं मूढमते ।
संप्राप्ते सन्निहिते काले न हि न हि रक्षति डुकृञ्करणे ॥

Birth unceasing! Death unceasing!
Ever to pass through a mother's womb!
Hard to cross is the world's wide ocean:
Lord, redeem me through Thy mercy!
Worship Govinda, worship Govinda,
Worship Govinda, foolish one!
Rules of grammar profit nothing
Once the hour of death draws nigh. (8)

पुनरपि रजनी पुनरपि दिवसः पुनरपि पक्षः पुनरपि मासः ।
पुनरप्ययनं पुनरपि वर्षं तदपि न मुञ्चत्याशामर्षम् ॥

भज गोविन्दं भज गोविन्दं भज गोविन्दं मूढमते ।
संप्राप्ते सन्निहिते काले न हि न हि रक्षति डुकृञ्करणे ॥

Day follows day, night follows night,
New moon, full moon, ever returning;

Summer and winter see the planet
Ever inclining on its axis;
Year follows year unfailingly.
But, though a changeless law of recurrence
Grips the world in relentless sway,
Still there is none who dare abandon
Expectation's empty promise.
Worship Govinda, worship Govinda
Worship Govinda, foolish one!
Rules of grammar profit nothing
Once the hour of death draws nigh. (9)

वयसि गते कः कामविकारश्शुष्के नीरे कः कासारः ।
क्षीणे वित्ते कः परिवारो ज्ञाते तत्त्वे कस्संसारः ॥

भज गोविन्दं भज गोविन्दं भज गोविन्दं मूढमते ।
संप्राप्ते सन्निहिते काले न हि न हि रक्षति डुकृञ्करणे ॥

Youth being fled, what good is passion?
Water gone, what use a lake?
Where to be found our friends and kinsmen
Once the money's all exhausted?
Where is the world, when Truth is known?
Worship Govinda, worship Govinda,
Worship Govinda, foolish one!
Rules of grammar profit nothing
Once the hour of death draws nigh. (10)

नारीस्तनभरनाभीदेशं दृष्ट्वा मायामोहावेशम् ।
एतन्मांसवसादिविकारं मनसि विचिन्तय वारं वारम् ॥

भज गोविन्दं भज गोविन्दं भज गोविन्दं मूढमते ।
संप्राप्ते सन्निहिते काले न हि न हि रक्षति डुकृञ्करणे ॥

Lust at the sight of a woman's body
Springs from ignorance, springs from error;
Inwardly reason, over and over,
Bodies are flesh and blood and fat.
Worship Govinda, worship Govinda,
Worship Govinda, foolish one!
Rules of grammar profit nothing
Once the hour of death draws nigh. (11)

कस्त्वं कोऽहं कुत आयातः का मे जननी को मे तातः ।
इति परिभावय सर्वमसारं विश्वं त्यक्त्वा स्वप्नविचारम् ॥

भज गोविन्दं भज गोविन्दं भज गोविन्दं मूढमते ।
संप्राप्ते सन्निहिते काले न हि न हि रक्षति डुकृञ्करणे ॥

Who am I? And who are you?
What is the place from which I come?
Who is my mother? Who my sire?
Pondering thus, perceive them all
As fancies only, without substance;
Give up the world as an idle dream.
Worship Govinda, worship Govinda,
Worship Govinda, foolish one!
Rules of grammar profit nothing
Once the hour of death draws nigh. (12)

गेयं गीतानामसहस्रं ध्येयं श्रीपतिरूपमजस्रम् ।
नेयं सज्जनसङ्गे चित्तं देयं दीनजनाय च वित्तम् ॥

भज गोविन्दं भज गोविन्दं भज गोविन्दं मूढमते ।
संप्राप्ते सन्निहिते काले न हि न हि रक्षति डुकृञ्करणे ॥

Every day recite from the Gītā;
Chant the thousand names of Viṣṇu,[1]
Cherishing Him within your heart.
Take delight to be with the holy;
Give your riches away to the poor.
Worship Govinda, worship Govinda,
Worship Govinda, foolish one!
Rules of grammar profit nothing
Once the hour of death draws nigh. (13)

यावज्जीवो निवसति देहे तावत्पृच्छति कुशलं गेहे ।
गतवति वायौ देहापाये भार्या बिभ्यति तस्मिन्काये ॥

भज गोविन्दं भज गोविन्दं भज गोविन्दं मूढमते ।
संप्राप्ते सन्निहिते काले न हि न हि रक्षति डुकृञ्करणे ॥

While man's soul remains in his body,
Fondly his family wish him well;
But when the life-breath leaves its dwelling,
Even his wife will flee in fear.
Worship Govinda, worship Govinda,
Worship Govinda, foolish one!
Rules of grammar profit nothing
Once the hour of death draws nigh. (14)

सुखतः क्रियते रामाभोगः पश्चाद्धन्त शरीरे रोगः ।
यद्यपि लोके मरणं शरणं तदपि न मुञ्चति पापाचरणम् ।

भज गोविन्दं भज गोविन्दं भज गोविन्दं मूढमते ।
संप्राप्ते सन्निहिते काले न हि न हि रक्षति डुकृञ्करणे ॥

1 Refers to a hymn which gives Viṣṇu's thousand names and accounts their significance.

He who yields to lust for pleasure
Leaves his frame a prey to disease;
Yet, though death is the final ending,
None forswears his sinfulness,
Worship Govinda, worship Govinda,
Worship Govinda, foolish one!
Rules of grammar profit nothing
Once the hour of death draws nigh. (15)

रथ्याकर्पटविरचितकन्थः पुण्यापुण्यविवर्जितपन्थः ।
नाहं न त्वं नायं लोकस्तदपि किमर्थं क्रियते शोकः ॥

भज गोविन्दं भज गोविन्दं भज गोविन्दं मूढमते ।
संप्राप्ते सन्निहिते काले न हि न हि रक्षति डुकृञ्करणे ॥

Rags cast off along the highway
Serve as a garment for the monk;
Freed from vice and freed from virtue,
Onward he wanders; in his sight
Nor I nor you nor the world exists.
Why, then, so give way to sorrow?
Worship Govinda, worship Govinda,
Worship Govinda, foolish one!
Rules of grammar profit nothing
Once the hour of death draws nigh. (16)

कुरुते गङ्गासागरगमनं व्रतपरिपालनमथवा दानम् ।
ज्ञानविहीने सर्वमनेन मुक्तिर्न भवति जन्मशतेन ॥

भज गोविन्दं भज गोविन्दं भज गोविन्दं मूढमते ।
संप्राप्ते सन्निहिते काले न हि न हि रक्षति डुकृञ्करणे ॥

Though, for the sake of his salvation,
Man may go a-pilgrimage to Ganga-sāgara[1]
Keep his vows, and give to the poor,
Failing the Knowledge of the Highest,
Nothing of this assures him freedom
Even in the span of a hundred lives.
Worship Govinda, worship Govinda,
Worship Govinda, foolish one!
Rules of grammar profit nothing
Once the hour of death draws nigh. (17)

॥ द्वादशपञ्जरिकास्तोत्रम् ॥

A CUDGEL FOR DELUSION

मूढ जहीहि धनागमतृष्णां कुरु सद्बुद्धिं मनसि वितृष्णाम् ।
यल्लभसे निजकर्मोपात्तं वित्तं तेन विनोदय चित्तम् ॥

Renounce, O fool, your ceaseless thirst
For hoarding gold and precious gems;
Content yourself with what may come
Through deeds performed in earlier lives;[2]
Devote your mind to righteousness
And let dispassion be your law. (1)

अर्थमनर्थं भावय नित्यं नास्ति ततस्सुखलेशस्सत्यम् ।
पुत्रादपि धनभाजां भीतिस्सर्वत्रैषा विहिता रीतिः ॥

1 Ganga-sagara—A place considered holy as the Ganges meets the sea here.

2 The results of action done in previous lives are reaped without much effort. A man's heart and soul should be devoted to contemplation of God and not to the accumulating of worldly profit.

Remember, riches bring out grief:
Truly, no joy abides in them.
A rich man even fears his son:
This is his position everywhere. (2)

का ते कान्ता कस्ते पुत्रस्संसारोऽयमतीव विचित्रः।
कस्य त्वं कः कुत आयातः तत्त्वं चिन्तय तदिह भ्रातः॥

Who is your wife? And who your child?
Strange indeed is this mortal world!
Who are you? And who is your own?
Where is the region whence you come?
Brother, ponder on these things. (3)

मा कुरु धनजनयौवनगर्वं हरति निमेषात्कालस्सर्वम्।
मायामयमिदमखिलं हित्वा ब्रह्मपदं त्वं प्रविश विदित्वा॥

Boast not of youth or friends or wealth;
Swifter than eyes can wink, by Time
Each one of these is stolen away.
Abjure the illusion of the world
And join yourself to timeless Truth. (4)

कामं क्रोधं लोभं मोहं त्यक्त्वात्मानं भावय कोऽहं।
आत्मज्ञानविहीना मूढास्ते पच्यन्ते नरकनिगूढाः॥

Give up the curse of lust and wrath;
Give up delusion, give up greed;
Remember who you really are.
Fools are they that are blind to Self:
Cast into hell, they suffer there. (5)

सुरमन्दिरतरुमूलनिवासश्शय्या भूतलमजिनं वासः ।
सर्वपरिग्रहभोगत्यागः कस्य सुखं न करोति विरागः ॥

Make of a temple or tree your home,
Clothe yourself in the skin of a deer,
And use the bare earth for your bed,
Avoiding gifts and sense delights:
Could any fail to be content,
Blest with dispassion such as this? (6)

शत्रौ मित्रे पुत्रे बन्धौ मा कुरु यत्नं विग्रहसन्धौ ।
भव समचित्तस्सर्वत्र त्वं वाञ्छस्यचिराद्यदि विष्णुत्वम् ॥

Be not attached to friend or foe,
To son or kinsman peace or war;
If you aspire to Viṣṇu's realm,
Look upon all things equally. (7)

त्वयि मयि चान्यत्रैको विष्णुः व्यर्थं कुप्यसि मय्यसहिष्णुः ।
सर्वस्मिन्नपि पश्यात्मानं सर्वत्रोत्सृज भेदज्ञानम् ॥

Viṣṇu alone it is who dwells
In you, in me, in everything;
Empty of meaning is your wrath,
And the impatience you reveal.
Seeing yourself in everyone.
Have done with all diversity. (8)

प्राणायामं प्रत्याहारं नित्यानित्यविवेकविचारम् ।
जाप्यसमानसमाधिविधानं कुर्ववधानं महदवधानम् ॥

Control the self restrain the breath,
Sift out the transient from the True,
Repeat the holy name of God,
And still the restless mind within.
To this, the universal rule,
Apply yourself with heart and soul. (9)

नलिनीदलगतजलमतितरलं तद्वज्जीवितमतिशयचपलम् ।
विद्धि व्याध्यभिमानग्रस्तं लोकं शोकहतं च समस्तम् ।

Uncertain is the life of man
As rain-drops on a lotus leaf;
The whole of humankind is prey
To grief and ego and disease: (10)

का तेऽष्टादशदेशे चिन्ता वातुल किं तव नास्ति नियन्ता ।
यस्त्वां हस्ते सुदृढनिबद्धं बोधयति प्रभवादिविरुद्धम् ॥

Why do all things distress your mind?
Has reason quite abandoned you?
Have you no guide to hold you firm,
Instructing you of life and death? (11)

गुरुचरणाम्बुजनिर्भरभक्तः संसारादचिराद्भव मुक्तः ।
इन्द्रियमानसनियमादेवं द्रक्ष्यसि निजहृदयस्थं देवम् ॥

Cherish your guru's lotus feet
And free yourself without delay
From the enslavement of this world;
Curb your senses and your mind
And see the Lord within your heart. (12)

द्वादशपञ्जरिकामय एषः शिष्याणां कथितो ह्युपदेशः ।
येषां चित्ते नैव विवेकस्ते पच्यन्ते नरकमनेकम् ॥

These dozen stanzas I have penned
To spur my pupils on their way;
Unless a man pursue the Real,
His pangs surpass the pangs of hell. (13)

॥ निर्वाणषट्कम् ॥

SIX STANZAS ON NIRVĀNA

ओं मनोबुद्ध्यहङ्कारचित्तानि नाहं न च श्रोत्रजिह्वे न च घ्राणनेत्रे ।
न च व्योम भूमिर्न तेजो न वायुश्चिदानन्दरूपः शिवोऽहं
शिवोऽहम् ॥

Om. I am neither the mind,
intelligence, ego, nor citta,[1]
Neither the ears nor the tongue,
nor the senses of smell and sight;
Neither ether nor air
nor fire nor water nor earth;
I am Eternal Bliss and Awareness
—I am Siva! I am Siva! (1)

न च प्राणसंज्ञो न वै पञ्चवायुर्न वा सप्तधातुर्न वा पञ्चकोशः ।
न वाक्पाणिपादं न चोपस्थपायू चिदानन्दरूपः शिवोऽहं
शिवोऽहम् ॥

1 The seat of memory.

I am neither the prāṇa[1]
nor the five vital breaths[2]
Neither the seven elements of
the body,[3] nor its five sheaths,[4]
Nor hands nor feet nor tongue,
nor other organs of action;
I am Eternal Bliss and Awareness
—I am Siva! I am Siva! (2)

न मे द्वेषरागौ न मे लोभमोहौ मदो नैव मे नैव मात्सर्यभावः ।
न धर्मो न चार्थो न कामो न मोक्षश्चिदानन्दरूपः शिवोऽहं
शिवोऽहम् ॥

Neither greed nor delusion,
loathing nor liking, have I;
Nothing of pride or ego,
of dharma or Liberation;
Neither desire of the mind
nor object for its desiring:
I am Eternal Bliss and Awareness
—I am Siva! I am Siva! (3)

न पुण्यं न पापं न सौख्यं न दुःखं न मन्त्रो न तीर्थं न वेदा न यज्ञाः ।
अहं भोजनं नैव भोज्यं न भोक्ता चिदानन्दरूपः शिवोऽहं
शिवोऽहम् ॥

1 The vital force that sustains life in a physical body.

2 The various functions of the prana, or vital force.

3 i.e., water, blood, flesh, fat, bone, marrow, and semen,

4 The sheaths of food, prana, mind, intelligence, and bliss. which conceal Atman, or the Self, as a scabbard conceals a sword.

Nothing of pleasure and pain,
 of virtue and vice do I know,
Of mantra or sacred place,
 of Vedas or sacrifice;
Neither am I the eater,
 the food nor the act of eating:
I am Eternal Bliss and Awareness
 --I am Siva! I am Siva! (4)

न मृत्युर्न शङ्का न मे जातिभेदः पिता नैव मे नैव माता न जन्म ।
न बन्धुर्न मित्रं गुरुर्नैव शिष्यश्चिदानन्दरूपः शिवोऽहं शिवोऽहम् ॥

Death or fear I have none,
 nor any distinction of caste;
Neither father nor mother,
 nor even a birth, have I;
Neither friend nor comrade,
 neither disciple nor guru:
I am Eternal Bliss and Awareness
 --I am Siva! I am Siva! (5)

अहं निर्विकल्पो निराकाररूपो विभुत्वाच्च सर्वत्र सर्वेन्द्रियाणाम् ।
न वासङ्गतं नैव मुक्तिर्न मेयश्चिदानन्दरूपः शिवोऽहं शिवोऽहम् ॥

I have no form or fancy:
 the All-pervading am I;
Everywhere I exist,
 and yet am beyond the senses;
Neither salvation am I,
 nor anything to be known:
I am Eternal Bliss and Awareness
 --I am Siva! I am Siva! (6)

GLOSSARY

GLOSSARY

Advaita	Non-duality: a school of Vedānta philosophy teaching the oneness of God, soul, and universe, whose chief exponent was Śankarācārya.
Agnihotra	A Vedic sacrifice in which oblations are offered to Agni, the Fire-god.
ahaṁkāra	Ego or "I-consciousness"; one of the functions of the inner organ. *See* antaḥkaraṇa.
ajñāna	A term of Vedānta philosophy meaning ignorance, individual or cosmic. According to Non-dualistic Vedānta it is responsible for the perception of multiplicity in the relative world, and also for man's bondage and suffering.
ākāsa	The first of the five material elements that constitute the universe; often translated as "space" or "ether". *See* Introduction, p. 69. The four other elements are vāyu (air), agni (fire), ap (water), and prithvi (earth).
Ānanda	Bliss.
ānandamayakośa	The sheath of bliss. *See* kosa.

annamayakośa — The gross physical sheath. *See* kośa.

antaḥkaraṇa — The inner organ, comprising manas (mind), buddhi (intellect or determinative faculty), citta (pleasure-seeking function) and, ahaṁkāra (ego).

Āraṇyakas — One of the sections of the Vedas. *See* Vedas.

Atharva-Veda — One of the four Vedas. *See* Vedas.

Ātmabodha — (*Lit.,* Self-Knowledge) The name of the Sanskrit work translated in this volume.

Ātman — The Self, or Soul: denotes also the Supreme Soul, which, according to Non-dualistic Vedānta, is one with the individual soul.

avidyā — A term of Vedānta philosophy meaning ignorance, individual or cosmic. *See* ajñāna.

Bhagavadgītā — A well-known Hindu scripture, comprising eighteen chapters (25th to 42nd) of the Bhīṣma Parva of the *Mahābhārata.*

Bhagavati — The Divine Mother.

Bhavānī — The Divine Mother.

Brahmā	The Creator God; the First Person of the Hindu Trinity, the other two being Viṣṇu and Siva.
brahmacāri	A celibate religious student who lives with his teacher and devotes himself to the practice of spiritual discipline. *See* p. 19.
Brahmajñāna	The knowledge of Brahman.
Brahmaloka	The plane of Brahmā, roughly corresponding to the highest heaven of the dualistic religions, where fortunate souls repair after death and enjoy spiritual communion with the Personal God.
Brahman	The Absolute: the Supreme Reality of Non-dualistic Vedānta.
Brahmaṇas	One of the two main sections of the Vedas. *See* Vedas.
Brahma-sūtras	An authoritative treatise on Vedanta philosophy ascribed to Vyasa. Same as *Vedānta-sūtras*.
Brahmavidyā	The Knowledge of Brahman.
brāhmin	A member of the priestly caste, the highest caste in Hindu society.
Buddha	(*Lit.*, The Enlightened One) The founder of Buddhism.
buddhi	The determinative faculty of the mind which makes decisions; sometimes translated as "intellect". *See* antahkarana.

Cārvāka	The founder of the well-known materialistic school of Hindu philosophy.
Cit	Consciousness.
citta	The function of the inner organ which seeks for pleasurable objects. *See* antaḥkaraṇa.
Code of Manu	A book on Hindu law by Manu.
devas	(*Lit,.* shining ones.) The gods of Hindu mythology.
dharma	Righteousness, duty. The inner constitution of a thing, which governs its growth.
Durgā	The Divine Mother.
Gaudapāda	A celebrated philosopher of Non-dualistic Vedānta whose principal work is a commentary on the *Māṇḍūkya Upaniṣad.*
Gaurī	(*Lit.,* One with complexion of gold.) The Divine Mother.
Gautama	The author of the Nyāya system of Hindu philosophy, or Indian Logic.
Govinda	A name of Śri Kṛṣṇa.
Govindapāda	The teacher of Śankarācārya.
guṇa	According to Sāṁkhya philosophy, Prakṛti (Nature or matter), consists of three gunas—usually translated as "qualities"—known as sattva, rajas, and tamas. Tamas stands for inertia or dullness; rajas, for activity or

	restlessness; sattva, for balance or righteousness.
guru	Spiritual teacher.
Indra	The king of the gods.
Īśvara	The Personal God. *See* Saguṇa Brahman.
Jaimini	The author of the Pūrva Mīmāmsā system of Hindu philosophy, which deals with the ritualistic portion of the Vedas.
japa	*See* mantra.
jiva	(*Lit.*, living being.) The individual soul, which in essence is one with the Universal Soul.
jīvanmukta	One enjoying Liberation while living in the body.
jñāna	Knowledge of reality.
Jñānakāṇḍa	The part of the Vedas that teaches philosophical wisdom.
Kailās	A peak of the Himālayas, regarded as the sacred abode of Śiva.
Kaṇāda	The author of the Vaiśeṣika system of Hindu philosophy.
Kapila	The author of the Sāṁkhya system of Hindu philosophy.
Kārika	A commentary on the *Māṇḍūkya Upaniśad,* ascribed to Gaudapāda.

karma	Action in general; duty; ritualistic worship.
Karmakāṇḍa	The part of the Vedas that deals with rituals and sacrifices.
kośa	(*Lit.*, sheath or covering.) The following are the five kośas as described in Vedānta philosophy: (1) the annamayakośa, or gross physical sheath, made of and sustained by food; (2) the prāṇamaya-kośa, or vital sheath, consisting of the five prāṇas or vital forces; (3) the manomayakośa, or mental sheath; (4) the vijñānamayakośa, or sheath of intelligence; (5) the ānandamayakośa, or sheath of bliss. These five sheaths cover the Soul which is the innermost reality or the jīva and is untouched by the characteristics of the sheaths.
Kṛṣṇa Śrī	An Incarnation of God whose life is given in the *Bhāgavata* and the *Mahābhārata*.
kṣatriya	A member of the warrior caste.
Madana	The god of earthly love.
Madhva	The founder of the Dualistic school of Vedānta philosophy (A.D. 1199—1276).
Mahābhārata	A famous Hindu epic.

Mahādeva	(*Lit.*, the Great God.) A name of Siva.
manas	The faculty of doubt and volition, sometimes translated as "mind"; one of the functions of the inner organ. *See* antaḥkaraṇa.
manomayakośa	The sheath of the mind. *See* kośa.
mantra	Holy Sanskrit text; the sacred formula used in japa, or repetition of God's name. Also one of the two main sections of the Vedas. *See* Vedas.
Manu	The celebrated law-giver of ancient India, who is supposed to be the author of the *Manusaṁhitā,* or *Code of Manu.*
māyā	A term of Vedānta philosophy denoting ignorance obscuring the vision of Reality; the cosmic illusion on account of which the One appears as the many, the Absolute as the relative.
mokṣa	Liberation.
Nārāyaṇa	The Supreme Godhead of the Vaiṣṇavas, or worshippers of Viṣṇu.
Nirguṇa Brahman	(*Lit.*, Brahman without attributes.) A term used to describe the Absolute.
Nirvāṇa	(*Lit.*, blowing out, as of a flame.) Annihilation of desire, passion, and

	ego; Liberation, characterized by freedom and bliss.
nirvikalpasamādhi	The highest state of samādhi, in which the aspirant realizes his total oneness with Brahman.
Om	The most sacred word of the Vedas; also written *Aum*. It is a symbol of both the personal God and the Absolute.
Pārvatī	Daughter of King Himālaya and Consort of Siva; a manifestation of the Divine Mother.
Patañjali	The author of the Yoga system of Hindu philosophy.
'rakrti	Primordial Nature; the material substratum of the creation, consisting of sattva, rajas, and tamas.
prāṇa	The vital breath, which sustains life in a physical body; the primal energy or force, of which other physical forces are manifestations. In the books of Yoga, prāṇa is described as having five modifications, according to its five different functions. These are; prāṇa (the vital energy that controls the breath), apāna (the vital energy that carries downward unassimilated food and drink), samāna (the vital energy that carries nutrition all over the body), vyana (the vital energy

	that pervades the entire body), and udāna (the vital energy by which the contents of the stomach are ejected through the mouth). The word *Prāṇa* is also a name of the Cosmic Soul, endowed with activity.
prāṇamayakośa	The vital sheath. *See* kośa.
prārabdha karma	Action done in a previous life which has begun to bear fruit in the present life. *See* Introduction, p. 31 n.
Purāṇas	Books of Hindu mythology.
Puruṣa	(*Lit.*, person.) A term of Sāṁkhya philosophy denoting the Conscious Principle. The universe evolves from the union of Prakrti (Nature) and Puruṣa. In Vedānta the word also denotes the Soul and the Absolute.
rajas	The principle of activity or restlessness. *See* guṇa.
rājasic	Pertaining to, or endowed with rajas.
Rāma	The hero of the *Rāmāyaṇa,* regarded by the Hindus as a Divine Incarnation.
Ramakrishna	A great saint of Bengal, regarded as a Divine Incarnation (A.D. 1836-1886).
Rāmānuja	A famous saint and philosopher of southern India, the founder of the

	school of Qualified Non-dualism (A.D. 1017-1137).
Rāmāyaṇa	A famous Hindu epic.
Rāvaṇa	The monster-king of Ceylon, who forcibly abducted Sītā, the wife of Rāma. His life and exploits are described in the *Rāmāyaṇa*.
Ṛg-Veda	One of the four Vedas. *See* Vedas.
ṛṣi	A seer of Truth; a revealer of the wisdom of the Vedas.
Rudra	An epithet of Śiva.
Sadānanda	A Vedantist philosopher, the author of *Vedāntasāra*, or *The Essence of Vedānta,* who lived probably during the middle of the fifteenth century.
Saguṇa Brahman	(*Lit.,* Brahman with attributes.) The Absolute conceived as the Creator, Preserver, and Destroyer of the universe; corresponds to Īśvara, or the Personal God.
samādhi	Ecstasy, trance, complete concentration, communion with God.
Sāma-Veda	One of the four Vedas. *See* Vedas.
Sambhu	An epithet of Śiva.
Samhitā	A section of the Vedas. *See* Vedas.
Sāṁkhya	One of the six systems of Hindu philosophy, ascribed to Kapila.
saṁsāra	The world of change and becoming; the relative world.

Sanātana Dharma	(*Lit.*, the Eternal Religion.) The religion of the Hindus, formulated by the *ṛṣis* of the Vedas. *See* Introduction, p. 6 n.
Śankara	A name of Śiva: also short for Saṇkarācārya.
Śankarācārya	The great philosopher of Non-dualistic Vedānta. (A.D. 788-820).
sannyāsa	The monastic life.
sannyāsi	A Hindu monk, who renounces the world in order to realize God. *See* Introduction, pp. 20-21.
sattva	The principle of balance or righteousness. *See* guṇa.
savikalpa samādhi	Communion with God in which the distinction between subject and object is retained.
Siṣya	Disciple.
Sītā	The consort of Rāma. Her life is described in the *Rāmāyaṇa.*
Śiva	The Destroyer God; the Third Person of the Hindu Trinity, the other two being Brahmā and Viṣṇu.
Smṛtis	The law books, subsidiary to the Vedas, guiding the daily life and conduct of the Hindus.
Śruti	The Vedas.
Suṣumnā	The hollow canal within the spinal column, through which the awakened spiritual energy rises.

Turīya — (*Lit.*, the fourth). A name of the Transcendental Brahman, which both transcends and pervades the three states of waking, dream, and deep sleep.

Umā — A name of the Divine Mother; same as Pārvatī, the Consort of Śiva.

upādhi — A term of Vedānta philosophy denoting a limitation imposed upon the Self or upon Brahman through ignorance.

Upaniṣads — One of the sections of the Vedas, forming, with one or two exceptions, the concluding chapters of the Āraṇyakas and containing the Vedanta philosophy. *See* Vedas. There are one hundred and eight Upaniṣads extant, of which eleven are the most important. *See* Introduction, p. 9 ff.

Vāmadeva — An epithet of Śiva.

Vedānta — (*Lit.*, the conclusion or the essence of the Vedas.) A system of philosophy ascribed to Vyāsa. discussed mainly in the Upaniṣads, the *Bhagavad-gita* and the *Brahma-sūtras*.

Vedānta-sūtras — *See Brahma-sūtras*.

Vedas	The most sacred scriptures of the Hindus and the ultimate authority of the Hindu religion and philosophy. They were arranged by Vyāsa into four books, namely, the Ṛg-Veda, the Yajur-Veda, the Sāma-Veda, and the Atharva-Veda. According to orthodox Vedic scholars the Vedas consist of the Mantras and the Brāhmaṇas. The Mantras include the Saṁhitās, and the Brāhmaṇas include the Āraṇyakas and the Upaniṣads.
vijñānamayakośa	The sheath of intelligence. *See* kośa.
Virāt	Consciousness limited or conditioned by the upādhi of the aggregate of gross bodies. *See* Introduction, p. 78.
Viṣṇu	(*Lit.,* the All-pervading Spirit.) A name of the Supreme Lord; the Preserver God, the Second Person of the Hindu Trinity, the other two being Brahmā and Śiva.
Viśiṣṭādvaita	The philosophy of Qualified Non-dualism, a school of Vedānta philosophy teaching that individual souls and the universe are parts of Brahman; its chief exponent was Rāmānuja.
Viveka	Philosophical discrimination.

Vyāsa	A celebrated sage, who is reputed to have arranged the Vedas in their present form: he is also believed to be the author of the *Mahabharata*, the eighteen Puranas, and the *Brahma-sutras*.
Yajur-Veda	One of the four Vedas. *See* Vedas.
yoga	Union of the individual soul and the Supreme Soul; the discipline by which such union is effected. The Yoga system of philosophy, ascribed to Patañjali, deals with the realization of Truth through concentration of mind.